TEACHING AND ITS PREDICAMENTS

For Vicki,
With best
wishes

Teaching and Its Predicaments

edited by
NICHOLAS C. BURBULES
University of Illinois–Urbana/Champaign

and

DAVID T. HANSEN
University of Illinois–Chicago

WestviewPress
A Division of HarperCollins*Publishers*

Published in 1997 in the United States of America by Westview Press, 5500 Central Avenue, Boulder, Colorado 80301-2877, and in the United Kingdom by Westview Press, 12 Hid's Copse Road, Cumnor Hill, Oxford OX2 9JJ

Library of Congress Cataloging-in-Publication Data
Teaching and its predicaments / edited by Nicholas C. Burbules, David T. Hansen
p. cm.
Includes bibliographical references and index.
ISBN 0-8133-2863-2 (hardcover). — ISBN 0-8133-2864-0 (pbk.)
1. Teachers—United States. 2. Teaching—United States. 3. Teacher-student relationships—United States. 4. Educational change—United States. I. Burbules, Nicholas C. II. Hansen, David T., 1952– .
LB1775.2.T475 1997
371.102—dc21 97-22269
CIP

The paper used in this publication meets the requirements of the American National Standard for Permanence of Paper for Printed Library Materials Z39.48-1984.

10 9 8 7 6 5 4 3 2 1

Contents

Acknowledgments

The editors wish to thank Dean Birkenkamp, who initially encouraged us to begin this project, and the staff at Westview Press who have worked with us to publish this book: Cathy Pusateri, Sarah Warner, Shena Redmond, Kathleen Christensen, and others who have seen it through to completion.

Nicholas C. Burbules
David T. Hansen

1

Introduction

David T. Hansen
Nicholas C. Burbules

A predicament is a problematic state of affairs that admits of no easy resolution. Predicaments require compromise and trade-offs. They do not necessarily paralyze human action; people can and do respond to them all the time. However, responses to predicaments tend to take the form of provisional, working resolutions: *provisional* because no response can permanently dissolve the predicament, but *working* because the response at least provides a strategy or a way of addressing the situation. Complex human endeavors, such as parenting, friendship, marriage, and teaching, all feature distinctive predicaments. Teachers cannot dictate what their students learn or the attitudes their students develop toward education. The reality of human individuality and the diversity of human interests means that predicaments such as these will persist for as long as parenting, teaching, and similar endeavors do.

Fortunately, life is not as daunting as the previous paragraph may suggest. Practices such as parenting and teaching do have their ongoing problematic dimensions. But they also yield incalculable fulfillment. Generation after generation would not willingly engage in those pursuits if they were not meaningful. Countless numbers of people have found a sense of self and identity in these very endeavors. For them, parenting and educating are purposeful activities that render human life into something other than random, aimless, or chaotic. Their work gives life form and direction and, in so doing, creates the possibility of growth, accomplishment, and joy.

Nonetheless, most people would probably agree that endeavors such as parenting and teaching are punctuated by difficulties and problems. Many would go further. They would suggest that misunderstandings, conflicting needs and values, unfulfilled hopes, and unmet expectations—in short, predicaments—are part of the ethos of such practices.

This book presents nine essays that identify and discuss predicaments in teaching. The authors are experienced researchers and teachers who are attuned to the nature of everyday classroom practice and to the kinds of pressures and problems teachers encounter in varied settings. The contributors take their point of departure from a shared perspective: that teaching is an invaluable, irreplaceable human endeavor, but one that is also indeterminate. The authors believe that teachers play a vital role in fueling the well-being of society, but they also argue that the teacher's world is characterized by uncertainty, ambiguity, and sometimes irreconcilable expectations. Those conditions make teaching unpredictable. Teaching at all levels of the educational system is alternately surprising, frustrating, delightful, and dispiriting. This indeterminacy holds in even the most favorable circumstances.

This book has been written for a broad audience: prospective teachers, experienced practitioners, teacher educators, researchers who study teaching, policymakers, and members of the public interested in learning more about conditions in the classroom. The contributors do not aim at resolving the predicaments of teaching—something the authors do not believe is possible. Rather, their purpose is to illuminate new ways of perceiving those dilemmas, to make them more manageable, less debilitating, and perhaps even a source of interest and inquiry on the part of teachers, prospective teachers, and others who care about the practice.

Each chapter can be read independently, depending on readers' inclinations and interests. However, the order in which the chapters appear is intentional. Chapters 2 through 4 examine predicaments generated by what might be called the culture of educational practice today. That culture produces a host of expectations and demands on teachers that can create difficult if not impossible challenges. Chapters 5 and 6 discuss predicaments that emerge from a broader origin, namely societal conditions writ large. Those conditions press down on teachers—who may not be aware of the source of the pressure—in ways that can trouble their classroom work. Chapters 7 through 10 illuminate predicaments that come more directly from within the practice of teaching. These are predicaments that, in some cases, simply cannot be avoided regardless of the prevailing educational culture or societal atmosphere.

This way of distinguishing the chapters, however, is neither hard nor fast. The chapters overlap considerably in terms of the authors' concern both for the broader circumstances in which teachers work and for the immediacies of everyday practice. Recurring themes cut across the individual contributions. We hope that readers find something of value in each of them.

* * *

In Chapter 2, Robert E. Floden points out that educational reforms often call on teachers to teach more than they know or understand. Floden focuses on contemporary calls for teachers not only to "deliver the goods"—the traditional image of what teachers do—but also to help students understand the logic and structure of subject matter. He points out that this expectation demands knowledge and experience that many teachers have never had. In many cases, their own education has not provided them an "insider's" understanding of, for example, the nature of historical thinking and interpretation. But they are suddenly asked to teach this very material to students. After describing some of the tensions and difficulties (and anxieties) this predicament engenders, Floden argues that teachers do not have to respond by taking on the Olympian task of mastering a subject inside and out, including its underlying epistemological and logical structures. There is no need, Floden implies, for teachers to assume the burden of what has been called the "Atlas complex," in which teachers perceive themselves as having to be all-knowing and all-wise.[1] Instead, Floden suggests, teachers can engage students more actively in learning and can also make enhanced use of curricular materials and computer technology. In other words, rather than feeling that they must be the exclusive source of knowledge, teachers can learn to assist students in their own inquiry. Floden contends that this kind of response, which he also compares with other possible responses, does not eliminate the predicament of having to teach more than one knows. But he argues that the approach provides teachers with a potentially enlightened method for dealing with it.

Nel Noddings, the author of Chapter 3, might respond to the difficult predicament Floden discusses by asking why teachers should be made to teach subject matter at all, or at least why they should be made to do so with the force and tenacity expected of them. Noddings poses a question that challenges many familiar educational assumptions: Must teachers motivate their students? At first glance, many educators might be startled by the question. Of course teachers need to motivate students. How else can they connect students and subject matter? Isn't that what teaching is about, at least in large part?

Noddings's reply is that this is not what teaching should be about. She urges the educational community to rethink what she regards as its well-intentioned but misguided emphasis on teaching common subject matter to all students. She suggests that, in practice, liberals and conservatives share this universalist posture, despite their being at loggerheads on many other issues. To construct her own position, Noddings explores notions of human freedom and also what it means to accept and interact with other human beings as genuinely "other." She applies this analysis to answer her opening question. In her view, teachers should not be put in the predicament of having to motivate students who may, in effect, not all want the same education. Rather, Noddings argues, "we must work more closely with students' own motives if we are to succeed in teaching them things we take to be worthwhile and in preparing them for democratic life."

Floden's and Noddings's chapters illuminate how much more challenging teachers' work is made as a result of externally defined pressures and expectations. In Chapter 4, Robert Boostrom treats another set of broad expectations—or better, assumptions—that cause problems for teachers. Boostrom recalls the familiar lament among educators that too much teaching consists of drills focusing on memorization, rote learning, and step-by-step skill building, all of which, so it is echoed, renders schooling mechanical and boring. Many educators complain that in the urgency to teach students how to read, we forget what it means to enjoy reading and that reading can be a path to new worlds and to changing people's lives. In short, we forget why human beings might want to read in the first place.

However, Boostrom suggests, while educators deplore what he calls "teaching by the numbers," they contribute to its ubiquity because of their own educational assumptions. Boostrom discusses widespread but often unarticulated views about knowledge, expertise, and student equality. He argues that those views, without anyone intending them to do so, conspire to entrench practices that emphasize both knowledge transmission and testing procedures designed to determine if the transmission has taken place. In a paradoxical sense, according to Boostrom, educators' fondest assumptions imprison their practice. Teachers find themselves at the very center of this predicament: They want to teach for meaning, they want to influence for the good the lives of the young, but despite themselves, they continue to fall into transmission-based pedagogical approaches. As do members of the larger educational culture, they find it difficult to abandon hardened assumptions about knowledge, expertise, and students. Boostrom offers no panacea for this predicament. How could he, he might point out, given the depth and breadth of the assumptions that created the predicament in the first place? What we can and must do, he suggests, is undertake the project of seriously questioning those assumptions.

Boostrom also writes that genuine or transformative teaching always implies "giving up" something. That is, to be educated is not just to "add on" information or skills, but rather to undergo a qualitative change in outlook, in attitude, in belief. Nicholas C. Burbules, in Chapter 5, describes the reality of having to give things up in the course of education as one of its tragic dimensions. Burbules focuses on the tragic as an inherent aspect of teaching. He suggests that the complicated, value-laden nature of education virtually guarantees that teachers face repeated trade-offs in their work. For example, Burbules writes, many teachers want to share authority with their students to empower them and create a sense of community in the classroom. However, society then turns around and blames teachers for poor student test scores because the teachers have not doggedly put students through their skill-building paces. Providing another example of a tragic dimension of teaching, Burbules points out that many educators work tirelessly to help students acquire knowledge of subject matter and the ability to perform well in a work environment. But the same educators often wonder about the quality of life in the "adult world," raising the deeper issue of what makes adulthood (as currently experienced in society) superior to childhood.

In analyzing these and other tensions in teaching, Burbules urges the educational community to temper what he calls its "utopian" expectations. Educators set themselves up for disillusionment by entertaining relentlessly overweening expectations of teachers and students. As a consequence, an unnecessary cloud of disappointment and failure sometimes hangs over the field. Burbules offers the idea of the tragic as a response to those conditions. A recognition of the tragic, he writes, can remind teachers what inspired them to enter their field in the first place. That recognition can help them embrace teaching once again as a terrain of the possible rather than accept it as a scene of the impossible, which it quickly becomes when burdened with unrealistic and contradictory societal expectations.

Burbules and Boostrom both address squarely, albeit in different terms, the fact of loss in education: that to "gain" an education means, at the very least, abandoning some of one's prior beliefs and assumptions. This dynamic of gain and loss creates a permanent predicament in teaching, but one that, according to both authors, need not lead to a pessimistic or dour assessment of educational practice. Far from it. Each author in his own way suggests that acknowledging loss in education opens the door to a more significant educational experience.

In Chapter 6, Jo Anne Pagano proposes what a meaningful educational experience might look like. Focusing on teacher-student relationships in the university, Pagano urges faculty and students alike to reconceive the terms of their encounter in the classroom. She argues that both parties are subject to intense if sometimes indirect pressure from the media and societal politics. Those forces cajole faculty and students alike into picturing the world in black-and-white terms, into believing there is only one truth, only one correct way to see the world, only one correct curriculum, only one correct approach to teaching.

Rather than accepting this harsh conception of education, Pagano urges, faculty and students should consider the idea of *generative criticism* as an orientation to teaching and learning. According to Pagano, generative criticism invites teachers and students to resist easy "isms" and to consider the possibility that university education can be a means of growth for all. Rather than bringing out hostility and suspicion, the premises of discourse that Pagano advances encourage empathy and compassion. The implications of generative criticism are like those of reflection as put forth by John Dewey: "Reflection also implies concern with the issue—a certain sympathetic identification of our own destiny, if only dramatic, with the outcome of the course of events."[2] Generative criticism can bring to life dispositions and ideas that help people see beyond the present conflictual terms of discourse, with an eye not on sidestepping disagreement—quite the contrary, Pagano argues—but rather on developing agreement and disagreement that acknowledges our too often battered and subdued hope of creating a more humane world in which to live. Pagano suggests that "troubled times" will recur and will continue to spark difficult predicaments for faculty and students in the university. But she shows how these men and women need not let their educational relations be determined by the oppositional terms in which the media and society as a whole often frame the problems of education.

What happens when teachers experience tension between their educational values and hopes and the philosophy embedded in a curriculum they are asked to teach? In Chapter 7, Elaine Atkins takes up this issue. Like Pagano, Atkins focuses explicitly on university-level education. She describes in detail the experiences of two pairs of faculty members, each of which was asked to teach a fused English/Humanities course embedded in a program whose philosophy Atkins describes as postmodern or poststructuralist. The philosophy assumes that no "fixed truths" reside in literature and that no single or "final" interpretations of a work of literature are possible. The program emphasizes writing assignments that emerge from students' own responses to the reading and entails considerable peer review and student interaction—rather than, for example, centering on a teacher's knowledge. In addition, the program urges attention to social and historical contexts in the exploration of literary materials.

Atkins shows how one team of teachers, practicing in harmony with the program's vision, enacted a rich version of the program's philosophy. The other team remained at best ambivalent about the program's aims, and each member more or less clung to a prior, more "traditional" set of values and beliefs about teaching and curriculum. Atkins explores the tensions and ambiguities in the teachers' curricular deliberations. She embeds her analysis of the two cases in a broader consideration of the often unappreciated power that values and assumptions play in curriculum deliberation. She suggests that teachers, like the rest of humanity, can never fully know or articulate their most deeply held views and beliefs—a fact that can trigger predicaments in curriculum deliberation and perhaps in other collaborative educational ventures as well. But Atkins writes that acknowledging the presence and potential influence of those basic values and beliefs can help teachers bring aspects of them to the surface. That process may generate other predicaments, particularly if a teacher finds that her newly uncovered values are out of sync with a curriculum. However, Atkins implies that such a teacher would be able to control her destiny more directly than would a teacher who was uncomfortable with a curriculum but could not articulate the sources of that discomfort.

In Chapter 8, Kathryn H. Au and Sheila W. Valencia examine curriculum deliberation as it pivots around the always problematic issue of assessment. As the authors report, portfolio assessment is a relatively new venture designed to replace exclusive reliance on instruments such as standardized tests and multiple-choice and fill-in-the-blanks examinations. Portfolio assessment makes possible an ongoing, cumulative record of student learning by drawing together in "folio" fashion students' work in areas such as reading and writing.

Au and Valencia describe this approach as more than just another tool of evaluation. They regard it as a curricular innovation. Taking portfolio assessment seriously, they argue, compels the teacher to think with greater care about her curriculum, her students' academic needs and capabilities, and her long-term goals over the school year. Consequently, this form of assessment is not an add-on package that leaves the rest of a teacher's practices untouched.

The authors walk the reader through a variety of dilemmas that portfolio assessment creates for the educational community and the public at large. For example, Au and Valencia report that it takes several years to develop an understanding of portfolio assessment and to integrate it into classroom practice. But administrators and the public, as we all know too well, often insist on more immediate evidence of "improvement." Another dilemma centers around teachers' openness to a new approach like portfolio assessment. Should reformers work, at least at the start, with only those teachers who truly want to learn the approach, or should they endeavor to promote more systemic change? How can reformers balance their democratic impulse to include all teachers with the practical realities of trying to implement a new, demanding approach to assessment? Au and Valencia strongly urge the educational community to keep itself open to thinking about such questions rather than close down a promising new idea—and, by implication, others like it—simply because it presents new challenges to educators.

In Chapter 9, Magdalene Lampert takes her point of departure from a remark by William James, which could also serve as a motto for many of this book's chapters: "Every real dilemma is in literal strictness a unique situation; and the exact combination of ideals realized and ideals disappointed which each decision creates is always a universe without precedent, and for which no adequate previous rules exist." In contrast with Atkins's focus, Lampert's is on predicaments that emerge when teachers are aware of rather than ignorant of or confused about their values, hopes, and goals as teachers.

Lampert analyzes three episodes from elementary classrooms in which teachers "reframe" their goals when they realize that two or more of them suddenly conflict. For example, in one case a teacher is delighted with a writing contribution from a normally reticent student—but then she notices a spelling mistake in his sentence. Two educational goals are involved here: student engagement (and all that it can imply for becoming educated) and correct spelling (and all that it can imply for literacy). As the teacher speaks with the boy, she realizes the fragility of the situation: To insist on the correct spelling of the word might plunge the student into his usual reticence. In this classroom scene, the teacher finds her aims in conflict. The other two cases Lampert analyzes feature similar moments in which two or more goals suddenly conflict in ways the teacher could never have anticipated. Lampert suggests that these everyday predicaments are endemic in teaching. She shows how all three teachers responded to their predicaments by reorienting their approach by means of strategies she calls social reorganization in the classroom, negotiation with students, and changing classroom materials in conjunction with negotiation. Lampert cautions that those and other strategies cannot function like blueprints. In contrast, she presents them as examples of how teachers can reconceive their aims in the moment of teaching, rather than straining dogmatically to fulfill objectives that might have been formulated even before the teachers met their individual students.

In Chapter 10, the final chapter of the book, David T. Hansen returns full circle to a source of predicaments that Robert E. Floden introduced: teachers and the knowledge they do and do not possess. Hansen focuses on the fact that teachers, while engaged in teaching, can never keep tabs on everything they are doing or on all the influences they are having on students. Teachers can never fully perceive the impact that their actions, their character, and their everyday habits of working have on students' learning, whether *learning* refers to academics or to attitudes and beliefs.

Teachers may wish to know what impact they are having on their students. They may question the students or even audiotape or videotape themselves to assess whether their everyday styles of working discourage students or promote a productive classroom environment. But such self-study, however useful it may be, will not eliminate the fact that teachers, if they are indeed attending to their students, cannot watch themselves while in the act of teaching. This condition creates a permanent "blind spot" in the practice of teaching. And the situation looks even more complex when we recall that a teacher's character, habits of working, and beliefs do not stand still. They evolve in ways that teachers cannot always monitor, much less control. Consequently, teachers can never know for sure if they are having the good influence they hope to have when they are in the presence of their students. Hansen suggests that if teachers reflect on their character and on their vision and aims as educators, they can build the confidence they need to respond to this predicament. But it remains a predicament nonetheless—a permanent feature of the work that calls on teachers to act on faith in their own possibility for growth rather than to strive for an unrealizable certainty.

* * *

Predicaments compel people to reconceive their circumstances and what they can realistically accomplish. Predicaments require compromise and trade-offs. People can always elect to sidestep predicaments, but that course of action usually means abandoning human possibilities rather than creating new ones. The philosopher Charles Taylor sheds light on the subject in a recent, pathbreaking study of the moral life. In analyzing different views of the moral, he poses the following concern: "Isn't there a danger of ironing out too quickly what is paradoxical in our deepest moral sense, of reconciling too quickly the conflicts, making a synthesis of what cannot easily be combined, in short of making our moral predicament look clearer, more unified, more harmonious, than it really is?"[3] Taylor's work is an inquiry into the difficulties human beings encounter in a world of contrasting and sometimes conflicting values, beliefs, and ethical understandings, many of which are rooted deep in the human past. He encourages his audience to ponder how to dwell within this condition, rather than to see it as artificial or unnatural or as a "problem" to be eliminated by means of the appropriate policies or political arrangements. Taylor argues that reconciling differences and disagreements is possible and is worthy of our very best efforts. But his basic assumption—one he invites us to consider—is that given the reality of human lives and communities, new differences, new disagreements, and new dilemmas will always emerge. He documents the perils, both potential and actual, of rejecting that assumption.

This book identifies and suggests ways of thinking about predicaments in teaching. As this introduction suggests, the focus of the book varies from the particular to the general, from problematic situations in the classroom to problematic conditions that characterize teaching as a social practice in our era. The authors share the conviction that such predicaments do not call for programmatic resolution—an elusive and possibly harmful aim, to echo Taylor's warning. Rather, the problems require continued reflection and concern. This book seeks to present not resolution but an orientation. It offers ways of perceiving the work of teachers that shift our focus from "problem-solution" to "condition-acceptance." That acceptance translates into acknowledging the predicaments in teaching rather than wishing them away or trying to ignore them. Predicaments accompany the work, and to pretend otherwise diminishes the teacher's own agency.

To "accept" the problematic conditions of the practice does not imply passivity. Rather, it suggests moving actively as a teacher to reframe and reconceive situations. This notion of reframing, which Lampert uses explicitly, or of reseeing or reexamining circumstances informs each chapter.[4] The book urges all who teach to take a broader view of their work, to see that predicaments accompany and constrain teaching but that they do not define it. Predicaments do not control teachers—unless teachers let them do so. As Boostrom suggests, teachers may be pulling upstream, but they have oars and can use them to make headway. Over the course of a career, that headway can be substantial and invaluable, as anyone who gratefully remembers a teacher can readily attest. We invite readers to approach the chapters from this point of view, to read them not for solutions to intractable dilemmas but for their orientation toward good practice.

Readers might also wish to identify and think about predicaments other than those presented here. We make no pretense of having "covered all the bases." Far from it. Our sense is that the predicaments that accompany the work of teachers are more numerous, more thorny, but also more intriguing, than research on teaching up to the present moment has shown. How might teachers think about the need to balance attention to individual students with attention to the whole class? How might they think about balancing attention to their work with attention to their own families, friends, and outside interests? How might they create ways to renew and reinvigorate their faith and hope in teaching, even as their society, and perhaps their own colleagues and students, sometimes give them cause for despair and pessimism? The human richness and depth of teaching, its almost indescribable social importance, its long history rooted in the very beginnings of culture—all suggest that we still have much to learn and to appreciate about the practice. We hope that this book will provoke readers to continue charting their own paths of exploration, understanding, and commitment.

Notes

1. See D. L. Finkel and G. S. Monk, "Teachers and Learning Groups: Dissolution of the Atlas Complex," in C. Bouton and R. Y. Garth (Eds.), *Learning in Groups* (San Francisco: Jossey-Bass, 1983), pp. 83–97.

2. John Dewey, *Democracy and Education* (New York: Free Press, 1966 [first published in 1916]), p. 147.

3. Charles Taylor, *Sources of the Self: The Making of the Modern Identity* (Cambridge: Harvard University Press, 1989), p. 98.

4. See also Margret Buchmann and Robert E. Floden, *Detachment and Concern: Conversations in the Philosophy of Teaching and Teacher Education* (New York: Teachers College Press, 1993); Nona Lyons, "Dilemmas of Knowing: Ethical and Epistemological Dimensions of Teachers' Work and Development," *Harvard Educational Review*, 60 (1990): 159–180; and Philip W. Jackson, *The Practice of Teaching* (New York: Teachers College Press, 1986).

2

Reforms That Call for Teaching More Than You Understand

ROBERT E. FLODEN

Reform is a perennial condition of schooling in the United States. Whether motivated by apparently poor performance in international comparisons, concerns about economic productivity, or changing conceptions about fundamental knowledge, the public repeatedly asks schools to improve. Reforms spring up to meet each request, often seeming to recycle recommendations from previous decades.[1] Although no reform ever achieves all it sets out to, each new movement gathers optimistic proponents, is embraced by many schools and educators, and is eventually replaced by a successor. The reforms often deposit a residue but leave the basic structure of schooling intact.[2]

The continual press to change has many sources. Some reforms are spurred by changes in knowledge about teaching and learning; others grow from changes in priorities for student learning. Americans see schools as the solution to a host of social problems, calling on them to train workers for tomorrow's jobs, develop character, empower a democratic citizenry, and build community. Schools cannot serve all those functions adequately, so priorities shift among them, swayed by changes in the political winds. The public's relatively short attention span also contributes to repeated changes in educational goals.[3] Educational leaders, both in the schools and outside the schools, make their careers by championing new initiatives, so the focus of reform changes as its leaders do.

Although any attempt to change schools must take teachers into consideration, some past reforms have sought to minimize dependence on teachers. Curriculum reformers of the 1960s, for example, often saw the development of "teacher-proof curricula" as a way to change schools while bypassing teachers. Experience with reforms based solely on new curricula was disappointing, so current reforms recognize that teachers must play a leading role in change. This shift, together with arguments that teachers can and should be seen as professionals, has convinced reformers that teachers are central to improving education.[4]

Although skepticism about the staying power of any one reform tempers teachers' enthusiasm, they are typically willing to embrace new content and instructional approaches,[5] at least early in their careers.[6] To make these changes, teachers need to learn new content, new approaches to teaching, and new information about how students learn and how to involve parents. The inevitable shifts in the focus of reform mean that such learning is always required; new expectations call for new learning, often before the expectations of the prior reform wave are met.

The need for teacher learning, prompted by reform, is thus repeatedly present. Sometimes the needed learning amounts to a brief review or study of a new topic or two. A "back-to-basics" reform, for example, may require teachers to review topics learned some years before that are once more appearing in the curriculum. At other times training in specific teaching techniques is needed. Teachers might, for instance, be encouraged to wait longer for student responses or to call on pupils in order rather than letting them volunteer.

Other reforms, however, ask teachers to make more radical changes in content, in classroom process, or in both. In such cases, the learning needed goes beyond a slight adjustment or a reminder of something once familiar. Some of the curriculum reforms of the 1960s were demanding in this way. The "new math," for example, asked teachers to teach the formal foundations of mathematics, with in-service preparation scarcely sufficient to cover spelling the new vocabulary. That reform failed, partly because teachers weren't taught enough of the new content. Teachers were asked to teach content they hadn't learned themselves, with results that satisfied no one.

The current reform again calls for teaching more challenging content. The goals seem more appealing to a broad audience this time around—teaching for understanding, solution of real problems, and application. Once again, however, the revised standards for student achievement call for students to master topics—within and about the subject area—that were not previously part of the K–12 curriculum or part of the content of teacher preparation. Understanding *why* the algorithms of arithmetic work, for example, was not a requirement when today's teachers attended elementary school, and their further studies in high school and college seldom returned to this topic. Preparation for teaching likewise stressed proficiency in using, but not understanding, those algorithms. How can teachers respond to this wave of reform, given that they will, once more, be expected to teach new content with little time and resources for their own learning?

A sharp discrepancy between the content teachers have learned and the content they are now expected to teach is found in many subject areas, not just mathematics. A teacher preparing to teach high school history, for example, might have completed a history major with honors and have earned strong ratings on the practical aspects of teaching, yet never have pondered questions about the nature of evidence and argument. Just such an appreciation for how historians know is, however, what some reformers hope high school seniors will learn.

The resulting predicament for teachers is that they are asked to teach content they have never learned. Teachers are expected to help students understand how historical evidence should be evaluated, but those teachers have not typically learned the procedures and criteria for such evaluation. Teachers are asked, in other words, to teach more than they understand.

This predicament would be of little consequence if the new instructional content could be learned quickly and easily. In mathematics, for example, if new standards called for teaching only a few additional algorithms, teachers could quickly expand their repertoires. Reforms would require teachers to work a bit more but would not create a predicament.

The difference between the old and the new instructional content, however, is not a simple increase in the list of skills and knowledge to be learned; instead, the changes introduce new and unfamiliar dimensions into old content. Mathematics must be understood, not merely performed. Historical interpretations must be justified using incomplete, contradictory records, rather than recalled from a standard text. Comprehension of scientific theories must be demonstrated by applying them to unfamiliar circumstances rather than by choosing which of four options is the best answer.

Teachers cannot acquire the content they are asked to teach simply by attending "brush-up" or "content-update" workshops for a few afternoons or even for a week's intensive study.[7] The time needed is measured in months and years, rather than hours and days. For a subject that a teacher feels confident about and is eager to learn, a college course or two might be enough to get a handle on the new content. That knowledge could then be brought to bear on K–12 instruction with further work and coaching. More is required, however, when teachers doubt that they will themselves ever achieve the deep understanding expected of their students. Many elementary school teachers, for example, are women whose experience as elementary and secondary school students led them to believe that they were poor students of science and mathematics. As a result, they stopped taking science and math courses midway through high school. They now feel that they might be able to memorize vocabulary and algorithms but despair of ever seeing the sense in those words and rules.

Those elementary school teachers, even more than other teachers, face the predicament: How can I teach what I don't understand? Addressing the predicament raises concrete questions such as: When students put forward ideas that I don't feel I can evaluate, should I give them general encouragement or raise questions about the grounds for their positions, grounds that may be equally difficult to judge? What should I do if a student's answer to a test question doesn't match the scoring guideline but seems creative?

Current policies give teachers little guidance about how those questions should be answered or about the initial directions in which changes in teaching are moving. The language of reform encourages teachers to move away from comfortable modes of practice, without clarity about what they should move toward. The reforms give general guidance, rather than specific suggestions. Teachers are told: "Listen more carefully to students," "Teach for understanding, not for recall," and "Create a community of learners." Teachers are to assess students by having them perform "authentic" tasks as part of instruction.

Knowing how to follow such advice depends on having a good grasp of central terms such as *understanding, community,* and *authentic.* So teachers face another version of trying to teach more than they know. They are asked to change to practices of which they have no clear images. Teachers with experiences of "understanding" and "community" in their own learning are in good shape; those without such experiences find little specific guidance.

Even if the prescribed ways of teaching were clearer, the proposed changes increase the uncertainties of teaching by revealing more of what students do and do not understand, by linking the progress of any given lesson to the unpredictable contributions of students, and by highlighting the uncertainties inherent in the subject matter.[8] The upshot is that this reform is not one in which teachers can simply be encouraged to implement specific changes in practice; they must become involved in creating a new practice.[9] If the new practice addresses both subject matter and student learning, teachers must understand how to learn as they teach, working with students when they encounter content neither they nor the students have mastered, and attending to what students are learning in deciding how teaching practices should be revised.

In what follows, I consider whether teachers can escape from their present predicament, a challenging version of the enduring problem of being asked to make changes with apparently insufficient time to prepare for them. Although I argue that the predicament cannot be completely dissolved, its force can be reduced by shifting from thinking of the teacher as the sole source of knowledge to recognizing that students themselves, curricular materials, and new technological tools are all teaching resources. An advantage of the current reform is that it highlights those resources, emphasizing classroom discourse as a source of learning and enthusiastically embracing information technologies. Teachers are still central, but their altered role means that what they need most is knowledge about how to find and evaluate answers to questions—questions about the subject matter and about teaching and learning. Traditional course work and in-service workshops have not been oriented toward helping teachers become better inquirers, but other professional activities, such as the development of new methods of student assessment, may give teachers the help they need.

Can We Conceive of Teaching What We Don't Understand?

Just how serious is this predicament? Is it true that teachers have no hope of teaching more challenging content until they have mastered it? Does this mean that educational reforms must be put on hold while teachers undergo a lengthy period of intensive study? One interpretation of "teaching" compels a discouraging answer to those questions. The necessity of understanding what you teach is the point behind Shulman's aphorism, "Those who understand, teach,"[10] and its relative, "Those who don't understand, can't teach." The strong link between understanding and teaching also undergirds the arguments for increased subject matter preparation for teaching.[11] What sorts of understanding are considered necessary or most important depends on the operating conception of teaching.

Commentators voice two major opinions on how strong the link between understanding and teaching should be. Each view is connected with a different idea of what constitutes teaching. One group holds that the link should be strong, that successful teaching for understanding is *impossible* for *topics* the teacher does not understand. This strong position implies that teachers should not bother to try to teach for understanding until they understand the material themselves, because they cannot be successful.

The other group claims that teachers' understanding of a topic helps them teach for understanding but is not necessary. This group acknowledges the importance of teachers' knowledge but emphasizes understanding how to approach new content, rather than concentrating on mastery of every topic to be taught. With a sense of what to do when they get "stuck," teachers may help students understand topics that are initially puzzling to the teachers and the students alike.

At first glance, the first viewpoint seems self-evident. How could a teacher effectively fulfill any instructional roles—offering information, answering student questions, designing learning opportunities, responding to student comments—without understanding the content students are to learn? How could a teacher offer the appropriate information without understanding what is offered? How could student questions be answered? How could the teacher devise learning opportunities or, more importantly, evaluate their appropriateness and effectiveness? How could the teacher decide whether to support a student response, suggest that it be modified, or recommend a sharply different perspective?

Although the first belief has surface appeal, it is grounded in the questionable view that teaching means having teachers transmit knowledge to receptive students. Proponents of this view hold that teachers cannot teach what they do not understand because teaching consists of moving knowledge from teachers to students. If teachers lack understanding, they cannot pass understanding on to their students. But this knowledge-transfer model of teaching and learning is now in disfavor.

How is it that teachers can teach more than they understand? Why, in other words, should we reject the idea that a strong link between understanding and teaching is necessary? The key is recognizing that teachers are not the sole font of information. Students have many other sources of knowledge, or more accurately, opportunities for learning. Although scholars do not agree on exactly how students acquire knowledge (for instance, on the degree to which it is constructed or assimilated), they agree that learning occurs by means of students' mental activity, not by means of passive reception. Students' opportunities to learn arise from encounters with other students, with curricular materials, and with adults other than their teachers as well as from listening to explanations teachers themselves offer.

Where Else Might Content Knowledge Arise?

Students can learn things the teacher doesn't understand from other sources inside and outside the classroom. Two important sources of knowledge are the students themselves and curricular materials. To what extent do those sources of knowledge extricate teachers from their predicament? In what ways do the limits of teachers' understanding continue to impede or limit student learning? What sorts of teacher knowledge are most important for helping students learn when educational reforms introduce content that goes beyond teachers' understanding?

Students as Their Own Teachers

The current wave of reform combines its call for student understanding with advocacy for greater student engagement in active learning. The reforms promote transforming classrooms into communities of learners, in which the teacher is only one of many participants. Cooperative learning is the topic of many in-service workshops. Construction of knowledge through discourse among peers is seen as a major route to understanding. Placing students more at the center of the classroom—active in creating knowledge as well as in learning—alters the terms of the predicament teachers face. Rather than having responsibility for providing answers, teachers must know how to guide classroom discussions so that the participants build appropriate, grounded understanding.

If classroom learning can rely heavily on interactions among students and on insights that students achieve independently, the need for teachers' content understanding is reduced, or at least revised. For concepts that the teacher feels shaky about, the students can serve as a resource. More importantly, the classroom community can, according to some constructivist theorists, build the understanding, from the bottom up, as it were. Students gain knowledge by working through problems and puzzles, much as would scholars. No one—including the teacher—needs to possess the understanding in advance; it is developed as a solution.

The teacher still has a role in promoting student understanding, however. Given the human propensity for errors in reasoning, classroom discourse may not lead to well-justified beliefs unless participants attend to rules of evidence and argument, such as those established by scholarly communities. Teachers can help their classes learn to follow such rules, even if the teachers themselves do not understand all the concepts and domains to which the rules may be applied.

Teachers may ask students to pursue topics on their own, applying intellectual tools they have acquired (with the teachers' help) to new content areas. A simple example makes the point: A teacher may use her understanding of literary analysis to help students learn how to study a poem, how to analyze its themes and structures. The teacher may then ask students to use their understanding of literary analysis to examine the work of poets the teacher has not herself read. By working on this assignment, students may come to understand poets and poems that the teacher does not understand. Although the teacher might be able to understand those poets if she took the time to do so (in other words, it is not that the teacher *cannot* understand the poems), the students have in this example managed to learn something the teacher does not currently understand.

One might ask whether, in this example, it is accurate to say that the teacher *taught* content she didn't understand, since it was the students' effort that produced the learning. That challenge begs the question, because it restricts "teaching" to those circumstances in which the teacher "gives" knowledge to students. The teacher helped the students acquire the tools to do the analysis, created an assignment in which the students read the poetry, and may even have checked whether the students used the analytic tools appropriately. The teacher thereby engaged in instructional activities that led to student learning. Barring some specific objection, this should count as teaching.

Moreover, teaching is not only about helping students acquire understanding. Reformers also hope that students acquire a desire to continue learning outside school, gain the ability to work cooperatively, and develop their powers of creativity. None of those attributes can simply be transmitted to students. Motivation, cooperation, and creativity can grow out of participation in activities that involve a variety of subjects. The teacher's role in promoting such learning is a combination of exemplifying those goals (for example, displaying her own eagerness to learn) and arranging classroom activities that encourage creative, cooperative efforts.

The poetry example can be extended to other subject areas. The teacher of a science class, for example, can teach students general principles of inquiry (such as how to measure accurately, how to analyze fluctuations in experimental results, how to control variables, and how to interpret graphs). The teacher might subsequently assign experiments involving light and prisms, then check to see whether students were measuring properly, representing their data accurately on graphs, and so on. By completing those experiments, students could gain an understanding of light and prisms that exceeds the understanding of the teacher. As the teacher in the poetry example does, the science teacher teaches the students things that she herself does not understand. By drawing on students themselves, teachers can teach more than they know; teachers' knowledge does, however, help to ensure that what students learn is well grounded.

The Roles of Curricular Materials and Information Technology

Teachers can also teach more than they know by using curricular materials that fill in the areas where teachers feel weak. With such materials, teachers need not understand everything students learn. If teachers know enough to follow the materials, even though they don't really understand the content of the lesson, the curricular materials can do the instructional work. The systems of "programmed instruction" created in the 1960s are examples of such "teacher-proof" curricula. In creating those systems, subject matter experts and curriculum developers took on the job of explaining concepts, devising student assignments, and creating tests to monitor student progress. The classroom teacher's job was to oversee a system in which students read assigned pages in a book, completed assignments and tests, and checked their answers against an answer book.

While such curricula were designed to convey subject understanding without depending on teachers' expertise, the typical experience with the systems demonstrated that teacher knowledge remained a critical factor. In the worst cases, attempts to bypass the teacher led to situations such as that described by Erlwanger, in which a student managed to progress through the curriculum despite his fundamental misunderstanding of the content.[12] Had a teacher with an understanding of the subject area been more closely involved with the student's work, a correction in course could have been achieved.

That misfiring of the system is one way in which teacher understanding continues to be important. Teachers' understanding may also continue to be important because instructional processes recommended in reforms involve students' learning to talk to one another in particular ways. To the extent that those ways are dependent on content accuracy, it is necessary to have someone there who does understand what the point is. Whether in print or in a more modern medium, curricular materials are not able to follow student discussions and decide how and when to interject, redirect, or summarize.

Teachers can also use information technology to supplement their knowledge or to connect students with experts and information. The technologies are rapidly evolving, building on network connections to people and data, multimedia resources on media with rapidly expanding storage capacities, intelligent tutoring systems, and systems for managing classroom investigations. Such tools do reduce student dependence on the teacher and the text as sources of information. The predicament for teachers does not disappear, however; it takes another shape.

The wealth of available information can also be a confusing welter. Information obtained from individuals outside the classroom can be misleading or inaccurate. Not everyone who responds to a query is an expert in the relevant field. Students need to learn how to make productive use of these tools, how to master these rapidly evolving information systems. Once more, teachers need to increase their understanding, with limited support for that learning.

Heaton's work includes an example that illustrates the problems with using tools (in this case, the curriculum) as the sole source of content understanding.[13] Heaton has a stronger background in mathematics than most elementary teachers do, including course work (and good grades) in college calculus and experience working with outstanding mathematics educators, such as Ball and Lampert, who focus their work on teaching elementary school mathematics for understanding. Moreover, Heaton has an outstanding record as a teacher, including recognition as Vermont's teacher of the year.

As part of her doctoral study, Heaton taught elementary school mathematics on a regular basis, using the CSMP curricular materials. The materials present addition and subtraction as functions, using arrows to represent operations such as adding 2 or subtracting 15, and ask students to work with the arrows rather than write computation problems in standard notation. The intent of the curriculum developers was to help children see arithmetic operations as particular cases of mathematical functions, a basic concept about the relationships among numbers. Although students practice computation, the materials are intended to get them to understand simultaneously such concepts as addition, subtraction, function, inverse, and number.

Partway through her work with the materials, Heaton realized that although she was following the directions in the teachers' guide and her classes seemed to be going well, she did not understand some of the basic ideas being taught. She was asking students to notice "patterns" in the results of their work with the function arrows, but Heaton found that she did not know which of the "patterns" students saw were mathematically relevant and which were mere superficial similarities. Despite her background in mathematics and her experience in teaching, she did not know what counted as a "pattern" and what did not. She found, to her surprise, that she was trying to teach something that she didn't understand.

The CSMP materials were constructed with the thought that they would carry the burden of "understanding" the mathematical content to be taught. The curriculum developers intended for students to understand basic ideas in mathematics, such as "function," but did not think that they could assume that typical elementary teachers already understood those concepts. So the materials and teachers' guide were written so that if teachers followed the directions in the guide and children did the problems, there was a good chance that students would begin to grasp the mathematical ideas.

As Heaton's example illustrates, however, an instructional approach that still involves the human teacher (as most do in elementary school mathematics) is likely (perhaps certain) to depend on some teacher judgments and comments to students. The teacher's guide suggested that Heaton ask students to look for patterns. For the students to make mathematical sense out of this exercise, Heaton had to make some indications of which "patterns" made mathematical sense and which did not. Given the unusually strong background Heaton possessed, it is likely that few teachers would have a better idea than she did. In other words, although the curriculum was carrying some of the burden of setting up experiences that would promote student understanding, the package required the teacher to have more than the usual degree of content understanding.

What and Where Should Teachers Learn?

If classrooms place student discussions more at the center, make use of the content explanations embedded in curricular materials, and use information technology for access to further content expertise, teachers need not understand all the content their students are supposed to learn. Teachers' content knowledge remains important, but emphasis shifts from transmitting knowledge to helping direct student learning, avoiding unproductive paths, and guarding students against alluring misconceptions. The additional resources of students, curricula, and technology ease the demands for teachers to learn some topics, but teachers continue to face the need to learn, with limited resources and time. Given that predicament, what opportunities for learning should they pursue? What learning should be given highest priority?

The typical occasions for teacher learning, college courses and in-service workshops, seldom focus on the learning that seems most urgent. Opportunities for learning also arise in activities, such as assessment, that blend learning about new subject matter with other professional work.

Learning to Inquire

I argued above that the predicament teachers now face should not be seen as a gap in their own understanding of the *topics* students are expected to learn. Because they are not the sole source of information on the topics, teachers can reenvision their role as helping students build understanding by participating in classroom discussions, working with curricular materials, and reaching outside the classroom for information. To organize such classrooms, teachers need knowledge about inquiry. To guide classroom discussions so that they lead to justified conclusions, teachers need to understand the criteria for evaluating arguments and conjectures. Some principles of evaluation are general, such as that plausible counterarguments should be recognized and addressed. Other principles are specific to individual subject areas.

As they try out the changes in pedagogy recommended by reforms, teachers need to understand how to adapt and extend their practice in light of its effect on students. Applying to teaching the habits and tools of inquiry—close observation, probing student understanding, reflection, imagining alternatives—will lead to better informed choices.

Assigning priority to habits of inquiry is not new. John Dewey argued for it in the first half of this century,[14] and Joseph Schwab later echoed Dewey, with a special emphasis on the knowledge teachers need.[15] The return to Dewey is appropriate, because the curricular emphases of the current reform resemble his emphasis on solution of real-world problems, drawing on accumulated understanding found in the disciplines. The challenges Dewey posed for teachers also seem familiar—to understand the subjects well enough to guide student learning, but not simply to transmit inert bodies of fact. Like the teachers who faced an "impossible role" (to borrow from Schwab's title) in trying to realize Dewey's vision, today's teachers feel as though they must learn much more. What opportunities do they have to learn, especially to learn about inquiry in their subject areas and in their classrooms?

Study in Courses and Workshops

College courses are commonly available opportunities for teacher learning. Most teachers continue to take courses while they are teaching, sometimes in pursuit of an advanced degree. Given the scholarly orientation of most colleges and universities, such courses seem promising places to learn more about inquiry and to gain greater understanding of the subjects to be taught.

Too often, however, teachers find it difficult to locate a course of study focused on their needs. College courses typically focus either on teaching methods or on subject matter intended for students preparing for graduate school in the field. Visits to the classes with the first focus suggest that they are likely to concentrate on general and specific methods for teaching certain topics, helping teachers see what their students might get out of particular approaches and giving teachers opportunities to exchange ideas to add to their bags of tricks. But teachers are unlikely to spend much time increasing their own understanding of either the subject matter they are learning to teach or its distinctive methods of inquiry.[16]

Content courses offer opportunities to learn about advanced topics but seldom focus on the topics included in the K–12 curriculum or on how to gain more understanding of those topics. Those courses, usually offered by the disciplinary departments, are oriented toward students preparing for careers in the disciplines. They focus instruction on content needed to pursue advanced degrees in the disciplines, not on content needed to understand the topics taught in elementary and secondary school. The result is that doing well in such course work is no guarantee that teachers understand the content they are expected to teach or how to guide classroom discussions that focus on those topics. Studies of subject area majors in mathematics, history, and English show that successful majors often have difficulty explaining content taught at lower levels.[17]

Many mathematics majors, for example, know what rules to follow in doing arithmetic but have difficulty explaining the logic behind the rules. They may think that the impossibility of dividing by zero is simply a rule one has to memorize, rather than seeing how it follows from the explosion of the quotient as the divisor approaches zero.

For workshops taught outside the higher education system, the situation is similarly mixed. It can be difficult to find in-service workshops that pay serious attention to content learning, though some do exist.[18] Information on in-service programs often takes the form of advertisements. General directories of available offerings are seldom available. Moreover, even activities intended to build subject matter knowledge sometimes skirt subject matter issues because of the fear that directly addressing misunderstandings may offend teachers or reduce their motivation to participate.[19]

In-service offerings are generally seen as lacking in substance, led by consultants with polished but superficial presentations. Popular programs for professional development often focus on structural changes, such as restructuring schools and creating career ladders. On close examination, it seems that such efforts seldom contribute much to the improvement of instruction, let alone focus on increasing teachers' subject matter knowledge.[20]

College courses and in-service workshops could be redirected to offer content that would help teachers with their predicament. If the topic focus were shifted to parallel the K–12 curriculum, teachers might have opportunities to fill the gaps in their understanding of what they are expected to teach.[21] If teachers could participate in guided discussions of unfamiliar topics, those teachers might learn how to guide such discussions in their own classrooms. By being engaged in inquiries into classroom practice, teachers could develop habits of inquiry to assist them as they figure out how reform pedagogy can be adapted for effective local use.

At present, such courses and workshops remain rare. In any case, they are unlikely to address all teachers' needs for greater understanding. Given the press of time, such learning opportunities outside the ongoing activities of professional life can make only a partial contribution to helping teachers teach more than they know. Other opportunities for teacher learning are needed.

Learning from Doing Assessment

Assessment systems are often used to check on whether teachers are being successful in helping students reach new learning goals. Dissatisfaction with multiple-choice tests has prompted many states and districts to adopt assessments in which students demonstrate in other ways that they have the hoped-for abilities, such as the ability to write or to solve mathematics problems.

Reformers argue that assessments should be "authentic," asking students to perform tasks representative of the desired learning goals, rather than completing test items that serve only as indicators of some related constituent ability. If the goal is for students to be able to write short stories, going through multiple drafts to reach a final version, then an authentic assessment would involve examining short stories written and revised over a period of time, rather than asking students to take a test of grammar and knowledge of story structure. Such authentic assessments are also claimed to solve the problem of teaching to the test. If the desired performance becomes the test, then teaching to the test is simply teaching to the hoped-for outcome—a virtue, not a vice.

Assessments that make new learning goals transparent, like the curricular materials discussed previously in this chapter, may help teachers teach more than they understand. If the assessment matches what students should learn, learning to assess student progress involves learning the content to be taught. Although a multiple-choice exam can be administered and scored without any understanding of the content being tested, teachers may not be able to carry out the newer type of assessment if they do not understand the content over which students are supposed to demonstrate mastery. It is difficult to gauge the chain of mathematical reasoning a student has used to solve a problem if the teacher has a weak grasp of mathematics.

Activities focused on learning to do the assessment may help teachers learn enough of the new content to evaluate the products of student work. The workshops and the teacher network organized in support of Vermont's performance assessment illustrate how attention to assessment can help teachers through their predicament.

In the early 1990s, the Vermont Department of Education instituted statewide assessment in writing and mathematics, focusing on the collection and scoring of student portfolios. In grades four and eight, teachers had students put samples of work into folders across the year. At year's end, classroom teachers scored those portfolios using state guidelines, and a sample of students in each district was selected for scoring by a statewide group of teachers. To be scorable, the work in the portfolios had to have certain general characteristics. The writing portfolios had to contain work from specific genres; the work in the mathematics portfolios had to include solutions to problems along with the steps used to solve the problems and the reasoning supporting those steps.

Since various statewide projects had supported elementary- and middle-school writing instruction for a decade or so before Vermont implemented the statewide assessment program, assembling the writing portfolios was not a great departure from previous practice. In mathematics, however, most elementary school teachers had previously used a traditional approach to mathematics, in which the only problems students solved were word problems matched to the computational skills being taught. Such problems did not lend themselves to inclusion in the portfolios, because they required little, if any, reasoning; students simply plugged the numbers from the problem into whatever mathematical procedure they had been practicing.

To inform teachers about the assessment process and to train them in the scoring rubrics, in-service sessions were held, followed by periodic meetings of regional networks, led by teachers.

Many teachers believed that having to do mathematics portfolios led them to change their practice. One teacher felt that portfolios were the most important education reform in the state. Another characterized the portfolios as "an effective way to get teachers to change. . . . I embrace the [Vermont] standards. . . . I might not have done it otherwise."[22]

As the Vermont teachers learned what was required for the mathematics portfolio assessment, they realized that they had to teach problem solving if students were to have scorable portfolios, let alone do well on the assessment. Like most elementary school teachers, they had little preparation for this new content and often little understanding themselves of mathematical problem solving.

In the initial years of the assessment system, the state offered four in-service sessions per year on the new assessment. In-service activities that focused on scoring the mathematics portfolios offered opportunities for teachers to learn about problem solving. Discussing whether a student response included a good strategy for solving a problem, for example, required analysis of different approaches to solving the problem and of how to decide which ways were better than others. As the teachers worked through those problems, they learned something about problem solving and a bit about how it might be taught.

Working on the portfolio assessment also led teachers to request sources of problems that would be suitable for their classrooms. In response, references to problem-solving materials were included in the handouts distributed at the in-service sessions.

Networks of teachers were also organized. Network leaders led the sessions preparing teachers to carry out the assessments and also served as resources for teachers who had questions about the assessment or the associated approach to instruction.

Embodied in the tasks of helping students produce solutions to problems and scoring those solutions according to guidelines demanding attention to the mathematics content, portfolio assessment serves as a support for mathematics instruction that stretches teachers' understanding. A teacher who knows what a good problem solution looks like is in a position to help students produce good solutions, even when the mathematics of some problems is challenging.

However, as with curricular materials, the support is limited. Some teachers need more than a few in-service sessions to learn how to assign valid scores to mathematics portfolios. Deciding whether mathematical terms are used appropriately, for example, may prove difficult for some. In-service workshops may give teachers a superficial understanding that is sufficient for generating a score for every portfolio and even that approximates the score given by a mathematics expert, but a shallow understanding can lead teachers to include inaccuracies in their instruction.

Furthermore, although a good understanding of assessment can be a valuable guide to instruction, it is not sufficient. Teaching students to be good mathematical problem solvers requires more than the ability to know whether the instruction has been a success. Additional knowledge about students and subject matter is needed to appreciate why a student repeatedly fails to find a solution or persistently arrives at incorrect solutions. Detailed knowledge of what a good performance looks like will be an aid in helping teachers teach more than they understand, but it cannot completely compensate.

Conclusion

Much is made of the difficulties teachers face in teaching the challenging content promoted in recent reforms. Quite accurately, commentators note that a major obstacle is that changes in content expectations make it impossible for teachers to draw on their own experience as students as they search for instructional solutions. In particular, they are asked to teach concepts that they never studied, let alone mastered. Given time, they may master the new content, but they face the acute predicament of trying to teach concepts they don't understand.

With the help of good curricular materials and students ready to be active participants in their own learning, that seemingly impossible goal can be achieved. Nonetheless, further teacher learning is important for ensuring that students move toward valid understanding.

Teachers' understanding of subject matter, in particular their understanding of how warranted understanding is developed and tested, is of particular importance. Although critics of contemporary education often press for more attention to learning substantive facts and concepts, teachers may be able to make better use of an understanding of the processes of inquiry. The substance of some fields is constantly changing, with additional discoveries and revisions of prior theories. The processes used for investigation change little, at least in comparison; thus, what is learned about the processes scholars use to develop and test conjectures is less in need of continual updating.

More important, when a curricular unit or classroom discussion goes beyond content that teachers have mastered, an understanding of how to find answers to questions or to test the accuracy of a claim can be used to help students build accurate understanding. With proper guidance, students can be encouraged to learn beyond what the teacher knows. A teacher may be able to ask telling questions without knowing the answers.

Notes

Suzanne Wilson provided insightful comments on an early draft of this chapter.

1. Larry Cuban, "Reforming again, again, and again." *Educational Researcher* 19, no. 1 (1990, January): 3–13.

2. David K. Cohen, "Teaching practice: Plus ça change." In *Contributing to educational practice: Perspectives on research and practice,* edited by P. Jackson, 27–84

(Berkeley: McCutchan, 1988); David Tyack and W. Tobin, "The 'grammar' of schooling: Why has it been so hard to change?" *American Educational Research Journal* 31 (1994): 453–479.

3. Anthony Downs, "The issue-attention cycle and improving our environment." (Chicago: Real Estate Research Corporation, 1971).

4. For example, Deborah Loewenberg Ball, "Developing mathematics reform: What don't we know about teacher learning—but would make good working hypotheses?" (East Lansing: National Center for Research on Teacher Learning, College of Education, Michigan State University, 1995); David K. Cohen, "Teaching practice: Plus ça change"; Linda Darling-Hammond and Milbrey W. McLaughlin, "Policies that support professional development in an era of reform." *Phi Delta Kappan* 76 (1995): 597–604; Gary Sykes, "Reform of and as professional development." *Phi Delta Kappan* 77 (1996): 465–467.

5. Robert E. Floden, Andrew C. Porter, William H. Schmidt, Donald J. Freeman, and John R. Schwille, "Responses to curriculum pressures: A policy-capturing study of teacher decisions about content." *Journal of Educational Psychology* 73 (1981): 129–141.

6. Michael Huberman, "The professional life cycle of teachers." *Teachers College Record* 91 (1989): 31–58.

7. Hilda Borko and Ralph Putnam, "Learning to teach." In *Handbook of educational psychology,* edited by R. C. Calfee and D. C. Berliner, 673–708. (New York: Macmillan, 1996).

8. Robert E. Floden and Christopher M. Clark, "Preparing teachers for uncertainty." *Teachers College Record* 89 (1988):505–524; Robert E. Floden and Margret Buchmann, "Between routines and anarchy: Preparing teachers for uncertainty." In *Detachment and concern: Conversations in the philosophy of teaching and teacher education*, 211–221 (New York: Teachers College Press, 1993).

9. Deborah Loewenberg Ball, "Developing mathematics reform."

10. Lee S. Shulman, "Those who understand: Knowledge growth in teaching." *Educational Researcher* 15, no. 2 (1986): 4–14.

11. Hilda Borko and Ralph Putnam, "Learning to teach."

12. Stanley H. Erlwanger, "Benny's conception of rules and answers in IPI mathematics." *Journal of Children's Mathematical Behavior* 1, no. 2 (1973): 7–26.

13. Ruth M. Heaton, "What is a pattern? An elementary teacher's early effort to teach mathematics for understanding." (East Lansing: National Center for Research on Teacher Learning, College of Education, Michigan State University, 1995).

14. John Dewey, *How we think: A restatement of the relation of reflective thinking to the educative process.* (Chicago: Henry Regnery, 1933).

15. Joseph J. Schwab, "The impossible role of the teacher in progressive education." In *Science, curriculum and liberal education: Selected essays,* edited by Ian Westbury and Neil J. Wilkof (Chicago: University of Chicago Press, 1978/1956).

16. See Robert E. Floden, G. Williamson McDiarmid, and Nancy Jennings, "Learning about mathematics in elementary methods courses." In *Preparing tomorrow's teachers: The field experience. Teacher Education Yearbook IV,* edited by D. J. McIntyre and David M. Byrd, 225–241 (Thousand Oaks, CA: Corwin, 1996). For an example of a course that does focus more on content, see Deborah Loewenberg Ball, "Breaking with experience: The role of a preservice methods

course." (East Lansing: National Center for Research on Teacher Learning, College of Education, Michigan State University, 1989).

17. Examples can be found in Deborah Loewenberg Ball, "The subject matter preparation of prospective mathematics teachers: Challenging the myths." (East Lansing: National Center for Research on Teacher Learning, College of Education, Michigan State University, 1988); Suzanne Wilson, "Understanding historical understanding: Subject matter knowledge and the teaching of history." Doctoral dissertation, Stanford University, 1988; Dianne Holt-Reynolds and G. Williamson McDiarmid, "How do prospective teachers think about literature and the teaching of literature?" (East Lansing: National Center for Research on Teacher Learning, College of Education, Michigan State University, 1994).

18. J. S. Krajcik, J. W. Layman, M. L. Starr, and S. Magnusson, "The development of middle school teachers' content knowledge and pedagogical content knowledge of heat energy and temperature." Paper presented at the annual meeting of the American Educational Research Association, Chicago, April 1991; M. A. Simon, "Towards a constructivist perspective: An intervention study of mathematics teacher development." *Educational Studies in Mathematics* 22 (1991): 309–331.

19. See, for example, Suzanne Wilson, Steve Mattson, and Sarah Theule-Lubienski, "Challenges of multiple commitments: The case of the California Mathematics Project." Presentation at the annual meeting of the American Educational Research Association, New York, April 1996.

20. Richard F. Elmore, Penelope Peterson, and Sarah J. McCarthey. *Restructuring in the classroom: Teaching, learning, and school organization* (San Francisco: Jossey-Bass, 1995).

21. For a description of one such course, see Pam Schram, Sandra Wilcox, Perry Lanier, and Glenda Lappan, "Changing mathematics conceptions of preservice teachers: A content and pedagogical intervention." (East Lansing: National Center for Research on Teacher Learning, College of Education, Michigan State University, 1988).

22. Margaret E. Goertz, Robert E. Floden, and Jennifer O'Day, "Studies of education reform: Systemic reform. Volume II: Case studies." (New Brunswick, NJ: Consortium for Policy Research in Education, Rutgers University, 1995), 118.

3

Must We Motivate?

NEL NODDINGS

Teachers today are urged continually to motivate their students, to make their subjects interesting and lively so that students will give their attention and learn. Further, teachers are to have high expectations for all students. Is it reasonable to expect teachers to induce interest in all their students? In this chapter, I explore the psychological and political paradoxes that have arisen in the area of motivation. My conclusion is that we must work more closely with students' own motives if we are to succeed in teaching them things we take to be worthwhile and in preparing them for democratic life.

Is Intrinsic Motivation a Reasonable Expectation?

The question of whether intrinsic motivation is a reasonable expectation embodies an interesting ambiguity. At whom is the expectation directed? We might mean: Is it reasonable to expect that students will be intrinsically motivated? If this is our question, the answer is almost certainly yes. Students are interested in some things for their own sake; they have intrinsic interests. However, they may have little or no interest in the particular subject a teacher tries to teach them. The challenge to the teacher, then, is to find some way to link students' interests with the official subject or, in difficult situations, to set aside the official subject and teach something else. This is the way John Dewey would have teachers work, and sound psychological and political rationales seem to support such an approach.

The question can also point to a currently popular expectation directed at teachers. The contention is that if they really know their subjects and bring energy and artistry to the task, teachers should be able to arouse students' interest in the subject. Is *this* a reasonable expectation? The empirical evidence available suggests that the expectation may in fact be unreasonable. Further, there are deeper questions to probe: Why *should* students be aroused to interest in mathematics, physics, or grammar? What makes such arousal desirable and justifies the enormous effort demanded of teachers?

Many teachers today believe their own propaganda—that is, they believe something is wrong with either students or teachers if students do not evince an interest in a given subject. However, after many years of teaching, I have come to believe that this is a great mistake. If I were teaching high school mathematics again, I would certainly work hard to be sure that students did not like the subject *less* because of my efforts. But, first and foremost, I would respect their feelings. Many very nice, highly intelligent people dislike mathematics. With some understanding and humor, a teacher can accept this dislike. The problem then becomes one of politics and socialization. If we are honest with our students, if we politicize our classrooms, we can help them to understand what is at stake in accepting or rejecting instruction in mathematics. We are ready to accept any legitimate motive that arises from a sound base of information. If intrinsic motivation develops from this attempt to inform, we rightly feel great satisfaction; if it does not, we work unflaggingly with the student's present motive.

For the most part, after an initial flurry of interest in the early grades, kids have little interest in the usual tasks of schooling. "*Boring* is students' most frequently used word to describe their schools."[1] Again and again, researchers, teachers, and students confirm the complaint, and usually teachers are blamed. They blame one another and sometimes themselves. Douglas Heath reports: "Distressingly, I have not found a single school in which the majority of teachers describe their colleagues as enthusiastic and intellectually stimulating. Two-thirds of the teachers in one reputedly excellent school actually wished that they themselves could become more intellectually exciting persons."[2]

However, it can be hard to hang on to intellectual excitement when one's subject is rejected and mocked, when even the teacher becomes an object of ridicule for showing interest in it. Lee C. Colsant has described the pain and despair he experienced in trying to teach French culture to inner-city high school students. He refers to his early success and what has happened since: "They [the early successes] trace back to my first years of teaching in Quebec when I was alive with teaching. I felt close to my students then. Now I live with distance. The rendezvous I had with teaching has changed. I barely noticed my cherished discipline being smothered."[3]

Trying to teach his usual curriculum in his usual way, Colsant suffers rejection and insult. Here's the start of one class period:

"'Students, would you open your books to the section on the use of the partitive article, p. 23,' my teaching begins.

"'Who the fuck cares about the partitive article?' emerges from their turf."[4]

Colsant knows better than to ask who said that. The wording is particularly nasty, but the sentiment is universal. Fortunately for both the students and Colsant himself, he finds a way to reach many of his students. He gradually scraps the beloved old curriculum and starts afresh. First he allows conversation about topics other than French and thus gets to know his students better. He talks to them frankly about what he is going through and takes an active interest in what they are going through. Little by little, taking time to develop relations of care and trust, he constructs a curriculum suitable for his students.

David T. Hansen tells the story of another teacher, Mr. James, who has to give up the idea of teaching a standard curriculum. Working with learning-disabled and emotionally disturbed high school students, Mr. James understands that students as well as teachers suffer predicaments.

He sees himself as a rival to the complex circumstances and forces that lead his often troubled students astray. He seeks to bring to their lives what he calls "order," "peace," and "clarity." He conducts himself as a moral agent—as a person, that is, who *can* have a positive influence on students—and as a moral educator, a person whose pedagogical obligation is to steer students toward the good.[5]

In Mr. James we see a teacher who gives of himself because it is just this that his students need most—someone who steadfastly respects them and tries to bring order, peace, and clarity to their lives. Unlike Colsant, who still teaches some French, Mr. James has almost given up the discipline in which he was trained. Both teachers work with their students' motivations; both try to introduce new motives, closely connected to existing ones, especially social motives.

There are other ways to treat students. In the nineteenth century and the early part of this century, coercion was the standard approach. George Orwell described his misery at Crossgates, the British elementary public school at which he was "prepared" for an elite preparatory school. One paragraph recounts memories of class with the headmaster, Sim:

> He would tap away at one's skull with his silver pencil, which, in my memory, seems to have been about the size of a banana, and which certainly was heavy enough to raise a bump; or he would pull the short hairs around one's ears, or, occasionally, reach out under the table and kick one's shin. On some days nothing seemed to go right, and then it would be: "All right, then. I know what you want. You've been asking for it the whole morning. Come along,

> you useless little slacker. Come to the study." And then whack, whack, whack, whack, and back one would come, red-wealed and smarting . . . to settle down to work again. This did not happen very often, but I do remember more than once being led out of the room in the middle of a Latin sentence, receiving a beating and then going straight ahead with the same sentence, just like that. It is a mistake to think such methods do not work. They work very well for their special purpose. Indeed, I doubt whether classical education ever has been or can be successfully carried on without corporal punishment. The boys themselves believed in its efficacy.[6]

Motivation, in the Crossgates model, comes at the end of a rattan switch. It is small wonder that thoughtful educators, reacting to the horrors of physically coercive schooling, often came to recommend an exactly opposite approach—complete freedom. Summerhill is probably the best-known example of a school in which the entire program was guided by students' own motives.[7] Must we choose between Crossgates and Summerhill? Coercion or permissiveness?

An alternative is seen in the work of Colsant and Mr. James. Mr. James describes his teaching as work on "a battleground of values." His students' motives have to provide the energy; his values have to guide the process and serve as possible ends for his students to consider. The whole enterprise is highly interactive.

Mr. James's teaching is not without its flaws. Indeed, Hansen suggests that Mr. James may have gone too far in abandoning a concern for academic achievement. Reasonable people can differ on this. Perhaps Mr. James could do more to help his students master basic subject matter. It is difficult for a reader-observer to judge. But his approach seems right; he works with a combination of students' motives and the needs he has uncovered through living with them. He neither ignores their motives nor accepts them without criticism, but (apparently tirelessly) guides them toward better social behavior. The process is clearly interactive.

What prevents the widespread use of thoroughly interactive methods? There are probably several answers to this question. No doubt many people still harbor considerable sympathy for the Crossgates model. Others find their own personal freedom and a degree of self-righteousness in adopting the Summerhill model (just leave the kids alone). However, the answer I want to explore more deeply here is political. The late-twentieth-century emphasis on equality has led many educators to insist that "all children can learn" and that all should have the same education. The recalcitrance of outcomes to conform with this ideal is a source of great frustration. But instead of reconsidering basic premises, educators keep toiling, planning, and dreaming to produce equal outcomes. Reconsideration might bring the realization that the equality prized in a democracy does not imply or depend on sameness. John Dewey, who consistently rejected permissiveness, nevertheless agreed completely with Rousseau on this:

> The general aim translates into the aim of regard for individual differences among children. Nobody can take the principle of consideration of native powers into account without being struck by the fact that these powers differ in different individuals. The difference applies not merely to their intensity, but even more to their quality and arrangement. As Rousseau said: "Each individual is born with a *distinctive* temperament. . . . We indiscriminately employ children of different bents on the same exercises; their education destroys the special bent and leaves a dull uniformity. Therefore after we have wasted our efforts in stunting the true gifts of nature we see the short-lived and illusory brilliance we have substituted die away, while the natural abilities we have crushed do not revive."[8]

What I want to explore next is why today's liberals, who belong to a lengthy tradition of freedom, have so often, in the name of equality, adopted a position of coercion with respect to schooling. Why all this interest in a national curriculum, national goals, universal requirements, and academic preparation for all students?

Education for Freedom

Sir Isaiah Berlin described two concepts of liberty (or freedom)—one negative, one positive. The negative concept is at the heart of liberalism. The basic question for liberals, Berlin wrote, is "What is the area within which the subject—a person or group of persons—is or should be left to do or be what he is able to do or be, without interference by other persons?"[9] Traditionally, the answer that gives the widest possible scope to noninterference is the one preferred by liberals, but two centuries of thought have produced much debate, and "liberals" have been scattered over the political spectrum according to where they stand on this issue. Those who place great value on equality often tolerate considerable interference; those who cling to freedom as the highest value permit considerable inequality.

Berlin described the positive concept this way: "The 'positive' sense of the word 'liberty' derives from the wish on the part of the individual to be his own master. I wish my life and decisions to depend on myself, not on external forces of whatever kind."[10]

As Berlin noted, the two concepts seem very close at first glance. "Yet the 'positive' and 'negative' notions of freedom historically developed in divergent directions not always by logically reputable steps, until, in the end, they came into direct conflict with each other."[11] The negative concept has developed into a theoretical position that emphasizes process and procedures. It insists that initial conditions be such that all persons have the opportunity to exercise their choice of legitimate goods. This insistence has led to a deep rupture in liberalism because it necessitates a large role for government in establishing conditions of fairness, and this large role is what classical liberals have traditionally opposed.

The positive concept, concerned as it is with *who* shall govern (rather than how) has produced concepts of the ideal leader, citizen, and state. From this perspective, certain goods must be posited and affirmed. A state, its leaders, and its citizens must stand for something, and the state has an obligation to mold its citizens in light of its legitimate ideals.

Criticisms have been directed at both positions. The negative view seems to describe a fictitious person—one with no loves, connections, or ideals—a "rational" agent concerned primarily with procedures, not ends. It has also been charged with neglecting community, overemphasizing autonomy, and promoting an arrogant universalism ("everyone is just like us"). For present purposes, we can see that a traditional liberal position does not yield much guidance on child rearing and education. Its subjects are fully competent, rational adults, and the question arises as to how such people are produced. Further, critics might well ask: Is this all we want of our citizens?

The positive concept, at its extreme, has been identified with totalitarianism. Under this concept, a person is free to become what he or she *should* be, not what he or she might mistakenly want to be. Philosophy, political ideology, and philosophy of education are closely linked in this view. Giovanni Gentile, a prominent Italian philosopher, fascist, and educator, described the individual this way:

> The language that every man uses is that of his fathers, the language of his tribe or his clan or his nation . . . he cannot use it to say "This is *my* view" unless . . . he can say "This is *our* view," for at the root of the "I" there is a "We." The community to which an individual belongs is the basis of his spiritual existence; it speaks through his mouth, feels with his heart, and thinks with his brain.[12]

Thus, in the total community, if the state or the nation is right, there is no room for dissent. All speak with one mouth, feel with one heart, think with one brain. Individuals *become* the individuals they *should be* by dedicated participation in the community.

Paradoxically, although most of us reject the positive concept when we see it set out in its extreme form, we accept something like it as educators and parents. We feel it is necessary to steer our children toward some ideal. Sara Ruddick has described three fundamental maternal interests: preserving the life of the child, fostering his or her growth, and shaping an acceptable child.[13] Although different parents may have different conceptions of acceptability, virtually all parents want their children to be acceptable by some definition. For example, even if we place a high value on intellectual growth (as a traditional liberal might), most of us still want our children to be not only bright and clever in reasoning but also decent and compassionate.

Positive and negative views converge on one point—that children must be guided (even compelled) in ways that would be, from the negative view, repugnant if directed at adults. John Stuart Mill, for example, insisted that no civilized community should exercise control over any individual except to prevent harm to others; it should not control a person for his or her own good. But he hastened to say: "It is perhaps unnecessary to say that this doctrine is meant to apply only to human beings in the maturity of their faculties. We are not speaking of children. . . . Those who are still in a state to require being taken care of by others, must be protected against their own actions as well as against external injury."[14]

How do we prepare children for a life of rational autonomy? This question has been a source of dispute among liberals, and the most familiar answer has been to teach children the subjects and skills that "well-educated" adults already have. In this response, advocates of negative freedom have not differed greatly from proponents of positive freedom. Whereas the second group of thinkers state ideals with specific content (for example, knowledge and virtues), the first speak in terms of rational competence. John Dewey recognized this similarity—that both groups assume

> that there must be a mental picture of some desired end, personal and social . . . and that this conception of a fixed determinate end ought to control educative processes. Reformers share this conviction with conservatives. The disciples of Lenin and Mussolini vie with captains of capitalistic society in endeavoring to bring about a formation of dispositions and ideas which will conduce to a preconceived goal.[15]

In contrast, Dewey insisted that, under an experimental method, "every care would be taken to surround the young with the physical and social conditions which best conjure, as far as freed knowledge extends, to release of personal potentialities."[16] However, it is not clear that Dewey himself was entirely free of an ideal conception. In many of his writings in which he is not talking specifically about the perversity of preconceived ideals, he reveals his desire to educate so that people will be able to formulate and solve problems, engage in consummatory experiences, develop religious attitudes (without religion), participate intelligently in democratic activities, and contribute generously to well-chosen communities. In his emphasis on process-like goals free of specific content, Dewey is closer to the negative liberal view than to the positive one, but in his wide-ranging discussion of human potentialities, he hovers at the edge of a positive view. He departs from both in his insistence that education is its own goal—that we cannot create an education that "prepares" children for a way of life they have not experienced in education itself. For Dewey, education must provide, in appropriate variations, the very forms of experience that constitute adult life.

Today, it seems that proponents of the negative view (mainly liberals) and the positive view (mainly conservatives) are caught just where they were when Dewey wrote. They both espouse preconceived ideals, and those ideals seem to be converging. Advocates of the positive view want all children to study a specific curriculum so that schools produce people with specific intellectual knowledge and specific virtues. Advocates of the negative view support a uniform curriculum in the name of equality. Possibly the more dangerous of the two rationales is now the negative one because it is so confused—recommending, for example, more and more coercion in the service of freedom, vacillating on whether it endorses equal opportunity or equal outcomes, unclear on its position with respect to equal capacities.

If we accept either of the classic views as they appear today, we are confronted with the question of motivation: How do we motivate students to do what *we* think they must do? If we agree with Dewey that this is an impossible task for education in a democracy, what are the alternatives? Is there another perspective that might suggest a way out of the motivational thicket?

The Equality Trap

A certain sense of equality has belonged to the liberal tradition from its inception, and it is accepted by both liberals and conservatives in today's politics. People are equal before the law, and any office or occupation should be open to all on the basis of qualifications relevant to the position. This is not the sense of equality that gives rise directly to the motivation problem, but it leads to another, more problematic concept of equality.

If positions in the society are to be open to all,[17] must not people have equal opportunities to qualify for those positions? How do we judge whether opportunities are indeed equal? If unequal outcomes persist—smaller percentages of Blacks in desirable professions, fewer women in mathematics and science—is that a sign that opportunities are still not equal, or is it a sign of something else?

Today's liberal position seems to involve the following assumptions:

1. All people have roughly equal capacities to handle academic material: "All children can learn."
2. Equal opportunity requires equal resources; this includes the same curriculum for all.
3. Disadvantaged students may require more resources until the "playing field is level."

If 2 and 3 are satisfied and 1 is true, then equal outcomes are the result. But of course, 1 may not be true, and 2 may harbor an error. Providing equal resources may not require that the *same* resources be provided for all. Further, it may be a mistake to regard curriculum as a "resource." Indeed, if we believe Dewey and Rousseau on this, we might protest that offering the same resources, particularly the same curriculum for all, gives rise to a gross inequality. Michael Apple comments:

> The "same treatment" by sex, race and ethnicity, or class is not the same at all. A democratic curriculum and pedagogy must begin with a recognition of "the different social positionings and cultural repertoire in the classrooms, and the power relations between them." Thus, if we are concerned with "really equal treatment," as I think we must be, we must base a curriculum on a recognition of those differences that empower and depower our students in identifiable ways.[18]

Apple is suggesting that curriculum and pedagogy must be sensitive not only to individuals (as recommended by Dewey and Rousseau) but also to gender, race, and class. However, this sensitivity might be adopted with or without the demand for equal outcomes; that is, we might launch into programs especially (and sensitively) designed to help Blacks succeed on the SAT and to promote the success of women in mathematics and science, or we might try to find out what individual people in those groups want and work with them to foster their own legitimate interests. The two responses are very different.

The liberal attitude, for all its generosity, inadvertently contains an arrogant set of assumptions. Underlying the surface assumptions laid out above is the assumption that all people *want* to be just like the people who created liberal political philosophy—that, if all people had a fair chance, they would want to go to college and obtain professional positions. Further, a tacit assumption, shared with conservative positive-concept advocates, is that people who have the prescribed form of education are thereby better citizens. Both of those assumptions are questionable.

The first disguises or glosses over the likelihood that although most people want at least a moderate level of material comfort, they do not necessarily want to do the kind of work usually implied by a college education. The politically correct emphasis on equal capacities, then, becomes a form of violence in itself. Insisting on equal capacities, it neglects entirely different interests and motives. Not everyone *wants* to do the kind of work that represents membership in the "overclass." Thus, a moral society needs to ask why such work should be a requirement for material security, not how everyone can be given an opportunity to enter occupations that require a college education. Paradoxically, the fear of creating a classed society seems to be driving liberals toward an educational program that ensures pernicious class distinctions.

The second assumption—that a universal curriculum based on traditional subjects will produce better citizens—is questionable on democratic grounds. Requiring all students to take academic courses (such as algebra and geometry) seems to be a move more compatible with authoritarian forms of government than with democracy. As Dewey pointed out again and again, democracy is a form of associated living, and young people need practice in its forms and processes if they are to be "prepared" for adult life in a democracy. But even if we set Dewey's pronouncements aside, there is something anomalous in the insistence of *liberals* on such requirements. One would expect a tradition of noninterference to allow considerable choice and to insist on procedures that would ensure the high quality of a great variety of educational programs.

The excessive emphasis on equality has created an interesting alliance of policymakers from both the negative and positive views of freedom. It has also helped to reveal something liberals have long tried to deny—that the negative view actually contains a strong positive ideal. The person Mill described as able to pursue his or her own goods freely and without harming others turns out to be highly educated, especially in the capacity for problem solving and critical thinking. This description is still compatible with liberal freedom if it is translated into the cooperative construction of curricula sensitive to individual and group differences. But construing equality in terms of a single ideal has contributed to the collapse of truly liberal positions in education and has also aggravated teaching's most pervasive predicament: how to teach adequately intelligent students material they do not want to learn.

An Alternative Perspective

We are living in an age when the great ideologies of the last two centuries are under threat of collapsing: Marxism totters under the practical failures of its models; liberalism threatens to lose itself to communitarianism or even to become indistinguishable from some forms of conservatism. Some thinkers—for example, Richard Rorty—offer hope in the revival of liberalism through renewed attention to Deweyan pragmatism.[19] But this may not be enough, because Dewey never really came to grips with the problems of vastly different groups struggling for material survival and social recognition in a society devoted to capitalism and individualism.

With patience, we might get some guidance from postmodern-dialogic philosophy. The temptation is to brush aside postmodernism as "subjectivist, half-baked neo-Nietzschean theories,"[20] but some of those "theories" yield powerful insights into how to meet and treat the "Other." Indeed, Richard J. Bernstein comments on Derrida, "Few writers have written with such nuanced understanding about the suffering, mourning 'other.'"[21] The fundamental insight is captured by both Derrida and Emmanuel Levinas: We must learn to respect the Other as other—different from ourselves but essential both to our own development as fully human persons and to the very possibility of ethics. Referring to thought on Being, the essence of all actual beings, Derrida remarks:

> It conditions the *respect* for the other *as what it is*: other. Without this acknowledgment, which is not a knowledge, or let us say without this "letting-be" of an existent (Other) as something existing outside one in the essence of what it is (first in its alterity), no ethics would be possible. . . . The "letting-be" concerns all possible forms of the existent, and even those which, *by essence,* cannot be transformed into "objects of comprehension."[22]

Derrida does not mean that we should ignore, neglect, or condescend to the Other. We may attend, offer to help, argue with, attempt to persuade, consult with, accept help from, live with, and so forth. But we do not either posit the Other as a mirror image of ourselves (as traditional liberalism so often does) or insist on the conversion of the Other (as conservatism does in adhering to its ideals). First and most important, we acknowledge and "let-be" the otherness of the Other.

This insight is found too in the ethic of care, an ethic that also puts emphasis on the Other, on the cared-for.[23] To receive the Other in a complete act of receptivity is to understand that, as Levinas puts it, "*we* is not the plural of *I*." In caring, the Other is primary, and everything that transpires in interaction is, at least in part, conditioned by the needs and desires of the Other.

Recognition of the Other, reception of the cared-for, rejects both coercion and permissiveness. On the one hand, we refuse to force the Other into a model of ourselves; on the other, we recognize a responsibility to the Other—we must respond. Again, this response-ability is a keynote of both postmodern (ethical) thought and caring.[24] It calls upon us to respond to the Other, but because it calls on *us,* we cannot relinquish ourselves. We enter the conversation full of values, knowledge, beliefs, and projects of our own. This constellation of "stuff" that constitutes us as individuals is not to be discarded as we respond to the Other, but it may be modified. As we respond, we inform and are informed, we give and receive, we talk and listen, we shape and are shaped, and we share.

As educators, then, we accept the responsibility identified by Martin Buber to present the "effective world" to our students; we do not let them do whatever they please on impulse. Buber put it this way:

> For if the educator of our day has to act consciously he must nevertheless do it "as though he did not." That raising of the finger, that questioning glance, are his genuine doing. Through him the selection of the effective world reaches the

> pupil. He fails the recipient when he presents this selection to him with a gesture of interference. . . . Interference divides the soul in his care into an obedient part and a rebellious part. But a hidden influence proceeding from his integrity has an integrating force.[25]

The raised finger, the questioning glance—both imply that the teacher has listened to the student. Caution is suggested; the student may anticipate an alternative to consider. The effectiveness of such gestures (and all they stand for as metaphors) depends on a relationship of care and trust already established. A well-loved and respected teacher can accomplish much with a raised finger. Both Colsant and Mr. James are so connected to their students that their gestures and facial expressions can be read instantly. Both teachers work hard to present a version of the world that inspires their students to something better than they have now. But both work with the present motives and expressed needs of their students. They have respect for their students as Others, and they have opened themselves to new experience. They have made dialogue possible.

Teachers who learn to work with students' own motives may transmit mountains of subject matter to students who want that subject matter, and indeed, it is one of the great ironies of today's demand for "high expectations" that teachers are often too exhausted from their futile efforts with resistant students to satisfy fully those whose interest—intrinsic or extrinsic—is high. Teachers can also accomplish impressive results with students who respond out of love for the teachers themselves. Orwell, in insisting that classical education could probably not be accomplished without corporal punishment, overlooks what can be attained by love. However, at bottom, he is probably right. For what loving teacher would impose such a curriculum on young children? At the persistent signs of recalcitrance, such a teacher would—like Colsant and Mr. James—begin to construct a new curriculum cooperatively with the students.

What emerges from the ethical thought of Derrida and Levinas is a great respect for the Other *as other*. Whereas Buber (whose work is highly regarded by Levinas) emphasized the positive, connecting aspects of relation, Derrida and Levinas offer us the deep insight that relation—face-to-face confrontation—with the Other always involves separation and difference. Derrida writes:

> Face to face with the other within a glance *and* a speech which both maintain distance and interrupt all totalities, this being-together as separation precedes or exceeds society, collectivity, community. Levinas calls it *religion*. It opens ethics. The ethical relation is a religious relation. Not *a* religion, but *the* religion, the religiosity of the religious.[26]

In attitude, in dedication, this religiosity is like that described by Dewey.[27] It pervades the life of the religious. In the work of Derrida and

Levinas, it is directed at the Other: "The only possible ethical imperative, the only incarnated nonviolence in that it is respect for the other himself . . . because it does not pass through the neutral element of the universal, and through respect—in the Kantian sense—for the law."[28]

Both Levinas and Derrida have considerable regard for Kant and agree with his dictum that "respect is applied only to persons," but both abandon Kant's dependence on universality. Attention is not on the moral agent who, because of adherence to an absolute law, sees all others as comparable moral agents deserving respect. Levinas and Derrida reject the totalization thus implied. Respect is immediate, and difference remains. There must be no coercion used to make the Other "just like us," nor may we murder or isolate the Other simply because he or she is "not like us."

These insights on difference, separation, and respect may contribute either to a revitalization of liberalism or to its being supplanted entirely. In an interview, Jürgen Habermas suggested a revitalization involving a revised concept of universality:

> What then does universalism mean? Relativizing one's own form of existence to the legitimate claims of other forms of life, according equal rights to aliens and others with all their idiosyncrasies and unintelligibility, not sticking doggedly to the universalization of one's own identity, not marginalizing that which deviates from one's own identity, allowing the sphere of tolerance to become ceaselessly larger than it is today—all this is what moral universalism means today.[29]

Whether liberalism can survive such changes remains to be seen. However, it seems clear that educators who identify themselves with the liberal tradition will have to reassess their views on equality, control, and positive ideals. At present, their policies too often endorse and even extend an ideology that deepens the predicament of teachers. Teachers are urged again and again to motivate students to work at tasks they dislike. If students were not so young and ignorant, we assume, they would agree with us; we would not have to coerce them. Believing that the "true selves" of our students want what we want for them, says Berlin,

> renders it easy for me to conceive of myself as coercing others for their own sake, in their, not my, interest. . . . Once I take this view, I am in a position to ignore the actual wishes of men or societies, to bully, oppress, torture them in the name, and on behalf, of their "real" selves, in the secure knowledge that whatever is the true goal of man (happiness, performance of duty, wisdom, a just society, self-fulfillment) must be identical with his freedom.[30]

Certainly Berlin's concerns apply, if not to elementary school children, to secondary students who have their own legitimate wishes, needs, and dreams. Must we motivate, or can we find a pedagogy and a political orientation that allow us to work effectively with students' own motives?

Notes

1. Douglas Heath, *Schools of Hope* (San Francisco: Jossey-Bass, 1994), p. 19.
2. Ibid., p. 21.
3. Lee C. Colsant, Jr., "'Hey, Man, Why Do We Gotta Take This?' . . . Learning to Listen to Students," in *Reasons for Learning,* ed. John G. Nicholls and Theresa A. Thorkildsen (New York: Teachers College Press, 1995), p. 64.
4. Ibid., p. 66.
5. David T. Hansen, *The Call to Teach* (New York: Teachers College Press, 1995), p. 68.
6. George Orwell, *The Orwell Reader* (New York: Harcourt Brace, 1956), p. 427.
7. See A. S. Neill, *Summerhill* (New York: Hart, 1960).
8. John Dewey, *Democracy and Education* (New York: Macmillan, 1916), p. 116.
9. Isaiah Berlin, "Two Concepts of Liberty," in *Liberalism and Its Critics,* ed. Michael Sandel (New York: New York University Press, 1984), p. 15.
10. Ibid., p. 22.
11. Ibid., p. 23.
12. Giovanni Gentile, *Genesis and Structure of Society,* trans. H. S. Harris (Urbana: University of Illinois, 1960), p. 82.
13. See Sara Ruddick, "Maternal Thinking," *Feminist Studies* 6(2), 1980, pp. 342–367.
14. John Stuart Mill, "On Liberty," in *Morality, Harm, and the Law,* ed. Gerald Dworkin (Boulder: Westview Press, 1994), p. 9.
15. John Dewey, *The Public and Its Problems* (New York: Henry Holt, 1927), p. 200.
16. Ibid., pp. 200–201.
17. See John Rawls, *A Theory of Justice* (Cambridge, MA: Harvard University Press, 1971).
18. Michael Apple, "The Politics of Official Knowledge: Does a National Curriculum Make Sense?" *Discourse* 14(1), 1993, p. 1.
19. See Richard Rorty, *Contingency, Irony, and Solidarity* (Cambridge: Cambridge University Press, 1989).
20. Charles Taylor, *Multiculturalism, and "The Politics of Recognition"* (Princeton: Princeton University Press, 1992), p. 70.
21. Richard J. Bernstein, *The New Constellation* (Cambridge, MA: MIT Press, 1992), p. 184.
22. Jacques Derrida, *Writing and Difference,* trans. Alan Bass (Chicago: University of Chicago Press, 1978), p. 138; see also Emmanuel Levinas, *The Levinas Reader,* ed. Seàn Hand (Oxford: Blackwell, 1989).
23. See Nel Noddings, *Caring: A Feminine Approach to Ethics and Moral Education* (Berkeley: University of California Press, 1984); also Noddings, *The Challenge to Care in Schools* (New York: Teachers College Press, 1992).
24. For a postmodern discussion of obligation, see John D. Caputo, *Against Ethics* (Bloomington: Indiana University Press, 1993); also Edith Wyschogrod,

Saints and Postmodernism: Revisioning Moral Philosophy (Chicago: University of Chicago Press, 1990).

25. Martin Buber, *Between Man and Man* (New York: Macmillan, 1965), p. 90.

26. Derrida, *Writing and Difference,* p. 96.

27. See John Dewey, *A Common Faith* (New Haven: New York University Press, 1934).

28. Derrida, *Writing and Difference,* p. 96.

29. The Habermas quote is from an interview reported in *Universalism vs. Communitarianism: Contemporary Debates in Ethics,* ed. David Rasmussen (Cambridge, MA: MIT Press, 1990), p. 6.

30. Berlin, "Two Concepts," p. 24.

4

Teaching by the Numbers

ROBERT BOOSTROM

A first-grade teacher was talking to me about a six-year-old boy in her class. Even before the first week of school had passed, she said, she had recognized that he was an exceptional reader, a child who could, for example, read and understand the instructions to the teacher printed at the bottom of work sheets, a child who could read aloud with fluency and feeling from books he had never seen before and who obviously enjoyed reading. Nevertheless, she insisted, it was appropriate and needful for him to work on the same array of word-attack skills that she worked on with the other students. She argued that he may never have mastered some skills. Moreover, he would be tested on his word-attack skills, and her lessons would enable him to do well on the tests. This was important, she explained, not only because high test scores were a tradition of the school but also because test scores would largely determine the boy's career in school.

How should we respond to that kind of talk? One response would be flat dismissal. After all, the curriculum of word-attack skills and the tests that measure those skills were devised to enhance the teaching of reading. That is to say that to teach students how to decode words is to teach a set of subskills that are intended to help students acquire the skill of reading. Word-attack skills are just a small part of the skill of reading; they are a means to a means, for the skill of reading is in its turn a means to a variety of ends, among which we would likely place the enjoyment of literature and the growth of an intellectual life. Word-attack skills lie at least two removes from the ends they were intended to support, yet in this teacher's talk, we hear them elevated to a significance of their own. They are themselves a thing to be acquired, a sort of merit badge, and their possession serves as a passport to open educational doors.

But what do I mean when I talk of the possession of word-attack skills? I mean, of course, a test score. Unable to measure in practice the operation of word-attack skills, we invent tests that to a greater or lesser extent predict the likelihood of the effective use in practice of word-attack skills. And it is this finely distilled end product, the probability that a subskill will enhance a skill that will eventuate in a desired outcome, that becomes the goal. Without a good test score, the student suffers, and the school looks bad.

Have I made too much of the offhand comments of one teacher? Perhaps she was merely casting about for a reasonable-sounding excuse for doing something that really had no rationale beyond the fact that it was her typical practice. Perhaps. But this line of thinking offers no escape from the irony. To argue that her comments sound reasonable is to say that in general we, the community of educators, have accepted the elevation of test scores from the status of a measure to that of an aim. And to say that this teacher is simply justifying her practice is to say that her practice itself embodies the vision in which means and ends are inverted, and the pinnacle of achievement is a high test score.

But before we shake our heads, wring our hands, and thank heaven that we at least are wise enough to see the error of such wrongheadedness, I would like to suggest the possibility that this teacher's views are encouraged by the educational community at large, even by many of those who decry the reduction of learning to a package of readily measurable subskills. Suppose I use a situation that is formally the same but involves different characters. This time I am the teacher; the subject is not reading, but educational philosophy; the test is the National Teacher Exam (NTE) or the Graduate Record Exam (GRE); and I have realized that in this undergraduate class I do not emphasize (or perhaps even mention) many items that are prominent on the test—say, schools of educational philosophy such as perennialism and essentialism. Let us stipulate further that my students have read some philosophers, have discussed their works with care, and have begun to think philosophically. Is the situation parallel? Is success on the NTE or the GRE an indicator or an aim? Should I change my course?

Now, it might be said that the course must be changed because those matters that I have left out really belong in it. That is, the subject matter in question (names of schools of educational philosophy) is intrinsically worthwhile. This is an arguable point that I do not intend to go into because it is irrelevant to the question I am raising. There are many topics for which a case can be made that they belong in my course. The question is, do I try to include them if I find them on the NTE or the GRE? Is the fact that a piece of information is likely to come up on a test (which many of my students will have to take to be licensed as teachers or admitted to graduate school) sufficient reason for attempting to teach that information in a course that deals with the general subject area?

Put in those terms, I think the answer has to be yes. Teachers of teachers are under many obligations, and adequate preparation for professional licensure is surely one of them. Similarly, teachers of first-graders are under many obligations, and preparing students for standardized testing is surely one of those obligations.

What happens to classroom life because the answer is yes is a story that has been often told and often lamented: "The crucial role of assessment is captured by the folk wisdom that you get what you assess and you do not get what you do not assess. . . . Topics on the test are what teachers most seriously teach and what students most seriously try to learn."[1]

Teaching for the test leads to the study of disconnected and often insignificant facts that are soon forgotten.[2] Moreover, the emphasis on a narrow range of readily testable facts and skills often increases until it takes over the whole of teaching.[3] Because "unmeasured outcomes often go untaught,"[4] classroom life is reduced to drills, reviews, and recitations in preparation for tests. The teacher's hands are tied. My hands are tied.

I find myself wondering, however, whether there is more to the story than a tale of well-meaning people caught in a machine they do not control. I wonder, for instance, what to make of the credentialing authority of tests. What assumptions lie beneath the surface of this seeming inevitability? What is concealed and disguised when educational choices are turned into bureaucratic processes? Why is it that what can't be measured tends not to be taught? Why does teaching for the test mean dull routine? My hunch is that Jerome Bruner was right when he said that "cultural institutions" (such as standardized testing for credentials) "are constructed in a manner to reflect commonsense beliefs about human behavior."[5] If we look closely enough at the institution, we may come to understand the beliefs. And if we understand the beliefs, we may be able to offer some relief for the predicament of teachers who feel forced to teach by the numbers.

The first problem I face in this search is to put a name to what I'm trying to look at. The credentialing authority of tests and the elevation of test results to the status of an end are symptoms of the phenomenon. The underlying condition is a perspective on teaching—a sort of teaching by the numbers. Another name that might be put to it is *mimetic,* a term I am borrowing from the work of Philip W. Jackson.[6] I am using the term somewhat differently than Jackson did, because only in its most technological form would mimetic instruction be what he would call teaching by the numbers. I believe, however, that the concept of the mimetic tradition is useful for understanding why teachers so often find themselves seemingly coerced into narrow and sterile teaching. To explain the mimetic tradition, I need to turn to Jackson's description of it.

The Mimetic and the Transformative

The final chapter of Jackson's *The Practice of Teaching* is an essay that describes two "educational traditions"—the mimetic and the transformative. Other names exist for the traditions—*subject-centered* and *child-centered, traditional* and *progressive*—but Jackson chooses "to avoid becoming prematurely embroiled in the well-known controversies associated with [those] phrases,"[7] so he chooses less-familiar labels.

In his essay Jackson sketches numerous distinctions between the two traditions (as well as noting their commonalities), but the central difference, the reason for writing the piece, is captured by the terms themselves. The mimetic tradition of teaching seeks imitation and reproduction; it seeks to add something (we call the thing "knowledge" or "skill") to a person who is, in a sense, already formed. The student is enhanced by the addition but is not fundamentally altered. We might think of the mimetic tradition (though Jackson does not employ this analogy) as adding a new room onto an old house.

The transformative tradition seeks a different kind of change—"a qualitative change often of dramatic proportion, a metamorphosis."[8] No one would claim that a butterfly is simply a caterpillar with a few parts added on, and from the point of view of the transformative tradition, students are caterpillars; they are in a state of becoming. The metaphors used to characterize this sort of education must be organic rather than mechanical.

The methods of the two traditions are distinctly different. Jackson divides mimetic instruction into five steps: (1) the teacher tests to see what the student already knows; (2) the teacher presents the material to be learned; (3) the student performs, or reproduces, what the teacher presented, and the student is evaluated; (4) correct performances are rewarded and "fixed," while incorrect performances lead to remediation; and (5) the student advances to a new unit of instruction. By contrast, transformative instruction tends not to sound like instruction at all. Instead of steps to follow, Jackson finds only "some characteristic ways of working," in particular, the use of personal modeling, soft suasion, and narrative.[9]

Mimetic instruction can be described in terms of a predetermined outcome—the possession by the student of propositions, facts, and theories, or the student's demonstration of a skill. The preeminent example of this approach today may be E. D. Hirsch's catalogs of what every child at a given grade level ought to know. The catalogs may be incomplete, the selections may be arguable, but the items are listable. Only sufficient time and discussion are needed to make the catalogs complete.

Transformative instruction cannot avail itself of a similar list. This is not because teachers in the transformative tradition (Jackson names Socrates and Christ as models) have no goals. Socrates, for example, sought to discover the nature of virtue; Christ sought to teach His disciples the nature of love. Like mimetic teaching, transformative teaching aims at outcomes; the difference lies in the ability of the transformative teacher to speak or write those outcomes. Socrates often insisted that he did not know what he was looking for, though he insisted that looking for it anyway is the right way to live. When asked whether virtue can be taught, he replied that he did not even know what it is.[10] One of the ironies of the transformative tradition that Jackson highlights is that it is not clear that the teacher knows more than the student; in fact, the relationship between teacher and student is "vexingly ambiguous."[11] The transformative teacher does not possess knowledge to be imitated by the student.

As different and distinctive as these educational traditions are, they can nevertheless be brought together, Jackson believes, in "those rare and memorable encounters with teachers that leave us doubly enriched, morally as well as intellectually."[12] This optimism about (or perhaps nostalgia for) a rapprochement of the mimetic and the transformative ironically underscores another important distinction between the two traditions. Apparently, mimetic teaching tends to focus on the intellectual, whereas transformative teaching focuses on the moral.

At first glance, this is a somewhat surprising claim. If we think of the mimetic tradition as typified by direct instruction and "objective" testing, we can readily come up with any number of examples of mimetic instruction in moral principles. In fact, it is arguable that teachers are increasingly seen as bureaucratic agents whose job is "the deliberate inculcation of the right societal values."[13] Such testimony seems to contradict flatly Jackson's claim that it is "teachers working within the transformative tradition" who aim to make their students "more virtuous, fuller participants in an evolving moral order."[14] What, then, does Jackson mean when he allies the transformative tradition with moral teaching?

Part of the answer may be that he is influenced by the concerns of his models of transformative teaching—Socrates and Christ. It hardly needs to be argued that the teaching of each is fundamentally moral. Nevertheless, the argument may be worth making because of what it reveals. For the significantly transformative element in the teaching of Socrates and Christ does not have to do with the content of instruction. That Socrates talked about virtue, and Christ about love, is not why either is a model of transformative teaching. It is the manner or method of each that places him in the transformative tradition.

The key element of transformation may lie in the emphasis on reflective thought that we find in Socratic or Christlike teachers. Jackson calls transformative instruction philosophical because it involves, he says, the use of "discussion, demonstration, and argumentation"; it has to do with asking questions; and it means "doing one's own thinking."[15] Transformative instruction is also interpretive—or perhaps it would be better to say that it calls forth interpretation from the student—because the use of narrative invites the hearer to make meaning of the story. As Bruner puts it, "To make a story good . . . you must make it somewhat uncertain, somehow open to variant readings, . . . undetermined."[16]

In three important ways, this philosophical/interpretive emphasis sets off transformative instruction from mimetic instruction. First, it helps to explain why the content of transformative instruction remains ineluctably unlistable. When the aim is for students to do their own thinking, it is not only possible but also desirable that they may think something unexpected by the teacher. Knowledge—instead of being a given as it is in mimetic instruction—is a variable. Second, because knowledge is a variable in the transformative tradition, it cannot be objectively tested, as it is in the mimetic tradition. Third, the philosophical/interpretive emphasis reveals how active the student must be in transformative instruction, for it is the student who philosophizes and interprets. Such activities have no place in the steps of the mimetic method.

One final word needs to be said about Jackson's analysis of the mimetic and the transformative traditions. Toward the end of his essay he says, "Teaching within our country and possibly within the Western world at large seems to be moving in the direction of becoming increasingly mimetic in its orientation."[17] Some observers of this trend applaud it, Jackson notes, whereas others deplore it. The concerns of the latter group center on the uses of "those practices most closely associated with the mimetic tradition—an emphasis on memorization, short-answer tests, copying, drill, and recitation."[18] I have, of course, placed myself among those who worry over the ascendancy of this mode of teaching, though my concern here is not to sing a jeremiad, but rather to probe the underlying beliefs that make possible the ascendancy of the mimetic tradition—what I am calling "teaching by the numbers." I will look at three beliefs that lie at the heart of that tradition—the idea of knowledge, the idea of expertise, and the idea of equality. Each of those, it turns out, is not only a constituent element of mimetic teaching but also an article of faith that most teachers would be loath to part with.

The Idea of Knowledge

Why does the mimetic tradition have such a powerful influence on educational practice? This is, of course, an old question. Eighty years ago Dewey asked it this way: "Why is it, in spite of the fact that teaching by pouring in, learning by a passive absorption, are universally condemned, that they are still so entrenched in practice? That education is not an affair of 'telling' and being told, but an active and constructive process, is a principle almost as generally violated in practice as conceded in theory."[19]

In the classes I teach (composed of teachers and people studying to become teachers), Dewey's lament moves the students to nod their heads in sad agreement and to affirm that children learn by doing, not by being told. An observer might conclude that among my students the mimetic tradition had been superseded by the transformative, but I suspect that what my students exhibit is not so much an acceptance of Dewey's perspective as it is an unwitting confirmation by example. The principle of an active and constructive education is readily conceded, but it is hard to let go of the practice of telling.

One reason for adherence to this practice can be seen if we return to Dewey's lament. His framing of the question leaves out what some would argue is the heart of the matter. "Teaching by pouring in," he says, "learning by a passive absorption." What is it that is supposed to be poured in? What is supposed to be absorbed? Of course, the answer to the question is so obvious that perhaps it does need to be stated: Knowledge is what the teacher is supposed to pour in, and knowledge is what the learner is supposed to absorb. Dewey, however, rejects this metaphor, and in so doing, he says, in effect, that we cannot put knowledge into students by telling. This startling assertion flies in the face of the conception of knowledge embodied in the mimetic tradition. As Jackson describes the mimetic, knowledge is seen as detachable and transmissible, as information and skills, which the teacher presents and the students reproduce or imitate. But if knowledge is indeed facts and bits of information, what else would we teachers do with it other than pour it in? The notion of information implies communication. Of course, the mimetic argument on behalf of telling does not restrict teachers to the Gradgrind position ("In this life we want nothing but Facts, sir; nothing but Facts!"). To believe that education involves transmitting facts does not preclude other dimensions of teaching. The mimetic tradition says merely that if there is information, if there is knowledge, it can be shared by telling.

What exactly is Dewey's problem with this seemingly sensible position? It is not that he rejects the importance of facts. Indeed, he writes that "mind is precisely intentional purposeful activity controlled by perception of facts and their relationship to one another."[20] His problem with the mimetic practice of "pouring in" seems to hang on his rejection of transmissibility. He describes knowledge as the outcome of an active process engaged in by the student, which is to say that, at best, teachers can stimulate the acquisition of knowledge, but they cannot cause it. This position might be described as a "constructivist" perspective, "with a view of knowledge as something created, discovered, and experienced."[21] It is the perspective that Dewey claims is "violated in practice" though "conceded in theory."

But is the transformative view as fully conceded as Dewey believed? "Students learn by doing" is often taken to mean that, in terms of how well students remember the content of a course, telling is less effective than showing, which is less effective than letting students do it for themselves. This reading of a supposedly Deweyan principle is more mimetic in spirit than transformative. Teachers who embrace Dewey in this way are actually contributing to the practice of "teaching by pouring in"; they have merely discovered more sophisticated methods of pouring.

Even those, however, who fully and reflectively concede Dewey's perspective "in theory" find it difficult to honor it in practice. For in teaching, there is no getting away from facts. The "perception of facts and of their interrelationships" controls the activity of mind. There is no study that can proceed without any taken-for-granted knowledge. Even if we turn to the most transformatively inclined subject matter and argue, for instance, that the evaluation of a work of art should draw on nothing but our perceptions of that work, we find ourselves treating as given facts such matters as what exactly constitutes that particular work: What is canvas and what is frame? What is the front of the picture, and what is the back? What is sculpture and what is pedestal and what is floor? When is the orchestra playing the symphony, and when is it tuning up? No mindful activity can ignore those sorts of shared understandings. We may counter that acknowledging such facts does not legitimate a pedagogy of pouring knowledge into the student's head; we may even insist that any of those facts might be treated interpretively in the constructivist mode. But the question is, do we really want to demand that they should be treated interpretively? How far can schooling go if no knowledge is ever taken for granted, if every step must be negotiated? Teaching is a practical business. Its practitioners cannot be expected to adopt a strict skepticism. They must, to some degree, deal in facts—knowledge that is not constructed by the student, but is rather presented to the student.

Because we believe in and rely upon the transmissibility of knowledge, we find that mimetic instruction, guided and shaped by tests, insinuates itself into our teaching, and we find practice ever drifting toward teaching by the numbers. Test scores are elevated in importance not because (as some would argue) they are objective or readily obtainable, but because they fit what we believe about knowledge. The heights and weights of students are objective and readily obtainable, but no one would use them to measure the outcomes of schooling. We may high-mindedly pronounce that standardized testing "encourages the teaching of a narrow set of measurable skills that often have little to do with what educators and parents value most," yet we also believe what those tests tell us.[22] Consider, for example, the educational reform in Kentucky, which has emphasized new forms of assessment (such as writing portfolios and performance events) and has dropped the practice of grading in the elementary years. An early evaluation of this reform looked at test scores—on paper-and-pencil achievement tests.[23] The reform that was intended in part to get beyond such forms of testing was measured by that testing. We measure all manner of educational outcomes with tests like those for the same reasons that we teach by telling. We believe in and depend upon the transmissibility of knowledge.

The Idea of Expertise

The mimetic tradition is based upon a triadic conception of teaching. The encounter consists of a teacher, a student, and a body of knowledge, and the aim of the encounter is for the teacher to transmit the body of knowledge to the student. The significant underlying assumptions tied up in this view include, first, that knowledge is separable from persons, and second, that the teacher possesses an abundance of the knowledge in question—at least, more than the student does. The first of those assumptions has already been discussed. The second, however, reveals another aspect of the hold that mimetic instruction has upon education.

The idea that a teacher must be knowledgeable in the field being taught is so commonplace, so self-evident, that it is what might be called an invisible assumption. It is thoroughly institutionalized. To become a public school teacher at any level above the sixth grade, one must have a college or a university certify a given level of knowledge about a field of study. It is arguable that this subject-matter specialization is one of the reasons that secondary school teachers have long enjoyed a somewhat higher status than have elementary school teachers. For my purposes, however, it is enough to point out what everyone already knows: To be a teacher of, say, mathematics is to claim to know more about mathematics than do those who present themselves as students.

To appreciate this bit of common knowledge, we must step back and consider its roots. In Plato's *Meno,* Socrates connects teaching and expertise. He observes that students who are looking for a teacher seek out a practitioner of the art they wish to learn. "Look at it in this way," he says, "if we wanted Meno to become a good physician, to what teachers would we send him? Would we not send him to the physicians? . . . And if we wanted him to be a good shoemaker, to shoemakers? . . . whenever we say that we mean that it would be reasonable to send him to those who practice the craft rather than to those who do not."[24]

At first glance, it may seem that Socrates is saying the same thing about medicine and shoemaking that I just said about mathematics: The teacher knows more about the field than do the students. But Socrates is making a somewhat different claim. The reason for choosing a person as a teacher isn't that the person knows more; it is, says Socrates, that the person is an accomplished practitioner of the art. According to Socrates, a necessary condition of teacherly expertise is accomplishment in the field.

How this condition would apply to the most rudimentary education (learning one's letters, learning to read, learning days of the week and seasons of the year, and so on) is an interesting question, for our first thought may be that there are no "practitioners" of such things. From another point of view, however, it turns out that all of the members of the community are practitioners. When Socrates speaks about the nurture and education of the young, he says that the key is that "music and gymnastics be preserved in their original form, and no innovation made. . . . And when they have made a good beginning in play, and by the help of music have gained the habit of good order, then this habit of order, in a manner how unlike the lawless play of others! will accompany them in all their actions and be a principle of growth to them." This beginning will, Socrates explains, direct the young toward "lesser rules" such as "when the young are to be silent before their elders; how they are to show respect to them by standing and making them sit; what honor is due to parents; what garments or shoes are to be worn; the mode of dressing the hair; deportment and manners in general."[25] In short, the rudimentary education Socrates describes seems to consist of the sorts of attitudes and practices that any civilized person would be expected to display. There is nothing arcane or specialized in it. Its content is possessed by all the members of the community, so that all are truly practitioners, and all are truly teachers.

The distinction between this view of expertise and that embodied in our modern public education rests, it seems, on differing standards—expert as practitioner versus expert as possessor of knowledge. The teacher, today, is one who knows. Writing about the characteristics of great and influential teachers he has seen at work, Ernest L. Boyer, president of the Carnegie Foundation for the Advancement of Teaching, says, "First, they knew their subjects. . . . Teaching deals with knowledge, and effective teachers are, above all, well-informed."[26] Some would say that being well-informed includes, in addition to subject matter knowledge, something that might be called pedagogical knowledge—that is, how to communicate subject matter knowledge. Others might argue that a teacher's subject matter knowledge is somehow different from a scholar's subject matter knowledge. What remains constant throughout those perspectives is the conviction that teachers deal in knowledge, and it is a notion of knowledge that does not include what Dewey calls "ability in action."[27] The predominance of this conviction (and of the mimetic tradition it supports) is perhaps necessary to the profession of teaching. If the people who claim to be teachers are not knowledgeable, what possible justification is there for them to remain in their jobs?

The deeper we dig, the tighter the connections become. Expertise is knowledge. Knowledge is what we measure on tests. Tests certify expertise. The system is closed, the conclusions unassailable. The beliefs that underlie the mimetic tradition not only guide instruction but also give authority to the profession of teaching. This is important in a profession that has often been accused of a lack of depth. Stephen Arons, a critic of public education, has written: "In education, the fragility of expertise is greater than in most professions and so is the profession's awareness of this fragility. As a result, educators respond to general social pressure for expertise by turning every human interaction into a matter of technique and every area of work into an arcane and inaccessible specialization."[28]

The specialization he is talking about is, of course, the increasingly elaborated expertise that results from dividing and subdividing knowledge. Without this expertise, teachers would lack the distinguishing mark that makes them teachers.

Interestingly, those beliefs about expertise also provide an explanation for classroom failure. Wrong answers, mistakes, empty blanks—those are what constitute failure with mimetic instruction. They are also, significantly, the phenomena of interest. The model Present-Practice-Test directs attention toward the shortcomings of students. The role of teachers is to seek out errors and remediate, a truth that has become a part of our folk culture:

"What do you do for a living?"

"I'm an English teacher."

"Oh! I'd better watch my grammar!"

From the mimetic perspective, two possible reasons account for student failure. The incorrectly reproduced information was either improperly presented by the teacher (it was incomplete, incorrect, or confusing), or else it was presented in the wrong sequence, which is to say that the student was not yet ready for the information. Instances in which the students were resistant or inattentive may be considered a third cause for failure, but they are perhaps better considered a category-one failure—improper presentation of the information. After all, the expertise of the teacher includes pedagogical knowledge, and pedagogical knowledge includes dealing with all sorts of students.

This explanation of failure may seem to put a great, or even unrealistic, responsibility upon teachers, but it should be remembered that what is at issue is not so much an individual instance of teaching as it is a system of teaching. That is, the failure lies not in the person who happens to occupy the role of teacher, but rather in the techniques or materials employed by that person. (Incompetents may exist—people who are not experts—but we assume they are exceptions.) The search for "what works" or "the one best system" is an expression of faith in the perfectibility of the mimetic method.[29] The creed says that with the right techniques, the right materials, the right organization, students will learn, which is to say that during the course of their schooling, their scores will rise on standardized tests because the number of their mistakes will lessen. The expertise of the teacher guarantees not only that errors will be caught but also that students making errors will be instructed in those areas in which they fall short. If some problem interferes with the student's ability to absorb the information, that too, falling within the range of the teacher's expertise, will be addressed.

What has the transformative tradition to offer in contrast with this view of expertise? Instead of a clear-cut program of instruction, it offers an enigma concerning the nature of educational influence. In Plato's *Meno,* Socrates questions whether virtue can be taught, because he cannot find any teachers of it. Surely, he says, if those who are virtuous could teach it, they would do so with their children, yet he can readily identify virtuous men whose offspring live mean, if not reprehensible, lives. We may want to take issue with Socrates and argue that it is possible to possess knowledge of a subject without possessing the ability to teach it, but this does not solve the problem he raises. For surely living under the same roof with an exemplar of virtue ought to lead to some of it rubbing off. How do we explain failures in transformative teaching?

Consider Jackson's other exemplar of transformative teaching—Christ. Of His twelve best-known students, how many truly learned the lessons? How do we account for Judas? Was Christ not as good a teacher as He might have been? Was it that He failed to recognize that Judas had a learning style different from that of the other students? Ought He to have seen that Judas needed some one-on-one instruction and a few remedial classes? Or do we simply shrug our shoulders and say that some students just can't get it?

If Christ had been a mimetic teacher, we might be content to blame His failure to teach Judas on the student's lack of talent (and a curriculum that didn't allow for individual differences), but the transformative model offers no place for this sort of explanation. Part of what Socrates shows Meno is that anyone can learn anything. He leads an untutored slave through a demonstration of geometry, and though we readers may doubt that the slave is "recollecting" geometric insight (as Socrates claims), little doubt remains that the slave's eventual grasp of the principles is genuine. In the same vein, Christ's teaching is thought to be within the intellectual reach of any listener. To argue that some students just can't get it is unacceptable.

The door seems to be left open, however, for a different kind of student failure—one of will rather than one of ability. We may wonder, in other words, whether Judas lacked motivation. Within the mimetic tradition, motivation is an eternal problem. The teacher enters the classroom with a clear-cut agenda and must find some way to get the students to attend to that agenda. The transformative tradition, however, takes a different perspective. When Dewey discusses motivation, he identifies it with affection, concern, and interest. He offers single-mindedness as the evidence of true motivation, and single-mindedness only results when the subject matter derives from a "situation having purpose."[30] The teacher working in the transformative tradition may propose subject matter and almost certainly must guide its development, but its true origin lies in the ongoing activities of the student. The transformative teacher presents, organizes, and demonstrates materials, but the student decides the purposes for which they will be used, and the student constructs the knowledge they make possible. A student may learn a lesson that the teacher never intended, and this outcome may be as highly valued as is any that was planned. Judas is not an example of a student who did not understand the lesson; he is an example of a student who learned an unexpected lesson. In other words, from the transformative perspective, we cannot talk about students who just can't get it because there isn't any "it." Instead of the triad of teacher, student, and body of knowledge, we have only the dyad of teacher and student. Knowledge is embodied rather than external. Within the transformative tradition, the problem is not how we account for failure, but rather how we define success. How do we know whether a student is, as Dewey would say, growing? Such a question is not without answer, of course, but the point is that the question is difficult, and the answer is not clear-cut. The expertise of the transformative teacher does not remove the ambiguities from instruction; in fact, it is not even clear what expertise means within the transformative tradition.

How many of us teachers are willing to relinquish our role as expert? How many can comfortably give up the triad of teacher, student, and body of knowledge? If those steps seem too extreme or too difficult, we find ourselves moving back into the arms of the mimetic tradition and its more reassuring idea of expertise.

The Idea of Equality

The belief of educational practitioners and of the public at large in equality is probably the strongest hold that the mimetic tradition and its teaching-by-the-numbers form of practice have on education. As long as we remain within the mimetic perspective, we assume that what teaching does to students is merely additive and that what is added to Student X in, say, ninth-grade algebra is equivalent, in its significant elements, to what is added to Student Y in the same class. The significant elements consist, of course, of knowledge about algebra. Students undoubtedly are affected in other ways, but the point of mimetic instruction is the transference of knowledge, and the knowledge to be transferred is the same for all. Admittedly, all students may not have equal access to all courses, but concerns about access merely echo the belief that the course content is the same for all who manage to be admitted.

To say that ninth-grade algebra is the same for all students is to express another implication of the ideas of knowledge and expertise that have already been discussed. If knowledge is separate from persons and if teaching expertise consists of the transmission of knowledge, then the aim and substance of any given course can readily be specified. It will be made up of a predetermined set of facts and skills to be transmitted from the teacher to the student. Since those facts and skills exist independently of the student (or of the teacher for that matter), it doesn't matter who takes the course—the content and purpose remain the same.

The idea of equality is built into mimetic instruction not only through the aims and substance of courses but also through related beliefs about students. However different students may be when they enter the classroom, they are assumed to be capable of adding on to themselves what the class has to offer—provided that they have been properly placed. Now, that proviso may seem to remove all substance from the assumption, but it is not quite as emasculating as it sounds. The assumption about the equality of students means that all differences are overlooked except for differences in knowledge. Passing grades in ninth-grade algebra (a measure of knowledge) are required for admittance to advanced algebra. A student who enrolled in advanced algebra without fulfilling that prerequisite would be improperly placed. But any students who complete the prerequisite are presumed to possess the knowledge to proceed to the next course. Differences among those students in their backgrounds or experiences are irrelevant; all of them are assumed to be capable of adding on to themselves what the class has to offer.

This assumption of student equality may sound so obvious (and appealing) that no alternative seems possible, but other points of view do exist. Aristotle, for example, says: "a young man is not equipped to be a student of politics; for he has no experience in the actions which life demands of him. . . . Moreover, since he follows his emotions, his study will be pointless and unprofitable. . . . Knowledge brings no benefit to this kind of person."[31]

In other words, Aristotle does not assume that those who come to him are equally prepared, nor does he assume that the important distinction between students is the amount of knowledge they possess. What he looks for in a student is a certain sort of background and upbringing: "to be a competent student of what is right and just, and of politics generally, one must first have received a proper upbringing in moral conduct. The acceptance of a fact as a fact is the starting point."[32]

Aristotle's views smack of elitism, of education for the privileged few. Anytime access to education is limited, the implication is that some people are better than others. The mimetic tradition deals with the need to control schooling by providing a basis for making the access to education formal and impersonal—a seemingly technical matter.

Because students are assumed to be equal when they enter the classroom and because the content of the course is assumed to be equal for all, we can also see that, within the mimetic tradition, students are, when they leave the classroom, still equal, except for their grades. Some students pick up more of the knowledge offered in the course than do other students. This is usually what teachers are remarking upon when they categorize a student as good or bad—the amount of knowledge the student took away.

Yet another aspect of equality is buried in the mimetic tradition. I have already said that a student who has learned a lesson has been improved only in that something new has been added on. The obverse of this is that a student who has been deprived of a lesson has been shortchanged only to the extent of that lesson. The differences between students who have had a course and those who have not are minor and predictable; they may be readily made up. E. D. Hirsch writes: "only a few hundred pages of information stand between the literate and the illiterate, between dependence and autonomy."[33]

In this sense, the mimetic tradition is much more optimistic than is the transformative tradition. Transformative teaching seeks to change students qualitatively rather than quantitatively. Jackson speaks of this as an emphasis on the moral, rather than on the intellectual, meaning. I think that teachers within the transformative tradition (think again of Socrates and Christ) are fundamentally concerned with how human beings treat one another. In other words, the transformative tradition is specifically concerned with outcomes that the mimetic tradition ignores. This is why transformative teaching cannot be summarized in "a few hundred pages of information." Consider two students of Christ—Judas and Peter. No amount of information, of however many hundreds of pages, suffices to turn Judas into Peter. But I needn't go to extreme examples to make this point. In the first chapter of *Untaught Lessons,* Philip Jackson discusses what he learned from his high school algebra teacher, Mrs. Henzi. His recollections consist of her dowdy appearance, the repetitions of a characteristic phrase, the practice of solving problems at the board, and his feelings of fear and anxiety in her classroom. Of the knowledge she transmitted, Jackson says, "I learned a lot of algebra that year," and he quotes some of the maxims he learned to help him solve for *x*.[34] Yet this knowledge was not, he wants us to believe, the most important thing he learned from Mrs. Henzi. She was, he maintains, a powerful influence on his life, the sort of person who is somehow tied up with beliefs about seeing a job through, paying attention to details, caring about one's work. How many hundreds of pages of information will be needed to convey such beliefs? The values can be stated, as I have stated them, but at what point does stating by the teacher become transformation in the student? Is there any amount of information sufficient to turn out a student like Jackson who does his work because he believes in the value of a job well done? Of course, the answer is no, and because it is no, the transformative tradition, which aims precisely at those outcomes, cannot guarantee the benefits that a student will accrue from a course of study. If we think transformatively, students who have been educationally deprived have lost something that cannot readily be made up. This does not mean that there is but one state of "being educated," nor does it mean that any schooled person is necessarily or in all ways superior to any unschooled person. What it does mean is that to be deprived of growth in the Deweyan sense—the enrichment in meaning of experience—is to lose more than the content of a few courses.

The full significance of a transformative change cannot be appreciated as long as we think of educational outcomes as merely additive. Perhaps the most important difference between the mimetic and transformative traditions is the loss that the transformative entails. We see it in Socrates' dealings with Meno and with the slave in the same dialogue. Both Meno and the slave are driven not only to confess ignorance but also to relinquish through that confession a former way of seeing things. Similarly, we see the loss in Christ's dealings with His disciples. They must give up everything to follow Him and have the chance of transformation. The difference between the educated and the uneducated (in this view) is like the difference between a hermit and someone who lives in society. The hermit cannot acquire the qualities of the social being without ceasing to be a hermit. One identity must be given up before the new identity can be acquired.

This transformative perspective makes teaching both exalting and frightening. Recall the moment in the play and movie *The Miracle Worker* when Helen Keller suddenly realizes what language is, suddenly sees that the confusion of objects and events around her can be named and ordered and that she can reach out of her darkness and silence to speak with another human being. The significance of this bursting insight is captured by Helen's need to learn the names for everything, to learn them right away, slapping impatiently on the pump, on the ground, on a tree trunk. Suddenly she stops and rests her hands on Annie Sullivan and insists on learning the name of the person who had given her language. Annie Sullivan spells into Helen's hand the word *teacher.*

Isn't this exactly what teachers do, or try to do, or hope they can do? Touch a student? Make a difference in someone's life? And doesn't this change mean a kind of loss? Helen must give up her wild isolation to take on a perspective that we believe to be fuller and richer.

But if education in the transformative mode means loss and growth, then it is a challenge to the idea of equality, especially in these times of racial, ethnic, and gender sensitivity, for it carries within it the seeds of what some call *deculturalization.* Joel Spring defines *deculturalization* as "the educational process of eliminating cultures."[35] He tells, for example, how George Washington was concerned about protecting "Native Americans from what were considered the worst aspects of European civilization—gambling, alcohol, fraud and stealing, and depraved sexual activities." Washington's concern became, during the nineteenth century, a national policy that aimed to turn Native Americans into Christians and farmers: "It was hoped that if the Europeans instilled Christian morality and the value of hard work, Indians could resist some of the corrupting influences of white settlers. Consequently, federal policies in the nineteenth century supported missionary and manual schools."[36] The problem with those schools, Spring says, is that they "were designed to change patterns of living among Indians and to replace their traditional economies."[37] Designed as institutions of social change, the schools corrupted tribal culture even as they failed to educate. Spring goes on to tell similar stories about the deculturalization of Puerto Ricans and the segregation of African Americans and Mexican Americans. He concludes, "Ethnocentric and bicultural education represent attempts to overcome the resistance of dominated cultures to public schools and to protect those cultures from the destructive forces of the dominant culture."[38] In other words, schooling ought not to take away the identity of the children who walk through the schoolhouse doors. Native Americans, Puerto Ricans, African Americans, Asian Americans, and Mexican Americans should not be force-fed an education that asks them to become white. Their schooling should add to what they are without removing anything.

The language of deculturalization lends itself readily to characterizing new situations. *The Miracle Worker* is a story of deculturalization. Annie Sullivan took from Helen her nonlinguistic understanding of the world and replaced it with the hegemonic perspective of the language users. This application may seem a fanciful excess or even a derisive attack on multiculturalism, but actually my point is that Spring's indignation has deep roots not only in the dominated cultures but also in the dominant culture. To the extent that education is transformative, we all find that schooling costs us something. The popular desire to resist this truth can be seen in a familiar element from the *Star Trek* mythology—the Prime Directive. This most important of all rules for Starfleet personnel says that representatives of the Federation must not influence the development of an alien culture. Although the ideal of noninterference is contravened in almost every episode, it continues to be extolled. The reason for the robustness of the Prime Directive is, I suspect, that the creators and fans of *Star Trek* believe in the idea of equality embodied in that impossible rule. We may not be able to follow faithfully the Prime Directive, but we affirm that alien cultures are to be left to themselves, because we define their right to exist as equal to our own. As long as we believe that cultures or individuals have an equal right to exist, we will be inclined to adopt an educational policy of noninterference, a form of schooling that is merely additive. The mimetic tradition affirms equality, while the transformative challenges it.

Keeping Our Bearings

Teaching by the numbers is widely perceived as wrongheaded, if not downright hazardous to society's well-being. "Our educational future," we are warned, "remains in crisis and the outlook is bleak as long as we insist on outmoded practices."[39] So familiar is the warning that we hardly need to have the phrase "outmoded practices" expanded, for it is the same old litany: "teacher-led blackboard lectures," "drill and kill, rote memorizing, and multiple-choice testing."[40] It is as if schooling has stood still since Dewey asked, "Why is it in spite of the fact that teaching by pouring in, learning by a passive absorption, are universally condemned, that they are still so entrenched in practice?" The answer Dewey offered when he posed that question was that the doctrine that says education is active and constructive was itself preached and lectured, but not enacted.[41] In other words, the people who championed transformative education did so in the manner of the mimetic tradition. The answer I have offered to Dewey's question is similar, for I too have argued that we are all responsible. Teaching by the numbers is not the result of outmoded practices being employed by a small group of well-meaning but misguided educators. Teaching by the numbers is a typical form of the mimetic tradition, and the mimetic tradition embodies ideas about knowledge, expertise, and equality that are widely shared. Although those ideas do not force us to teach by the numbers, they make it easy to focus on the transmission of knowledge measured by scores on objective tests, and they make it hard to remember what educators and parents value most.

What all of this adds up to is the realization that teachers who feel trapped in a routine of narrow and sterile schooling are not really responding to a particular problem at a particular time, but rather to an ongoing predicament of schooling. Schools will tend toward teaching by the numbers as long as we believe that students need facts, that teachers possess an abundance of those facts, and that students are (in the important ways) equal to one another. The inclination to tell and test will be with us as long as we strive to educate our young toward what Dewey calls "like-mindedness" with ourselves.[42] Because those beliefs and aims are not likely to be abandoned anytime soon (and I would not argue that they should be), we will continue to work in schools that constantly drift toward rote instruction, drill, memorization, objective tests of narrowly defined skills, and all the other phenomena captured by the phrase "teaching by the numbers."

If a way exists to resist this ceaseless current, I suspect that it requires us to remain skeptical about what we know and what we can do in classrooms. Confidence and certainty are the colors of those who teach by the numbers. Above all, this means rejecting the arrogant conclusion that we have seen for all time the hazards of the mimetic tradition and have permanently risen above teaching by the numbers. Our predicament as teachers is that we can never escape the downstream current toward narrow and sterile teaching. All we can do is row against it.

Notes

1. Hyman Bass, "Let's Measure What's Worth Measuring," *Education Week* (October 27, 1993), 32.

2. David F. Lohman, "Teaching and Testing to Develop Fluid Abilities," *Educational Researcher* 22 (1993): 12–23. Holt, quoted in Laurence J. Stott, *Essays in Philosophy and Education* (Lanham, Md.: University Press of America, 1988), 91.

3. Jonathan Kozol, *Savage Inequalities* (New York: HarperCollins, 1991), 143–144.

4. Lohman, "Teaching and Testing," 15.

5. Jerome Bruner, *Acts of Meaning* (Cambridge, Mass.: Harvard University Press, 1990), 38.

6. Philip W. Jackson, *The Practice of Teaching* (New York: Teachers College Press, 1986), 115–145.

7. Jackson, *Practice,* 115.

8. Jackson, *Practice,* 120.

9. Jackson, *Practice,* 119–120 and 124–125.

10. Plato, *Meno,* translated by G. M. A. Grube (Indianapolis: Hackett Publishing Co., 1976), 3, 14, and 20.

11. Jackson, *Practice,* 126.

12. Jackson, *Practice,* 144.

13. Goldstein, quoted in Stephen Arons, *Compelling Belief: The Culture of American Schooling* (Amherst: The University of Massachusetts Press, 1986), 47.

14. Jackson, *Practice,* 127.

15. Jackson, *Practice,* 127–128.

16. Bruner, *Acts,* 53–54.

17. Jackson, *Practice,* 131.

18. Jackson, *Practice,* 142.

19. John Dewey, *Democracy and Education* (New York: Free Press, 1966/1916), 38.

20. Dewey, *Democracy,* 103.

21. Jon Snyder, Frances Bolin, and Karen Zumwalt, "Curriculum Implementation," in *The Handbook of Research on Curriculum,* ed. Philip W. Jackson (New York: Macmillan, 1992), 415.

22. Iris C. Rotberg, "Chapter 1 Testing: It's No 'Field of Dreams,'" *Education Week* (September 29, 1993), 40.

23. Reported in an article in *Education Week,* October 13, 1993, 15.

24. Plato, *Meno,* 23.

25. Plato, *The Republic,* in *The Portable Plato,* trans. Benjamin Jowett, ed. Scott Buchanan (New York: Viking Press, 1948), 419–421.

26. Ernest L. Boyer, "Rediscovering the Center," *ASEE Prism* (September 1993), 24.

27. Dewey, *Democracy,* 185.

28. Arons, *Compelling Belief,* 109.

29. U.S. Department of Education, *What Works: Research About Teaching and Learning* (Washington, D.C.: U.S. Department of Education, 1987). David B. Tyack, *The One Best System: A History of American Urban Education* (Cambridge, Mass.: Harvard University Press, 1974).

30. Dewey, *Democracy,* 125 and 176–178.

31. Aristotle, *Nicomachean Ethics,* trans. Martin Ostwald (New York: Macmillan, 1986), 5–6.

32. Aristotle, *Ethics,* 7.

33. E. D. Hirsch, *Cultural Literacy* (New York: Houghton Mifflin, 1987), 143.

34. Philip W. Jackson, *Untaught Lessons* (New York: Teachers College Press, 1992), 4.

35. Joel Spring, *Deculturalization and the Struggle for Equality: A Brief History of the Education of Dominated Cultures in the United States* (New York: McGraw-Hill, 1994), 1.

36. Spring, *Deculturalization,* 5.

37. Spring, *Deculturalization,* 8.

38. Spring, *Deculturalization,* 105.

39. H. Eric Branscomb, "Review of Odyssey—Pepsi to Apple: A Journal of a Marketing Impresario, by John Sculley and John H. Byrne," in *Thought and Action* V (Fall 1989): 118.

40. Branscomb, "Review of Odyssey," 118.

41. Dewey, *Democracy,* 38.

42. Dewey, *Democracy,* 11.

5

Teaching and the Tragic Sense of Education

NICHOLAS C. BURBULES

Over the past several years, I have written about a perspective toward education, and its possibilities and limits, that I have called "tragic."[1] This is, admittedly, an unusual perspective to offer on education, an endeavor that seems to be intrinsically about hope, possibility, and progress. Given the connotations of tragedy as something bitter, miserable, or hopeless, one might argue, "Be constructive. Teachers are under assault already from so many quarters, so overworked and overstressed, underpaid and underappreciated, that they hardly need any new occasion for pathos. Talented teachers quit every day over the frustrations and limits they encounter in their work. They don't need a sense of tragedy. They need a reason to stay." To this I reply, Fair enough, but whether teachers are just starting out or are struggling with the cynicism of burnout, if we try to persuade them of the value of teaching on the basis of hopes and possibilities that cannot be sustained, we do them no favors.[2]

The tragic perspective, I suggest, argues *for* a strong sense of hope in education, but one tempered by an awareness of the contradictory character of what we might count as "success," an understanding that gains can always be seen also as losses, and an appreciation that certain educational goals and purposes can be obtained only at the cost of others. The tragic perspective argues *against* a hope that is utopian, against a belief in personal or social perfectibility, against the idea that our educational endeavor always does good and never harm. The tragic perspective discourages a focus on minimal, incremental improvements, instead encouraging reflection on the conflicted aims and values inherent in any educational activity. For me, the tragic view of education provides a positive, constructive way to think about teaching and what it can and cannot accomplish. In this essay, I try to show how this is so.

* * *

When we view or experience events, what gives us a sense of tragedy is not the fact of unhappiness or suffering itself, however strongly these are felt; it is the recognition that, given other circumstances, things might have transpired differently (if only she had known . . . , if only the letter had arrived in time . . . , if only . . .). The tragic sense is the point of tension between seeing the necessity of things as they are and the persistent imagining of them turning out otherwise. The tragic sense depends on this dual perspective—of seeing at the same time the possibilities and the limits, the gains and the costs, the hopes and the disappointments, of any human endeavor. By helping us accept the inevitability of doubt and disappointment in much of what we do, the tragic sense also frees us to take those moments of failure as occasions for new learning. On the other hand, by helping us stubbornly refuse to abandon hope in the face of cynicism, the tragic sense gives us a reason to care, to persist in our efforts. We could make our view of life simpler by adopting one view to the exclusion of the other (hope over an awareness of failure, cynicism over a sense of possibility), but for reasons I spell out in this essay, either option makes us a worse educator—indeed, makes us a worse person. In the essay in which I first laid out these ideas, I alluded to Herbert J. Muller's call to pass "all the way through tragedy" to a different orientation toward life.[3] However, I never explained what that means, and Rene Arcilla rightly asks, "How is tragedy itself an educative force?"[4]

My starting point, like that of the other contributors to this book, is the idea of a *dilemma*—not just a difficult choice between two options, not just a balancing act between alternatives, not just our second-guessing about a decision we might have made differently, but a recognition of a deep, intractable contradiction between competing aims and values.[5] What makes dilemmas most disturbing and challenging is not just that we are recognizing at a distance the trade-offs that most complex human activities inevitably entail. No, what makes them *tragic* is that we see conflict and contradiction reflected in our own hopes and desires—a reflection that throws into doubt some of the very values that inspire our educational endeavor in the first place. What we do not know how to reconcile are dimensions of our own beliefs and motivations, and to recognize conflict in those is to unsettle the very basis of any confidence that such conflicts can be overcome.[6]

Five such conflicts surrounding teaching carry a sense of force and immediacy for me. They are important because they touch upon unavoidable conditions of teaching as a practice. We can question or doubt those conditions, but we cannot continue to teach without continuing to struggle with them.

First are the ambivalent benefits and costs of *authority*.[7] Authority is inherent in any teaching-learning relation; it cannot be abrogated or denied even when one wishes to minimize its significance. But authority carries certain costs: It can foster dependency; it implies certain privileges of position that interfere with egalitarian social commitments; it becomes too easily taken for granted in the minds of both student and teacher. Encouraging students to question authority, even inviting challenges to one's own authority as a teacher, can foster valuable learning—but only a person in authority can do that. In one sense, the very purpose of authority in teaching is to make itself ultimately superfluous (because the students themselves become independent learners and knowledge creators). Balancing such tensions is a skill of good teaching. But the terms of success are not entirely within one's control. Institutional customs arrogate dimensions of privilege to teachers that conflict with our attempt to manage authority gracefully. Student habits and expectations, or those of their parents or the larger community, place demands upon teachers that are not compatible with the maintenance of a self-questioning authority. At a still deeper level, we who have chosen teaching as a career must acknowledge in ourselves the desires that motivate us. However modest we might endeavor to be, the influence that comes with authority and the pride of seeing our plans and intentions (sometimes) come to fruition are seductive pulls back into the temptation to exercise our authority—though only for the "best" of purposes, of course.

The second conflict is a skepticism toward the idea of *progress*. I have been persuaded, by the arguments of Dennis Carlson[8] and others, that the idea that history marks a human journey of becoming more and more knowledgeable and humane relies on an oversimple, linear view of history, an unproblematized effort to judge the past in terms of the present's standards, and the tendency to look with blinders at our present failings. I do not doubt that certain specific comparisons of historical advantage "before and after" can be made with some justification, but doing so always abstracts that comparison from a larger web of social contingencies and consequences that—if faced honestly—vastly complicate such judgments.

What is true at the level of human history is also true, I think, at the level of personal development and growth. Is there any way to argue, for example, that it is better, overall, to be an adult than a child? Are we clearly better off with the understanding *and* burdens, the knowledge *and* uncertainties, the freedoms *and* responsibilities, and the successes *and* disappointments that constitute an "educated," "mature" life? And even if some of us feel comfortable deciding that we are better off, is this a decision that would have been made, could have been made, from an alternative point of view (since we are already a product of such learning)?

What does the educational endeavor look like without such a faith in progress? It would mean grounding our investigations in the needs, problems, and questions of the present. It would mean doing less "for the sake of" prospective future attainments. It would mean questioning certain models of development, especially stage theories that assume normative improvement as well as change over time.[9] On a larger scale, it would mean abandoning the link between education and a vision of social perfection—a link that has been central to many Western educational theories.

The third conflict relates to the great amount of criticism that—as part of the so-called multiculturalism debates—has been leveled at the hegemony of *canonical texts.* Without revisiting all those arguments, I think that the debates raise another intractable dilemma. It is certainly justified, I believe, to argue that the master texts in many areas of the curriculum, at all levels of education, have tended to favor the outlooks and values of a dominant sociocultural group. Recent trends to diversify those sources, to encourage the exploration by students of other sociocultural outlooks and experiences as well as their own, have had the effect of broadening the range of perspectives that teachers and students can consider in their exploration of ideas and issues. This seems all to the better. But should this process simply result in a new, albeit more diversified, set of canonical texts, or should it result in a continually changing and contested set of resources, with no claims made to their being better or more influential or more representative than the alternatives?

The first option, in the long run, recreates all of the problems with canonicity in the first place, for any criteria of inclusion and exclusion, however pluralistic, will leave out *someone.* The second option is either disingenuous or antieducational—disingenuous because it tacitly invokes criteria of inclusion and exclusion (based on different standards but based on standards nonetheless) that are not out in the open for reflection or debate, and ultimately antieducational because any and all sets of standards are given equal place, or no set of standards is proposed at all. It is incoherent to encourage or require the reading of *anything* in an educational setting without being able to explain or justify why one has chosen those items and not others. As soon as one does require readings, however, the same objections raised against the canon come to bear. The dilemma lies in recognizing and accepting the responsibility of selecting texts for others to read, discuss, and yes, criticize (and the responsibility of requiring other kinds of assignments involved in teaching) while also recognizing the constraints and prejudices inherent in making any such selection or assignment.

The current "canonicity" debates are merely the latest version of a perennial dilemma intrinsic in teaching: the tension between the need to make choices, by whatever criteria one favors, that prioritize and mandate what learners must study, and the recognition that their needs, interests, and long-term preferences might have been better served by other choices, including matters of which one might personally be ignorant. This is not an argument against making such choices—as noted, they are unavoidable—but against settling complacently for "essential," "expert," or "institutionally mandated" materials. A general curriculum inevitably draws from and reinforces common cultural sources and reference points, yet if it is taken for granted, it suppresses the possibilities of difference and challenge to such norms.

The fourth conflict, which follows from the last point, flows from current views of education and society that stress the centrality of *diversity* and tolerance. But any educational practice, however fluid and multifaceted, has the inevitable effect of making people more alike, in at least some respects. One can label this phenomenon favorably as the "melting pot," or one can label it critically as Foucauldian "normalization."[10] Either way, diversity is lessened to the extent that a common syllabus, a common set of evaluation criteria, a common classroom culture, have an effect. That effect may be felt especially strongly and poignantly by learners who feel increasingly alienated from their own cultures, traditions, families, and communities as a result. To be sure, there may be ways in which learning makes people different, as well. However, intentional or not, the overall effect of any common system of education must be to draw students gradually away from their personal and cultural differences into a common culture. There are beneficial aspects of this, for the individual as well as for society, and there are detriments as well. My point is, we cannot have one without the other.

Put in more general terms, education *requires* diversity. The value of conversation and debate in schools depends upon the mutual enrichment and challenge of alternative perspectives. And to an extent, education *promotes* diversity when the mandates of a "canon" or of other centripetal forces, discussed previously, are not enforced in ways that override cultural and other kinds of difference. Yet at the same time, education *threatens* diversity, because of the normalizing effects of practices that by their very nature bring students under the sway of common, homogenizing influences.

The fifth conflict is the uncertainty involved in assessing outcomes, the uncertainty about what constitutes "success" as a teacher. Every human action has multiple outcomes, most of which are unforeseeable and unintended; at least some of those actions will result in some degree of unhappiness or harm to someone. We act in a complex web of contingencies (increasingly, with ramifications on a global scale) that frustrate the simple, linear cause-and-effect responsibilities entailed in moral consequentialism. In the context of teaching, that insight can have several results. We might say, roughly, "Good teaching results in learning," but that will not do: learning what? Teaching tends to focus on the knowledge and skills fostered by the teaching-learning relation. The dominant trend in school reform, in fact, is to focus narrowly, even obsessively, on such outcomes, as defined and measured by standardized tests—a truncated outcome, indeed. But that focus is deceptive, because it artificially excludes all other outcomes, which may be more ambivalent, uncertain, and difficult to reconcile: What kinds of people are students becoming? What do they value? How do they treat one another? The teacher at ground level is often aware of those considerations but has less and less room in which to address them. Certain outcomes, only the learner will know. Others, the learner may never recognize or attribute to the teacher. Some changes will be apparent only long after the teacher's influence has been felt; certain benefits are apparent only subtly, indirectly, in future accomplishments that teachers make possible today. Hence, there is a Kierkegaardian "leap of faith" in teaching—one not of religious belief but of persistent effort in the face of uncertain outcomes. For Kierkegaard, we do not leap once and for all; we leap, and we keep leaping, never knowing for sure what we will find on the other side.

The effects of teaching are too varied, too mixed between the beneficial and the harmful, too delayed, and too indirect to be the subject of any simple utilitarian balancing of costs and benefits or any simple abstracting of intended from unintended effects. One does the best one can, but how does one maintain a commitment to teaching when one is aware of such profound ambivalence?

The five dilemmas, I am suggesting, are at one level or another intrinsic to the teaching endeavor. One response to such dilemmas, of course, is to abandon teaching or to reject the value of education entirely. Yet education, in some form, seems an integral aspect of human culture. We can go about it differently, but we cannot refuse to do it at all. We must educate, and we must take responsibility for our choices and priorities. Even our desire for students to question or challenge us is an educational goal, one that has its own values and limitations. We have to take certain things for granted so that others might be questioned. This suggests, among other things, a serious limit to what any critical or reflective approach to pedagogy can achieve. Moreover, although obviously we can, as individuals, choose to do something besides teach, we must recognize that one consequence of doing so is to turn over the conduct of education to others who may not feel the force of those dilemmas.

* * *

Another typical response to dilemmas is to seek a way to resolve or reconcile them. Here I consider a few of the more common ways of attempting to do so. The simplest and least abstract way is to allow one perspective to dominate one's understanding and to try to ignore the other or rationalize it away. No dilemma remains, because one views the issue with one eye covered. Another strategy is to seek some sort of "compromise" or middle ground; this route assumes that the terms of the dilemma fall upon a single continuum. Yet another resolution is a synthesis, Hegelian or otherwise, in which the apparent opposites are viewed as aspects of a common interactive relation. Tensions are reconciled in the genesis of some new form that combines elements of both sides into a new mix. Still another approach can be called Deweyan: One denies the apparent terms of the dilemma by adopting a third point of view, rejecting the two opposing alternatives. And one other approach exists: to assume an incommensurability between the alternatives, so that they do not engage one another. This approach does not dissolve or reconcile the dilemma but elides it.

Each of those perspectives can illuminate both conceptual and practical problems. The views can provide understanding, a sense of possibility, and a way out of the difficulty. Different dilemmas are amenable to different approaches. But I suggest another way to approach certain dilemmas: *Don't* seek a way of making them disappear, but keep the tension alive—a dialectic that does not move toward resolution but yields creativity out of the sustained movement back and forth between the two (or more) alternatives.[11] In part, this creativity arises from respecting the distinct advantages of each perspective and from learning to look both ways. In part, too, it arises from the state of uneasiness that accompanies not being settled into a comfortable, singular point of view. In part, finally, it arises from the open-ended outlook that such an attitude forces upon us—not simply the sense that *any* belief should be open to new information, challenge, and modification, but the sense of open boundaries, of unfinished business.

I do not mean to minimize the difficulty, the unsettled state of uncertainty, that accompanies such an orientation to the world. But as I have discussed elsewhere, certain narrative tropes—including tragedy, irony, and parody—can lend to this sense of dilemma a certain attitude or tone that makes it livable.[12] A narrative trope can help us formulate a *version* of events that grants them some coherence and meaning. Each of those tropes (and perhaps others as well) can help us regard the world through a dual lens without reconciling the different perspectives, and each affords a distinctive *mood* to that tension. In the case of tragedy, irony, and parody, the mood may be one of dramatic urgency or of wry regret or of arch comedy. There is no reason why different tropes and moods might not be overlaid on different issues, and there is nothing more true or more fundamental about the tragic trope, which is my focus here. The educational endeavor, in other words, could be regarded just as fruitfully as ironic or parodic.

But through tragedy, we see an aspect of urgency in our educational successes and failures. We carry the full weight of disappointment but at the same time try to move forward with the lightness of hope. Such a perspective speaks directly to the five dilemmas discussed earlier in this essay. Through tragedy, we wear authority uneasily, neither denying it nor taking it for granted. Through tragedy, we hope for progress but acknowledge that the path is neither straight nor smooth; indeed, it is not even *one* path, but many, and progress along one path can always be viewed as a detour or a retrogression from the perspective of another. Through tragedy, we take on the responsibility of identifying more and less worthy subjects of study, but always with a sense of doubt—a doubt we should share with our partners in teaching and learning—that those are necessarily the best or most worthy or most true subjects of study. Through tragedy, we come to believe that we are doing well by our students, trying to represent to them a perspective on events that respects contrasting points of view. Yet we recognize also that this very process tends to normalize, to converge, views—that with everything we give, we take something away. Because the tragic perspective does not seek a convergence of all differences (not even around the merits of a uniquely tragic perspective), it draws our tendencies as teachers into more provisional, tentative postures. Through tragedy, we accept the uncertainty of short-term and long-term consequences and the varied perspectives from which any teaching-learning encounter might be viewed either as a success or as a failure.

My concern is with a certain complacency to which teachers can fall prey and with which I myself struggle. The authority and privilege that institutions grant to teachers (yes, even though underpaid and underappreciated in many contexts, especially public school contexts), the fact that one is typically older and more experienced than one's students, the fact that in most classroom settings one is likely to be among the most articulate and well-informed participants—all can lead to a certain settling into the teaching role and taking for granted that what one knows is best. Any teacher reading this will understand such inclinations and will understand, as well, the moments of real doubt that one is up to the challenges of this vocation.[13] Complacency is not the only danger of the teaching role; a paradoxical doubt that one is expert enough to deserve the position often arises as well. But I want to suggest that those twin concerns are offspring of the same underlying attitude. Complacency assumes a certain givenness to one's status as a teacher; the search for legitimacy as an "expert" demonstrates a desire for the same result. Instead, I am suggesting the benefits of a conception of teaching, and an attitude toward oneself as a teacher, that is more unsettled and hence more difficult to sustain; we can't be constantly tragic or ironic or parodic. Those are not new metanarratives. I see the tragic sense not as a universal orientation toward life, but as a corrective that comes upon us, if we are open to it, when we acknowledge the irreconcilable tensions among different aspects of who we are trying to be and what we are trying to accomplish as educators.

* * *

The "benefits" of the tragic sense (such as they are) are not limited to effects on our own attitudes and motivations as teachers. I believe that the tragic sense inclines us to approach teaching in a different manner.

First, by abandoning the expectation that we will be expert in all matters pertaining to our subject, we are more open to new opportunities for discovery. We are less likely to insist upon our conclusions as the best or only ones and more able to adopt an inquiry orientation with our students. We expect to learn with and from them (whatever age they happen to be), and we feel less threatened by occasions in which we need to admit to them that we do not know or understand something. It is educationally important to model for learners what it is *not to know,* and what to do next. Yet how often do we actually say to students, "I don't know" or "This is difficult for me"?

Second, an openness to the unexpected creates a real dynamism in the teaching-learning encounter. It fosters the type of dialogue, for example, that I have elsewhere called *nonteleological*—exploratory, without a preconceived (by the teacher, that is) end point or conclusion.[14] This attitude respects deep complexity, not only in the sense of a complicated puzzle to be worked out or solved but in the sense of a perpetually open question, always susceptible to new perspectives, new pathways, new discoveries. This suggests a transient and provisional sense of knowledge and understanding. Questions for which we feel that a "true" answer has been established are *dead* questions—educationally less useful questions.

Third, the attitude and approach I describe accept as a condition of exploration and discovery the occasional state of being lost, confused, and unsettled. I believe, in fact, that this state of *aporia* is an underexplored educational moment. Too often, we regard such puzzlement or uncertainty as merely a transitional state between ignorance or misconception and a more complete or "truer" understanding. This is the sense of *aporia* in Plato's dialogue *The Meno,* for example. But what if *aporia* is not simply a transitional state but a rich fertile moment of educational potential itself? Exploring this topic is a separate project,[15] but my point is that we need to prepare learners for such an experience, not as a moment of frustration or failure but as a moment of possibility. We can do so authentically only when we make clear to them that this difficult state is one we experience and struggle through ourselves. I believe that a great deal of insight can be gained by reflecting on the educational centrality of making mistakes, of being wrong, of feeling doubt or puzzlement. We seek to settle or satisfy those shortfalls, but in doing so we only create the conditions for new mistakes, errors, doubts, puzzlements. The tragic sense helps us maintain a humble respect for such experiences and accept them as a condition of life rather than as something to be transcended, avoided, or explained away.

A fourth benefit of the tragic sense—one that can also be a major educational challenge, especially for teachers who value critical thought—is to help students *think differently*.[16] What does this mean? It does not mean replacing wrong answers with different, correct ones. It does not even mean, or mean only, helping students to explore or consider alternative perspectives or hypotheses about some problem, with the intent of comparing them to find the best of them. At a deeper level, learning to think differently means standing outside a particular set of assumptions, categories, and values to consider the possibility of how the world is, given a different set of them. It is a disproof at the level of practice of radical incommensurability, to the extent that we and our students can entertain the possibility that the paradigms we happen to take for granted do not define the horizons of the universe. Sometimes cross-cultural study can play a role in this, as can certain works of literature, but this places a great weight on our talents of imagination. Other times, dialogue with others not like us, undertaken in a spirit of curiosity and respect, can do more for us, because the engagement itself supports the possibility of understanding across that difference—there can be explanations and examples provided that directly respond to our questions.[17] There will be limits in our capacity to imagine a way of life utterly foreign to us, but the tragic sense prepares us for such limits, even as we push against them.

The fifth benefit of this orientation to teaching is that it suspects *method*, especially the search for any single method. I believe that conservative and progressive educators, mainstream and radical educators, all have been tempted by this quest. From direct instruction to whole learning, from progressivism to critical pedagogy, the modern history of education can be studied as a succession of new prescriptions about the one right way to teach—the most effective, the most humane, the most politically correct. Yet if there is anything that the practical experience of teaching shows us, it is that there is no single approach that works with every student, every subject matter—or (for that matter) that works *for us* every single day. How many have had the experience of trying an activity with a group of students with disastrous consequences, when we had wonderful results with the same activity and another group, sometimes even earlier the same day?

To me, such experiences yield two "tragic" insights. The first is that the search for one right way to teach must be supplanted by a deep pluralism of approaches and perspectives. One becomes an experienced teacher not by mastering a single method but by acquiring the good judgment and sense of security to adopt alternative approaches and to change midstream when necessary, as circumstances and student reactions warrant. But such pluralism implies judgment and choice, and that implies errors—*our* errors, not the shortcomings of some "method." The second is that the very metaphor of "method" is a trap. Drawing from Heidegger, I think it is better to think not of a *method* of teaching but of a *way* of teaching—not a technique, but a path, a direction. Of course we need to have purposes and expectations as we plan a teaching-learning situation, but our relation to those is not means-ends efficacy but an orientation, a reference point against which we can judge our present position and course. And if we are lost—*when* we are lost—we need to find a new way and not be hampered by the habit of simply persisting with "what works." (I am reminded of the old joke that when a child is given a hammer, everything needs hammering. Some educators are like that child.)

The sixth benefit of the tragic sense is that it undermines our sense of self-sufficiency and independence. It makes clear our need to seek out with others (our colleagues, our friends, our students, and their parents) alternative ideas and different problem-solving approaches as well as seek from them a sense of common purpose and possibility. Nothing is as good a remedy for complacency as the recognition that one has erred, fundamentally and without recourse. I do not mean to romanticize the discouragement and unhappiness caused by such failures—or to treat lightly the crises of confidence that can result. Like most teachers, I have felt them. But letting their effect sink in teaches us something as well—that we are not the only ones to have experienced them, that they are something intrinsic to the teaching endeavor itself. That way, the most debilitating consequence of such experiences—the sense of isolation—need not paralyze us, since we have recourse to others who have experienced these crises as well. And in case it needs to be emphasized, this uncertainty is something we need to be willing to share with our students also. How can we expect them to admit their questions and uncertainties to us if we are unwilling to admit any of our own? Here, too, I believe, the tragic sense has a constructive, enabling potential as we pass "all the way through" a sense of disappointment and loss to the recognition of different possibilities on the other side.

* * *

Why teach? If we adopt the tragic view, what is to sustain us as educators? How do we maintain a sense of purpose and hope—a sense of courage, I would say—in full recognition of the occasions of difficulty, uncertainty, error, and failure that we will encounter? As Arcilla asks, what can support one's sense of decency and integrity as a teacher?[18]

In finding provisional answers to such questions, we should avoid some tempting but false paths, I believe. If we base our hopes on unrealistic, utopian dreams, what we might gain in the short term in terms of a feeling of momentary inspiration can lead, in the end, to greater frustration and disappointment. For me, this is not the way to go, is not what I seek for myself or what I try to offer students.

The core of an alternative attitude is what Foucault calls "the care of the self."[19] The phrase refers not to selfishness or self-centeredness, but to an appreciation of the conditions that allow us to maintain an identity and a sense of efficacy. We must act out of and respect our own sense of dignity and integrity, not because those are ethical absolutes but because not to do so is to undermine our capability as ethical agents. For teachers, I believe, this means more than just the platitude "You need to take care of yourself before you can take care of anybody else." We should ground our teaching and our motivation for teaching in the things that we can influence and determine ourselves, in our relations to others, not in the transcendent or the altruistic.

What I want to say is something more like this: "Teach for the pleasure of doing something you are good at, not out of a sense of duty. Teach for the satisfaction you feel at seeing others succeed, not out of a desire to 'help' them. Teach for the joy of the subject matter you are discussing, not to attain 'standards' defined by others. Teach out of the love you feel for students, not out of some abstract mission of social transformation."

I do not know if such a vision is robust enough to sustain anyone else's commitment to teaching. But this vision of teaching grounds our sense of purpose in what we can do, and do well, in what gives us a sense of satisfaction and joy. Of course we mean for this to benefit students, to help them, to make society better. But those aims, I am afraid, are not only exaggerated in their aspirations but also ephemeral in their ability to move us. On many occasions, we must (if we are honest with ourselves) doubt whether we can attain those larger aims without their being contradicted by just as many countervailing effects. The tragic sense keeps us honest and modest; it forces us to ground our commitment to teaching in what our ability and will can sustain. We often ask students to love learning for the sake of learning; we never consider what it might mean to love teaching for the sake of teaching.

Notes

Earlier versions of this paper were presented at the University of Auckland and the University of Otago, New Zealand, and at the University of Sydney, Australia. I want to thank the participants in all of those sessions for their constructive comments. Thanks especially to David T. Hansen for suggesting improvements to this chapter.

1. Nicholas C. Burbules, "The tragic sense of education," *Teachers College Record,* Vol. 91 No. 4 (1990): 469–479; Nicholas C. Burbules, "Authority and the tragic dimension of teaching," *The Educational Conversation: Closing the Gap,* James Garrison and A. G. Rud, eds. (New York: SUNY Press, 1995), 29–40. See the thoughtful analysis of this essay by Rene Arcilla, from which I have learned much: "Tragic absolutism in education," *Educational Theory*, Vol. 42 No. 4 (1992): 473–481.

2. See also Robert W. Floden and Christopher M. Clark, "Preparing teachers for uncertainty," *Teachers College Record,* Vol. 89 No. 4 (1988): 505–524 and Philip W. Jackson, *The Practice of Teaching* (New York: Teachers College Press, 1986), 53–74.

3. Herbert J. Muller, *The Uses of the Past: Profiles of Former Societies* (New York: Oxford University Press, 1957), 23–25.

4. Arcilla, "Tragic absolutism in education," 480; see also Friedrich Nietzsche, *The Birth of Tragedy and the Genealogy of Morals,* trans. Francis Golffing (New York: Doubleday, 1956), 8.

5. For a helpful discussion of a range of dilemmas in education, see Ann Berlak and Harold Berlak, *Dilemmas of Schooling: Teaching and Social Change* (New York: Methuen, 1981), chapter 7. Unfortunately, this book, having laid out sixteen dilemmas, proceeds to try and find a resolution to each and every case. See also Karl Hostetler, *Ethical Judgment in Teaching* (Boston: Allyn and Bacon, 1997).

6. Nicholas C. Burbules, "Postmodern doubt and philosophy of education," *Philosophy of Education 1995,* Alven Neiman, ed. (Urbana, Ill.: Philosophy of Education Society, 1996), 39–48.

7. See also Burbules, "Authority and the tragic dimension of teaching."

8. Dennis Carlson, "Progress, progressivism, and postmodernism in education," in Dennis Carlson, *Making Progress: Education and Culture in New Times* (New York: Teachers College Press, 1997).

9. See, for example, Erica Burman, *Deconstructing Developmental Psychology* (New York: Routledge, 1994), 18. Thanks to John Morss for this reference.

10. Michel Foucault, *Discipline and Punish: The Birth of the Prison,* trans. Alan Sheridan (New York: Vintage Books, 1977), 177–184 and elsewhere.

11. A slightly similar idea is explored in Peter Elbow, *Embracing Contraries: Explorations in Learning and Teaching* (New York: Oxford University Press, 1986). Yet for Elbow, contraries are embraced within the context of a "larger, more inclusive view" (240), which is of course a way of reconciling them.

12. See Burbules, "Postmodern doubt and philosophy of education."

13. See also David T. Hansen, "Teaching and the sense of vocation," *Educational Theory,* Vol. 44 No. 3 (1994): 259–275; David T. Hansen, *The Call to Teach* (New York: Teachers College Press, 1995).

14. Nicholas C. Burbules, *Dialogue in Teaching: Theory and Practice* (New York: Teachers College Press, 1993), 5–7, 17–18.

15. Nicholas C. Burbules, "Aporia: Webs, passages, getting lost, and learning to go on," in Susan Laird, ed., *Philosophy of Education 1997* (forthcoming).

16. Nicholas C. Burbules and Rupert Berk, "Critical thinking and critical pedagogy: Relations, differences, and limits," in Thomas S. Popkewitz and Philip Higgs, eds., *Critical Theory in Educational Discourse* (Butterworth's, forthcoming).

17. Nicholas C. Burbules and Suzanne Rice, "Dialogue across differences: Continuing the conversation," *Harvard Educational Review*, Vol. 61 No. 4 (1991): 393–416. Republished in *Teaching for Change: Addressing Issues of Difference in the College Classroom*, in Kathryn Geismar and Guitele Nicoleau, eds. (Cambridge, Mass.: Harvard Educational Review, 1993), 1–25.

18. Arcilla, "Tragic absolutism in education," 477.

19. Michel Foucault, *The Care of the Self*, trans. Robert Hurley (New York: Vintage Books, 1986).

6

The Problems of Teacher-Student Relationships in Troubled Times

Jo Anne Pagano

Despite the obvious influence of critical educational studies in colleges and universities and on the practices of many public school teachers and administrators, the public discourse on education remains innocent of the ideas and arguments of critical educational theorists and their analyses of the social, political, and ethical consequences of the forms and functions of schooling. When members of the press and the public are aware of the more than two decades of critical scholarship in education, they are likely to see it as a benign irrelevancy or a threat to life as we know it. This results in public debate and legislation that defy commitment to democratic forms of life even while claiming to defend those forms of life against the depredations of the late twentieth century. In most instances, the debate even manages to ignore the profound differences between the late twentieth century and the late nineteenth century, holding the future hostage to a past that never was. A commitment to democratic living requires that critical educational theorists engage public debate and try to change its terms.

In public discourse, education is a "problem," the symptoms of which are falling test scores, teenage pregnancy, drug use, and violence. The solution to the problem is vigilance, discipline, "family values," and a kick in the behinds of progressive educators. Even the president of the United States apparently believes that teen curfews, school uniforms, and the further impoverishment of young women and their children are the answer to the massive educational crisis that critical theorists have identified as both cause and effect of a general social, political, and ethical callousness threatening democratic structures.

Educational scholarship seems caught between the claims of equality and empowerment, or nurture and acceptance, as they have been shaped in critical discourse, on the one hand, and the claims of our culture and disciplines, on the other. In exploring the continued marginality of critical discourse in the public sphere, we may locate two tendencies within that discourse itself. The first is the acceptance and adoption of prevailing and inherited forms of intellectual discourse unfamiliar to the culture in general—the intellectual isolation and autonomy of disciplinary communities. We do not seem to speak to any but ourselves, so the public and our students see us as irrelevant at best. The other is the related tendency, common to all disciplines, to spend a great deal of time correcting one another while the so-called culture wars decimate our credibility and enfeeble our efforts to teach.

As an academic discipline, housed in colleges and universities, educational studies observes the rituals and expectations of other disciplines. This means that we publish in professional journals, attend professional meetings, and tend to gather in groups of like-minded people. At the same time, the study of education is notably different from studies in other disciplines. In other disciplines, the object of study is clearly delimited, while scholars in education have turned their attention to the range of disciplines as they are constituted and sustained in educational discourse and practice. Another important difference is the intimate connection between scholarship in education and curriculum development and teaching. Educational scholars do not enjoy the same protections of professional expertise as scholars in other disciplines, although recent onslaughts of popular criticism against historians and literary critics suggest that such protections for other scholars are being eroded as well. Still, unlike other scholars, scholars in education must be sensitive and responsive to audiences outside their professional community. Moreover, the audiences to whom they must be responsible—teachers at all levels, legislators, parents, and employers, not to mention children—may have conflicting interests. Perhaps we have not been as sensitive and responsive to the conflicts among those interests as we should be. We need to find ways of talking within and across groups if we are to teach our students and make a public difference. And we must always remember that our students are in the process of becoming "the public"—a public that will be hostile to us tomorrow if our students are today. We must look first to our own educational practices as classroom teachers and as scholars.

My focus in this chapter is on university education because the university is where I teach. As I write *university,* I am troubled by prevailing criticisms of universities from within and without. I am troubled by students' hostility to their universities. I am troubled because these conflicts will finally have no winners; I fear that only ignorance and intolerance will prevail. You must not infer that I oppose conflict and resolve in bringing about change. You must not infer that I mean to insist on a unified front. Teaching is necessarily an act of cultural criticism, which we must teach our students, and we must teach our students that the purpose of cultural criticism is to generate and not destroy. The ordinary forms of academic discourse and media writing do not make that obvious. Through our teaching and our criticism, we intend to generate ideas and dispositions that sustain a humane world.

We teach because we think it is important to teach. We teach because we believe that *what* we teach is important. Those of us who teach in education departments do so because we believe that *how* we teach is as important as *what* we teach. Many of us believe that knowledge leads to empowerment, and that power, critically understood, can have a positive transformative effect on individuals and their communities. Many of us believe that human relationships are implicated in knowledge and its forms, and that knowledge is implicated in human relationships. Our students seem tired of hearing this. They don't believe us, or they choose not to believe us. Of course, in the current political climate, such knowledge is frightening. It demands more of us than praying in schools and placing metal detectors at their doors. It is more reassuring to dismiss concepts such as "empowerment" as liberal claptrap.

The year 1990 was an interesting one. We might even mark it as the year in which Allan Bloom's war against something he called the university escalated, the battle joined by a motley crew of academics, journalists, politicians, and students.[1] With the arrival of Bloom and his followers in the academy, it seemed that finally the professors and intellectuals were saying something people wanted to hear. Book after book, article after article, informed us of a crisis in the university. The daily newspapers broadcast the news promiscuously. The *New York Times* was suddenly interested in the depredations on moral and intellectual life made by participants at the annual meetings of the MLA. The efforts of teachers attempting to reconceptualize teaching and learning were ridiculed. Students became a generic "they," a fiercely contested territory in the culture wars.

Perhaps none joined the battle more eagerly than our students. Here was a whole world of public opinion to support their suspicion of professors. But why should they be so suspicious of professors? What have *we* done to earn that suspicion? After all, the turn to a new critical feminist, antiracist, and postcolonial scholarship and the efforts toward progressive pedagogies emerged from concern for students and their lives. Postmodern criticism and progressive pedagogy demonstrate that critical and pedagogical practices are deeply political. Critics of such practices understand this to mean that scholarship is *only* political. And the public has been persuaded that classrooms across the nation are under the control of "tenured radicals"[2] practicing "politics by other means."[3] Even if this were the case, why should our students be so ready to join the attack? We might expect them to be flattered rather than suspicious. We might expect them to join eagerly in criticism of entrenched ways of thinking and acting. In exploring the question of pedagogy, Elizabeth Ellsworth argues that we delude ourselves but not our students. She says that so-called critical pedagogies sustain teachers in their roles as the owners of knowledge, and students think they are being lied to. While teachers talk about empowering the students, students know the power is the teachers'.[4] Similarly, postmodern criticisms, just as preceding criticisms did, sustain the authors' power to subdue and exclude. Both critical pedagogy and postmodern criticism take oppositional stances that ironically maintain the structures and relations they seek to undo. Rather than *generate* new ways of reading and teaching, their oppositional nature simply gives point to the old ways. We need instead a generative criticism that supports a generative pedagogy, rather than simply repeating the old forms of attack.

I read the student press conscientiously, because my students are so very different from myself. This is a different time, and theirs is a different world. From the students who write, I learn that feminist women feel beleaguered, that other women are for equal rights but against feminism, that many women, feminist and not, feel victimized by the sexual politics of social life at our college, and that all tenured members of the faculty are said to be liberals. I learn that faculty are ignorant, and administrators venal. A sample of this sentiment appears in a student op-ed piece entitled "Self-Censorship at Colgate." The writer laments the demise of the value of rationality in the university and the limitation of free choice and goes on to say:

> I am concerned about an administration which applies law according to its own values, and condemns Greek letter organizations (rightly or wrongly) but fails to condemn in the same terms those who commit crimes against those organizations. I am concerned about a university that makes it abundantly clear that exclusive organizations will be eliminated by the year 2000, but which contains a building that claims to be a "cultural center" which is exclusively non-white in its orientation. . . . Is a somewhat less exclusive system legitimized simply because it espouses values and concerns which coincide with currently fashionable thinking? . . . It takes tremendous courage to speak one's mind on this campus.

Another student, responding to a classmate's antiwar position, wrote under the following headline: "New Standard Set for Absurdity." Another article, under the headline "Asinine Attack Envisioned," criticizes political correctness, intellectual acceptance of "reverse racism and reverse sexism," the residential-life staff, general education, dumb teachers, and faculty who think they have a right to enforce attendance policies, demand that students prepare for classes, and develop curriculum requirements. Complaints come at us from students across the lines of student divisions. We are reviled by everyone from students of color and feminists to fraternity and sorority members. You name them, they hate us.

Another issue of the school paper published so many negative articles that no faculty member could read it without feeling beaten up. One article promises to examine student evaluation of teaching. Its headline, "Forms [referring to evaluation-of-teaching forms] Influence Decisions," might lead one to expect an article reporting on the importance of student judgments. Not so. Readers are informed that their evaluations are not confidential, as claimed, since in classes of more than fifteen students, the evaluations are not typewritten. The writer suggests that students are, therefore, vulnerable to vindictive grading by faculty members who recognize their handwriting. Students are reminded that a teacher popular among some was not renewed despite his popularity. To such a degree are faculty perceived as arbitrary and tyrannical, and students as their victims.

Another article claims that students' constitutional rights are denied by a policy delaying fraternity rush until the sophomore year. Two trustees petitioned the courts for a restraining order on the grounds that students are being denied their right of association.

A letter to the editor carries the headline "Silent Agony." The writer says, "I have spent the last three years of my life being indoctrinated in the teachings of the all-powerful political correctness at Colgate." Referring to another student's complaint against offensive posters in one of the residences, the writer says, "the point you and the rest of the P.C. zombies have missed is that Colgate SHOULD NOT [protect people from un-P.C. activities]. The University already tells us when we can rush, where we can tailgate, and when the people in the apartments can have hot water. I do not want them to tell me what I can and cannot say. I am an adult."

"Currently Out of Touch" reads another headline. In this article, faculty are accused of teaching Socrates, Chaucer, and Marx while failing to inform students of events in Russia. This writer saw fit to observe that he had had to go home for vacation before he learned of the centrality of grunge in the fashion world. We apparently can't do anything right.

Another student writes that she will "not regret leaving an institution that cares so little for the safety or the human rights of the communities which exist within its borders." How can we teach in such an atmosphere? How can we teach students who hate us? And why do they hate us?

We might be tempted to dismiss the complaints as whiny and adolescent. We might be tempted to respond to them with trenchant analysis pointing out the incoherence of their positions, noting the gaps in their information and their failure of analysis. If we do so, we fail to acknowledge that large issues are at stake for them. We fail to understand that running beneath all of the complaints is a current of disappointment. We fail to acknowledge the anger provoked by students' sense that we have failed to take them seriously.

The guests on the *Sally Jessy Raphael* show the first time I saw it had all been abducted by space aliens. They were there together, members of a support group for former space alien abductees, to tell their stories. A married couple had met after joining the group, evidence that some good comes from everything. The stories themselves were uninteresting—the routine experiments and white and blue lights, the usual threats of environmental disaster and pleas for world peace. What *was* fascinating was the audience response. They were furious, and they were hostile. They were angry because they *knew* that space aliens do not exist. I was more bemused than amused by this response. I was even a little frightened. It just didn't seem to me worth getting so worked up over the whole business. Perhaps the guests *were* abducted by space aliens. I certainly have no way of knowing for sure. But the audience was very certain, indeed. But even if the guests *had not* been abducted by aliens, the fantasy of abduction strikes me as more interesting than infuriating.

Interested, I tuned in again a few days later. This time all the guests were recovering from multiple personality disorder or, perhaps more accurately, were learning to cope with their condition. Once again the audience responded with intense anger and hostility, knowing for certain that such a condition is an ontological and epistemological impossibility and probably an ethically pernicious hoax—that is, except for the few who claimed the distinction of multiple personalities for themselves, noting that their mothers, lovers, brothers, and friends often remark that they sometimes seem to be two different people. Multiple personalities get translated in this case into self-indulgent moodiness. Both of the responses are fascinating—the one that rejects unconditionally the possibility of an experience that is not one's own and the one that assimilates voraciously that experience.

The dynamic of this response is similar to the uproar regarding "political correctness" in schools and universities. We must be astonished by the violence of response to the annual meetings of the MLA and to curricular revisions in public schools and colleges and universities. In no less a place than page one of the *New York Times* on October 28, 1989, Richard Bernstein, indefatigable watchdog over the excesses of the academy, assures us under the screamers "ACADEMIA'S FASHIONABLE ORTHODOXY," "MAKE TENURE NOT WAR," and "THE RISING HEGEMONY OF THE POLITICALLY CORRECT" that "some even question the very notion that there is such a thing as disinterested, objective scholarship." He informs his readers that political correctness has its roots in a 1960s radicalism that unites commitments to affirmative action with what some scornfully refer to as the "Studies." As evidence of this, he provides us with a list of titles from recent meetings of the MLA: "Jane Austen and the Masturbating Girl," "Brotherly Love: Nabokov's Homosexual Double," and "A Womb of His Own: Male Renaissance Poets in the Female's Body." Such scholarship, he suggests, along with environmentalism, support for Palestinian self-determination, and the use of biodegradable garbage bags, is responsible for the decline of civility and the decline of the West, the demise of academic freedom, subversion of the First Amendment, and the general philistinism of the young everywhere. We might expect to find this piece on the op-ed page, but we do not.

On January 1, 1990, Bernstein returns to the "Week in Review" section of the *New York Times,* fresh from the 1989 meetings of the MLA, to inform us that "LITERARY CRITICS FIND POLITICS EVERYWHERE." He is followed on February 10, 1991, again in the *New York Times*, by Anne Matthews, a self-proclaimed survivor of the 1990 meetings, who provides us with another list of titles to be taken as evidence of the decline of education and civilization. The title of her essay is "Deciphering Victorian Underwear and Other Seminars." She also provides a list of titles: "The Detective as Pervert," "Strategies for Teaching a Feminist Political Latin American Culture Course," "The Repulsive Woman as Poet," "Lord Peter Wimsey: A Member of the Neighboring Sex," "Self-Consuming Fictions: The Dialectics of Cannibalism in Recent Caribbean Narratives," "M.L.A.: It's My Party and I'll Cry If I Want To," and many more. Whether she attended any of those sessions is unclear. Perhaps no one ever told her not to judge a book by its cover. The mania for list making and the assurance that merely presenting those lists stands as an argument for or against anything is itself an interesting phenomenon. This is the sort of writing emulated in the student press.

A former student of mine, thinking me more naive than evil or stupid, pressed on me his copy, well annotated and underlined, of Roger Kimball's *Tenured Radicals*. His friend, also one of my students, wrote in the campus press:

> I'm also glad that GNED [general education] really punches up the problem of deconstruction in American education. I'm really sick of always having to read the works of bad white female authors and dead black authors. I hear that this trend will continue and that for my graduate work in English I'll have to read live Caribbean and Nigerian authors and unknown female authors who hate men. I'm not sure this is English, but since it goes along with the concept of GNED it must be good. I hear it's also liberal and that's always, without question, good.

Richard Bernstein was heard from again in the *New York Times* on June 11, 1991, when he lambasted the *Random House Dictionary* for "spelling out rudeness." He was so appalled by the dictionary's inclusion of new usages that he called all the way across the ocean to editor John Simpson in London. Simpson joined in with a lament about the association of the word *gay* with *homosexual,* which, he said, "deprives the word of its former primary meaning of happy, bright, merry." Well, perhaps. It probably depends on who you are.

Writing in the *New York Times* on May 5, 1991, Donald Kagan observes:

> At present, however, the study of western civilization is under attack. We are told we should not give a privileged place in the curriculum to the great works of its history and literature. At the extremes of this onslaught, the civilization, and its study, is attacked because of its history of slavery, imperialism, racial prejudice, action to war, its exclusion of women and people not of the white race from its rights and privileges.

The assumption shared by all those writers and their readership is that universities and curricula have, until now, been steady purveyors of a fixed commodity, easily and unproblematically identifiable as the "best that has been thought and said" in some mythic land of Western civilization. The attacks on the MLA, for example, betray the authors' ignorance of the history of colleges and universities. The very idea that one would study literature in one's own language was once thought to be an assault on academic integrity and educational standards in the minds of many nineteenth- and early-twentieth-century critics.

We might point out that we need not choose between a common culture and a land of diversity or between particularism and pluralism. The law of the excluded middle seems wrongly invoked here. We might also point out that what is really at stake is symbolic power and its role in the economy of cultural and political power. The curriculum, then, becomes a proxy for the real issue, as was argued by Mike Bygrave in his analysis of political correctness in the *Guardian Weekly* on May 26, 1991. He says:

> Political correctness is Marxism without the economics, a revolution made with words instead of weapons. . . . P.C. . . . only makes sense against the background of the Reagan/Bush decade. In a sense, P.C. is the politics of despair, or even of irrelevance. Changing the curriculum is what you do when there is no hope of changing the government. We might add that a cultural assault aimed at the body of political correctness is similarly an expression of a politics of despair.

The culture wars are not about the facts of the case. They are about who we are and about our relationships with one another. The culture wars are about perceived challenges to personal identity. They are about what it means to be a responsible, educated person at the end of the twentieth century.

Several years ago, a publication distributed to college students across the country depicted on its cover Macbeth's three witches. The witches are stirring an evil broth in a large kettle in which young people are screaming and floundering. The witches are named Feminism, Multiculturalism, and Deconstruction.

At the same time, those students who align themselves with the political and cultural left are no more tolerant or generous in their understanding of others. It was with a clear sense of her own moral superiority that a student in one of my classes informed another that calling an African American Black is insulting.

Nor are hostilities restricted to the press and to cocurricular events. A few years ago, a student of mine wrote a midterm paper entitled "The Emersonian Myth of Consciousness and Historic Perspective." At the heart of the author's reading is resentment toward Ralph Waldo Emerson's moral criticism of Daniel Webster's voting for the Fugitive Slave Law and toward my criticism of an editorial by the Southern Democrat John L. O'Sullivan urging the annexation of Texas. His argument was that we can't judge the past by present moral standards. Even if we now all agree that slavery is an evil, we cannot criticize those who once supported that institution. His argument was not an expression of *simple* moral relativism. The author maintained that Emerson himself was arrogant in applying absolute standards of moral judgment to the fugitive slave issue. But Emerson was not the real issue for him. More interesting is the heart of the matter, what may seem a non sequitur but is in reality the occasion for this particular essay. Here is the author announcing his real concern:

> While historic hindsight gives us a qualified view that Emerson was right and O'Sullivan wrong, there is a dangerous and often ignored myth associated with Emerson's consciousness theory [*sic*] that haunts American education in its close-mindedness even today. This is the worrisome, uppity attitude now associated with the academic elite, that they now have some sort of moral monopoly on political issues of "consciousness."

The conclusion of this paper is a recommendation of tolerance, an insistence that there are two sides to every issue. That the student is clearly confused in his reading worries me less than his obvious sense of powerlessness.

Another student in that same class insisted that teachers have no right to express their own views because asymmetries in power necessarily result in students' being either brainwashed or silenced. The students stand divided along ideological, racial, ethnic, and sexual lines. They stand against faculty and administrators. And the way they talk to, or past, each other is what they have learned from us.

As faculty, we barricade ourselves from each other and from our students in armed ideological camps. Prominent among opposing camps are the scholars versus the teachers, and the defenders of excellence against the promoters of diversity. A colleague informed me that there are two kinds of people in the university—those who adhere to standards of universal and timeless truth, and intellectual terrorists. Moreover, those two cannot talk to one another. Another colleague published a plea for objectivity in which he attacked "MTV intellectuals," and we knew who we were. He and others, he says, believe in standards and values. But who does not? Some of us are even willing to acknowledge that there may be eternal standards and values, just as there may be space aliens abducting human beings with surprising frequency. I get nervous, though, around people who think they know what those standards are. Reading academic journals and popular magazines alike, I am struck by the too-frequent absence of civility, by the viciousness and smugness with which we dismiss all claims and arguments but our own. I too feel endangered by the impulse to self-censorship. I regret the absence of open-mindedness. I regret even more the anxiety that prevents our talking together about what really matters to us.

I am not against disagreement, criticism, and opposition. But our critical postures may forestall the possibility of the sort of disagreement and opposition that, by truly engaging all positions, leads to the growth of knowledge and the enlargement of perspective. It seems that we can only validate our own work if that of others is seen to be invalid. My stature requires you to be dwarfed. My intelligence depends on your idiocy. Only in education and politics does this seem an acceptable way of talking with one another. This is how we teach our students to talk, and clearly they have learned their lessons well.

Certainly the struggle for the curriculum, if not a proxy for larger political struggles, is at least an expression of those larger struggles. But it is also more than that. The struggle is not one to be negotiated by means of rational argument or demonstration only, because it is more than that. For those of us who would teach the young, it is important that we recognize that we are confronting a question of identity—the fundamental problem of who we are.

This problem is met and engaged in the field of curriculum because it is the office of education to teach us who we are. As Stanley Cavell once said, all education is political education, for through education we discover who speaks representatively for us and for whom we can speak representatively.[5] The education wars currently being waged across the country are political wars; they are wars of representation. They are also moral wars. At issue is who we are and with whom and with what we identify. Our very sense of "we," and consequently our sense of self, is at stake. And this is one of those indurate psychological and moral problems recalcitrant to rational resolution.

The question of who we are is necessarily related to the question of Western culture, as Christopher Hitchens notes in the *Times Literary*

Supplement, March 4–10, 1988. Is Western culture only white, male, and European? Or is it simply the case that white, male, and European is Western culture as we know it? Some of us would argue that the project of the new fields and studies is one that honors Western culture by practicing the traditions of inquiry and analysis that enhance our self-understanding. Recent studies of *The Tempest,* for example, exploring the imperialist dimensions of Shakespeare's play, do not diminish Shakespeare or Western culture. No one recommends, as D'Souza claims, that we "expel Shakespeare" from the curriculum.[6] Such a conclusion seems willfully ignorant. New readings, even contesting readings, add to our knowledge and enjoyment of Shakespeare. This seems so self-evident that the denial of the legitimacy of new studies and new information seems as absurd as the fantasy of a "political correctness movement."

Many, stung by the charge of political correctness, take pains to point out that the political correctness movement is an invention of the right-wing press. They insist that when the term *politically correct* is employed by those on the left, it is meant as an ironic check on possible excesses attendant on moral smugness. My denial that I am a member of a "political correctness movement," or even a fellow traveler of proponents of such a movement, is beside the point. This is all beside the point.

Our passion for ignorance is the point. It is worth noting that those who defend the integrity of the Western culture canon most enthusiastically, including my students, are probably more ignorant of it than its critics. Shoshana Felman argues that teaching is possible only because it is impossible, that it involves us with others who do not lack knowledge, but who actively resist it. Teaching involves us with our own ignorance, a desire to ignore, a passion to resist acknowledging our complicity. Ignorance is not opposed to knowledge; it is a condition of the structure of knowledge. Teaching creates the condition through which knowledge and ignorance enter a dialogue, a dialogue between teacher and students in which their mutual resistances become the point of exploration.[7] What is it that critics of the university and their student followers resist? The picture of Macbeth's three witches contains a map. The witches may be read as the Witches of Otherness. Like the original Other, the primal mother who threatens to devour her children, the Witches of Otherness mean to eat those helpless students.

It would be tempting and easy to see the present situation as *merely* an outcome of the Reagan/Bush years, as a product of the increasing scarcity of economic and social goods for more and more people, of shrinking university budgets, and so on. The financial condition of universities and colleges around the country is infelicitous, certainly, and disciplines and departments compete for space, positions, and equipment, often basing their claims on the relative prestige of disciplines and departments. But more is going on here. We are in a crisis of knowledge, and the routines and rituals of intellectual life provide us with no models to help us in meeting this crisis. The various "post" languages identifying this crisis give us no help either, defying, as they do, experience.

Terrence Des Pres, in an essay entitled "On Governing Narratives: The Turkish Armenian Case," anchors this crisis in knowledge to a global politics of power. He takes by way of illustration the Turkish government's denial in 1986 of the occurrence of the Armenian genocide of 1915, and our own government's willingness to acknowledge, despite the facts, a possibility that there was a legitimate Turkish "side." Des Pres argues that the pressures of cold war politics, combined with a two-sides-to-every-story rationality and the historical revisionism everywhere in the air, made possible the American government's failure of moral courage and its revocation of its earlier attitude toward the genocide.

According to Des Pres, we come to ourselves and make sense of the social and historical worlds through "presiding fictions" or "governing narratives." One pervasive narrative of our Enlightenment heritage is a narrative of knowledge. The protagonist of this narrative is the hero of knowledge who, armed with the two-sides method, effectively challenges the authority of church and monarchy. This narrative is presently opposed by the postmodern narrative of Armageddon, the hero of which is the hero of power. Whereas the older narrative is founded in optimism and faith, replete with a sense of destiny, the narrative of Armageddon, or power, is "founded on conditions almost systematic in their negativity." In this narrative, "destiny gives way to fate." The narrative of power gains strength from the increasing inefficacy of the two-sides method. The hero of knowledge attaches a corollary to the proposition that there are two sides to every story. The hero of knowledge knows that one of them must be wrong.[8] In the hands of present-day champions of the narrative of knowledge, the two-sides method has become weak and flabby, leading merely to an anemic relativism.

As our students oppose each other and us, as we oppose each other, both outside and inside our respective camps, we situate ourselves within one of those narratives, although with a curious inversion and an odd sort of moral contradiction. Those of us who cast ourselves as heroes of knowledge are those who cling to standards, to certainties, to traditions—precisely those things opposed by the original heroes of knowledge. At the same time, our two-sided method of critical inquiry logically commits us to a narrative of power. And power certainly enables the continued enforcement of regimes of truth.

Those of us dismissed by the heroes of knowledge as "politically correct," as "thought police," find ourselves, in Des Pres's schematic, uncomfortably situated. If pushed, some of us would have to admit that we have become, indeed—although unwittingly—heroes of power. We are now caught, says Des Pres, between the two governing narratives, both of which appear inimical to the liberal and moral interests of education.

Narratives are anchored in political and historical circumstances, Des Pres argues. They are also expressions of desire. The social and historical worlds that figure in our narratives are the worlds that we desire, and we learn, from the particular stories included in the canons of our governing narratives, that we desire power. Even stories of empowering others are expressions of our desire for our own power.

Governing narratives in education are about finding and forming identity. People are educated, and in the process of education, they take their places in the cultural conversation. Our understanding of ourselves as participants in this conversation is implicated in the ways that we identify others and in the identifications we forge. Discussions of identity have tended to divide neatly along lines of cultural and identity politics. The literature of identity politics, for example, neglects the complexity of identity, either reducing identity to the self or collapsing identity into a set of positions and social practices. Relationships between self and others, or between students and objects of study, are oversimplified because identity itself is oversimplified.

The version of this reductionism found in literary theory lodges meaning solely in the text or solely in the reader. Like reductionist literary theory, the implicit psychology of our two opposing governing narratives is bipolar. Bipolarity undermines the educational project of dialogue. Missing from such bipolar constructions is a term that nourishes and sustains dialogue between unity and multiplicity.

Psychological theories tend to stress the perception of difference as critical to the development of identity, a development on which all knowledge is said to depend. Now, the acknowledgment and nature of difference are precisely what are at issue in many of our educational debates and are a principal bone of contention between proponents of the narrative of knowledge and proponents of the narrative of power. I suspect that our students need us but that their own project of identity development requires a disclaimer of that need, a need that makes us as uncomfortable as it makes them. But the need persists. And we need their acquiescence in order to confirm our own identities. Being denied by them and avoided by ourselves leads to anger and to distance. That this should be the outcome of education speaks to the danger of unacknowledged need.

I do not suggest, however, that we all get together and talk about how we need one another. I propose a third narrative, one that acknowledges the claims of each of the others, even as its purpose is to tell a different tale. I call it a generative narrative. Its protagonist is a protagonist of compassion.

If there are two sides to a story, one of them must be wrong. If there are two sides to a story, one of them must prevail. Well, yes and no. Of course we desire to win others to our positions. Teaching and scholarship have as one of their aims the persuasion of others to different points of view. We want not simply to describe the world but to change it. But when we make sense of ourselves and our histories and politics within a generative narrative, we ask different questions of the world we criticize. Our knowledge that we are connected as well as separate, our identifications, our differences—all lead us to a sense of the importance of the other's identity. In a generative model of teaching and criticism, we want to understand who is speaking and under what conditions. We want to know under what circumstances certain assertions and positions would make sense. We want to know under what circumstances sense might fail. Critics engaged in generative criticism, by virtue of their own connections and identifications, are changed, even as the object of criticism is changed. We make new connections.

Generative criticism is not prescriptive, and it serves to enlarge discourse communities. Generative criticism operates to bring various interest groups and discourse communities into a single conversational circle by acknowledging the legitimacy of seemingly competing claims. It neither effaces the claims of others nor succumbs to the lure of personal relationship. Generative criticism is both a method of scholarship and a method of teaching that operates simultaneously within two discursive universes: that of relationship and the necessity of acknowledgment, and that of the public world and the claim of knowledge. Generative criticism is a method of attention and a method of teaching attention. It acknowledges the claims of relationship, among colleagues as well as among teachers and students, while asserting the importance of a mediating term in this relationship—the French Revolution, perhaps, or democracy and education—to prevent collapse either onto the pole of unreflective didacticism or into equally unreflective personal relationships, without succumbing to the seduction of either the hero of knowledge or the hero of power. The object of generative criticism is change—change that affects all participants in a scholarly community or in a classroom as we fix our attention on our diverse responses to the third term of our relationship.

We bring always to educational situations not only ourselves but also our previous identifications, and as those shift and are reconfigured, we shift and reconfigure our identities. Identification is a process by which we learn to share the desire of the other—to make it, at least for the moment, our own. But we do not thereby lose our identities. The curriculum we create reflects our identities and identifications both. As we work together, colleagues and students, we are changed. We learn to read and reread our own identities and others as we shift in our relationships with each other and in our relationships with the transitional object of the curriculum. Reading and rereading—understood as a serious business, not as a process of decoding or encoding—is the root of identity, a process of acknowledging and claiming the world in which we live. Education may be rendered as a series of triangles in which identity, identification, and object constantly shift along some axis of desire. Liberatory education requires spaces in which the identities we bring to our work as teachers and students meet the identifications we will make. If our work is to be generative, it must be generous as well.

Notes

1. Allan Bloom, *The Closing of the American Mind* (New York: Simon & Schuster, 1987).
2. Roger Kimball, *Tenured Radicals: How Politics Has Corrupted Our Higher Education* (New York: Harper & Row, 1990).
3. David Bromwich, *Politics by Other Means: Higher Education and Group Thinking* (New Haven: Yale University Press, 1992).
4. Elizabeth Ellsworth, "Why Doesn't This Feel Empowering? Working Through the Repressive Myths of Critical Pedagogy," *Harvard Educational Review* 59:3 (August 1989), 297–324.
5. Stanley Cavell, *The Claim of Reason* (New York: Oxford University Press, 1979).
6. Dinesh D'Souza, *Illiberal Education: The Politics of Race and Sex on Campus* (New York: Free Press, 1991).
7. Shoshana Felman, "Psychoanalysis and Education: Teaching Terminable and Interminable," in *The Pedagogical Imperative: Teaching as a Literary Genre,* ed. Barbara Johnson (New Haven: Yale University Press, 1982) 21–44.
8. Terrence Des Pres, "On Governing Narratives: The Turkish Armenian Case," in *Writing into the World* (New York: Viking Press, 1991) 249–262.

7

Predicaments in Curriculum Deliberation

ELAINE ATKINS

Over a quarter of a century ago, Joseph J. Schwab attempted to turn the curriculum field's attention to the practical, contextual nature of curricular decisionmaking.[1] He was only partially successful; the literature on what happens when teachers collaborate to design new curricula is still sparse. Although researchers such as Ian Westbury,[2] William A. Reid,[3] Decker Walker,[4] Lynne M. Hannay,[5] and myself[6] have devoted considerable attention to examining the implications of a deliberative approach, and in some instances have studied actual cases, the field still does not have a sufficiently rich body of literature examining how curriculum teams go about making joint decisions about what to teach. In particular, very little consideration has been given to the role that tacit knowledge and submerged values play in making those decisions.

This chapter is part of a continuing effort to reveal and examine the influence that such values and assumptions have on the deliberative process. In previous works, I looked at how tacit values and assumptions undergird and bolster the conscious decisions made by teachers as they work within pedagogically driven programs.[7] In this chapter, I examine how individuals' submerged epistemological and ethical commitments are coexistent, compatible, or in conflict with the philosophy of such a program. More specifically, I focus on the extent to which long-held but often hidden beliefs about the importance of teaching the canonical content of a discipline hold sway over competing pedagogical interests. For some teachers, an academic discipline consists of, and is defined by, a finite set of principles and body of knowledge, rather than, say, a mode or a language of inquiry. Often, essentialist beliefs undergird and shape those disciplinary conceptions. I am particularly interested here in how disciplinary concerns and underlying essentialist beliefs conflict with a perspective that may be loosely defined and readily identified as a "poststructural" perspective.

The term *essentialism* is used flexibly in educational discourse. For the purposes of this paper, it suffices to define essentialism as a reliance upon an irreducible body of true knowledge, whose innate worthiness is both ahistorical and decontextualized. For essentialists, the world contains fixed and stable meanings. As Richard Rorty points out, to assume such a stance is to view the life of reason as an "illuminated state of consciousness."[8] Language is used to capture the intrinsic nature of reality, and truth is defined as accuracy of representation.[9] In Rorty's words, "truth, goodness and beauty [are regarded] as eternal objects which we try to locate and reveal."[10] William E. Doll shows how essentialists reject the postmodern era of doubt and its reliance on contingency; instead, they draw on science and theology to reinforce one another, maintaining that God is the stable and permanent center of a well-ordered universe.[11]

The concept of tacit knowledge is also loosely defined in current educational literature; it is frequently tied to or used synonymously with expert knowledge. Again for the purposes of this paper, a broad definition suffices: Tacit knowledge refers here to that which we know but cannot readily tell and that which we value but no longer recognize we value. I borrow Michael Polanyi's definition of it as an "immense mental domain" of laws, manners, and arts that we use but whose contents we cannot specifically know.[12] It is so complex because it refers to both practical and theoretic knowledge and exists on many levels of consciousness, from the subliminal to the almost fully conscious.

It is my contention that helping teachers become more aware of the differences between their avowed pedagogical commitments and the resilient, silent values and assumptions that permeate their curriculum planning will enable them to make more consistent decisions. By examining the ways in which curriculum deliberators in specific contexts engage in the dynamic interplay between tacit and explicit knowledge, teachers can become sensitized to the benefits of uncovering, examining, and perhaps changing their own values and operating assumptions. Case studies of how teachers go about constructing curricula as they draw both from what they know they know and from what they have forgotten they know or value thus can contribute to a growing understanding of the curriculum-development process. It is important to keep in mind here the paradoxical and messy nature of such deliberations. The power of tacit assumptions and values should not be underestimated.

In more concrete terms, this paper is a case study of two pairs of instructors who each plan and teach a six-credit, fused English/Humanities course at Community College of Philadelphia (CCP), an urban institution with over 40,000 students. The four teach within the Humanities Enrichment Program (HEP), a project based upon and dedicated to a small set of post-structural commitments summarized later. From its inception in the summer of 1985 as a staff and curriculum-development workshop funded by a grant from the National Endowment for the Humanities, the project has assumed an interpretive, or hermeneutical, stance. However, it is important to emphasize that this stance has never been articulated in print; there exists no document that links its pedagogical commitments to a broader philosophical or theoretical framework. Instead, HEP's agenda must be deduced from its written "guiding principles" and from the language used by faculty at seminars and workshops. Although the leadership of HEP considers the program postmodern in both philosophy and practice, those individuals have never closely examined or even explicitly discussed with their colleagues what that means. As a result, it is conceivable that a few faculty members who do not attend HEP meetings regularly may have only the sketchiest idea of what the term refers to in either a popular or an academic sense; it is also conceivable that others who do have a well-formed conception would ultimately reject it as descriptive of their own worldview. This contributes to the predicament that I describe later.

When the project's leaders, who also wrote the grant, planned the original 1985 summer workshop, they brought in visiting scholars (including a hermeneutical philosopher) who shared their own postmodern[13] leanings, and they attracted and recruited colleagues whom they thought shared similar perspectives. In the past ten years, over thirty new faculty have joined HEP. The incentives for teaching within the program are predominantly intrinsic. Each instructor volunteers three hours a week of unpaid time to remain in the classroom during his or her partner's assigned hours. The students who are invited into the program have slightly higher reading scores than average for the college and the same entry-level writing scores; their morale appears to be higher, perhaps because they are pleased to have been "selected." The rewards for the faculty, in addition to working with motivated students, are the opportunity to collaborate with a respected, self-chosen partner and to participate in stimulating, informal staff discussions and workshops with like-minded colleagues.

The fused course that each HEP team plans gives students three credits each in English 101 (Basic Expository Writing and English Composition) and History 245 (The Individual in Society).[14] The only commitments to guide course development are the following:

1. The close interpretation of primary texts in the humanities.
2. Substantive writing assignments that emanate from course readings and discussions (as opposed to, say, isolated skills approaches).
3. The development of a learning community based on inquiry, reflection, peer review, and revision of written drafts.

4. Discussions and classroom activities framed within a cultural, social, and historical context.

Those four commitments are explained to students when they are recruited into the program, and a written summary of them is available for collegewide use by counselors and administrators.

Although, as I mentioned previously, there is no public or articulated philosophy that explains how the four principles cited above reflect a post-structural approach, a closer look at them reveals such an affinity. The careful reading of a primary text, for example, focuses on tacking back and forth between its parts, moving between general claims and supporting details, finding evidence to form a reasonable interpretation; it avoids general, definitive claims about what the text "really means." Assigning writing that emanates from and is shaped by a response to class discussion and readings also assumes that there is no formula "out there," no sure rules to follow when writing an expository essay. The reliance on peer-review groups similarly assumes that the quality of a piece of writing depends on the effect it has on its intended audience, rather than on a set of inherent traits. Finally, the program's dedication to placing the study of humans within their social and historical contexts reflects an emphasis on social contingency, on understanding people in terms of the cultures that shape and define them.

This postmodern stance permeates staff workshops and seminars. The language used at HEP meetings over the past ten years reflects the shifting emphases among and within poststructural movements. Several years ago, "deconstructing texts" was a familiar term; today, "hegemonic influences" are given careful attention. Race, class, and gender concerns are on the rise. A recent self-study of the project indicated that faculty thought that a dual benefit for their students was their growing ability to arrange and create categories of information, and their awareness that such categories are intellectual constructs and therefore arbitrary.[15] In short, most of the faculty are comfortable at least with the surface language of poststructuralist thought.

As I mentioned previously, however, it is also clear that some teachers don't draw from this lexicon at all and that others, especially new participants, are oblivious to its pedagogical implications. The deliberations of the two teams studied reveal two levels of buying into the dominant posture. A careful scrutiny of their planning sessions demonstrates how a member of one team struggles with the tension between disciplinary content and intellectual processes, while at least one member of the other team embraces an essentialist position, at the same time believing that she is working within HEP's parameters.

What follows is an account of the early planning workshop that I conducted with each team (in my role as codirector and curriculum facilitator of HEP as well as researcher) and the conversations we had when they met with me a year later (this time with me solely in my role as researcher) to reflect back on their initial course design and its classroom implementation. The four participants understood that they were participating in a research project and gave me permission to tape their sessions. Drawing from those taped interviews, I looked closely at the language each team used to tell its story. My method was hermeneutical in the sense that I interpreted the interviews by tacking back and forth within and among the transcripts, looking for themes and trying to understand each team on its own terms, including sudden disjunctures and inconsistencies. My focus, as I indicated previously, was on disjunctures between HEP's poststructural stance and privately held disciplinary or essentialist claims and concerns.

Rebecca and Kevin

Rebecca and Kevin are part-time instructors at CCP who have had extensive teaching experience at other colleges. Both hold Ph.D.'s in folklore. Rebecca, who also has an English degree, teaches in the English Department, whereas Kevin is a member of the Anthropology Department. When a new member joins HEP, he or she must work with a colleague who has taught in the program before. Rebecca is the veteran HEP teacher in this partnership.

Planning Session

Kevin is one of the first social scientists to teach in this project. With one other exception, the rest of us are English, history, art history, and philosophy instructors. At the beginning of our meeting, I mention that we still don't have a good sense of whether or not HEP should "move" into the social sciences. Kevin points out that anthropology belongs to the humanities just as much as it does to the social sciences, noting that "anthropology is one of those disciplines that straddle both worlds" and that he and Rebecca "come out of an ethnographic discipline in the Folklore Department, which is even more heavily influenced by the humanities and interested in an evaluation of the general human condition." We talk briefly about the anthropologist Clifford Geertz, and I remark that HEP has been influenced by the concept of social contingency and human creation of meaning. We agree that whatever the team works out, it will use History 245 as the generic label for, as I vaguely put it, "a fused English-anthropology-history interdisciplinary approach."

Rebecca and Kevin have come to the meeting with a rough plan for their course. With copies in hand, we begin to discuss it. It is organized into themes based on cultural anthropology courses Kevin has taught before.

The second theme, for example, focuses on a particular anthropology text. Rebecca has added reading material to "fit in" with the various themes. She comments that Kevin "basically had a very ambitious course that covered . . . cultural anthropology very thoroughly." When I suggest that they reconsider whether they really want to cover so much territory, Kevin acknowledges that the two have been talking about eliminating some content or simplifying it in some way.

They take a look at their preliminary sketch of the course, especially at its first part, which deals with culture contact. Kevin begins to describe one of their texts, explaining that it consists basically of writings by Native American authors from five Native American cultures. He thinks it is a superb fit for the class because it "looks at that moment when Europeans who arrived in the New World and elsewhere had contact with peoples they had never seen before. So this is a historical volume; it would really fit in with the fact that this is History 245. And it looks at that moment of contact . . . and it doesn't look at it as just a historical issue but as a cultural artifact. That is, what were the perspectives that Cortés brought and his expectations as a conquistador?"

When I ask him what he is going to teach his students to do, he replies that the "idea was to have students read some of this." Rebecca adds that both she and Kevin like to confront their students "with a culture that's radically different. . . . They're very myopic. . . . Even though they're studying with and possibly even living in close proximity to people in different cultures, . . . they still . . . perceive the world . . . how everyone perceives the world. They don't think of perception as something that's mutable."

It soon becomes clear that this concern for cultural content is going to permeate the course. As Kevin puts it, "that topic is important for introducing to students the very idea, not just of culture, which is something they can readily absorb, but the issue of cultural difference and the perspectives we hold within ourselves." But at this point in the planning, he wants to do much more: "I usually then go on to introduce more of anthropology." When I question this, he laughs, stops to consider the possibility of limiting the content, and then replies, "Well, the glib but still serious answer is that there is more to anthropology than just cultural difference." When I remind him that he is not teaching, covering, or providing students with an introductory anthropology course, that he is liberated from that, he appears to be caught off guard and repeats, very slowly in a bemused tone, "I—am—liberated from that."

Rebecca picks up on the idea of focusing the entire course on "culture contact." She begins to talk about "assimilation . . . exploitation of different cultures, the compromised position of Third World peoples." Kevin returns to texts, suggesting that they throw out their original textual choice, go on to another book for the first three weeks, and then move to *The*

Forest People: "There's a lot of stuff there on contact. . . . Well, we could make it a whole course on the matter of culture contact and . . . the lack of cultural communication."

Rebecca once again moves back to talking about themes: "Well, you know what would be interesting actually. . . . You could deal with discontinuity, but you could deal in a number of these themes [with] how people structure meaning and continuity and how they derive meaning out of seemingly disjunctive situations." But Kevin returns to content, suggesting a film that addresses the issue of cultural meaning. Examining a particular craft tradition (painting window screens) in Baltimore, the film demonstrates, in his words, "how a material tradition overcomes difference. In other words, you have a variety of different ethnic groups that utilize the screens." Referring to their original curriculum sketch, he suggests that they could then "do the thing with culture contact and language, which is week five" [of the original plan]. After Rebecca adds that she thinks the film would be important "in terms of both the verbal and nonverbal," Kevin suggests that they substitute a new topic for another already in the sketch and shift others around, moving week four's topic to a later date.

When I remark that they are going very quickly in terms of covering areas as opposed to engaging in an in-depth examination of issues, Kevin explains that "each theme would be used to highlight a different issue. It's not like you're going to be covering the same thing . . . in all of these topics, but rather each one kind of highlights a different facet."

It is at this point that Rebecca focuses again on their students, remarking that it is very hard for them "to get a handle on a culture that's totally foreign to them. You have to remember that they don't have any theoretical framework to hang this on . . . and basically all they've got, from my experience, is content. . . . If the content is interesting, that's what they're going to retain. They're going to retain some interesting cultural details. But they may not. . . . They're going to have a very hard time drawing a thread through these various cultures."

The conversation soon turns to writing assignments and ways to share the responsibilities of assigning and grading essays. Suddenly, Kevin asks, "My dumb question is, what is History 245? I now realize that I don't have a clear sense of how HEP views History 245." I answer that History 245 is a placeholder for a course that focuses on human beings and their place in society, and I stress its broad, flexible nature. I reiterate the program's emphasis on cultural context, writing-group revision, and the close interpretation of primary texts. Kevin repeats the words "of texts" and remarks that the "interesting problem of incorporating the social sciences into the HEP thing is the matter of social process as opposed to texts."

Eventually Kevin brings the session to a close by admitting that he needs "to take a step back from this and revamp it a little bit . . . and what's helpful is that what I didn't understand was I thought that History 245 was a kind of flexible catchall for courses from other disciplines. And that's not really the case, and now that I understand that, it makes it easier to revise the weekly assignments."

Planning Session Analysis

At this first session, it becomes obvious that, in spite of their deep understandings and agreements, the partners are in different places in terms of curriculum planning. Rebecca, after all, has taught with HEP before and has attended curriculum and staff development workshops. She also has read pedagogical literature extensively and may well have been influenced by the field's concern for intellectual processes and the language of student activities and outcomes. In any case, the first meeting finds Kevin talking mostly about themes, topics, and issues, and Rebecca mostly about changing student perspectives.

They come to this first session with a plan that replicates previous anthropology courses taught by Kevin; up to now, their collaboration primarily has consisted of Rebecca's incorporation of reading materials into Kevin's numerous themes. When I challenge them on what I perceive as their inclination to cover too much territory, Kevin stresses the importance of essential issues, such as "cultural difference and the perspectives we hold within ourselves." Rebecca, on the other hand, speaks primarily in terms of how she wants to influence her students; she is concerned with their myopia and wants to change the ways in which they perceive themselves and others.

In spite of Kevin's concern for teaching the corpus of "anthropology," he expresses a willingness to look for other means of organizing the course. When asked if he would consider devoting the entire course to the first theme, he remarks that he usually goes on to introduce more of anthropology, "that there is more to anthropology than just cultural difference." Yet when I persist, he appears genuinely surprised and reflective. His response to my suggestion that he does not have to teach an introductory anthropology course, the way he slowly repeats, "I—am—liberated from that," gives some indication of his careful consideration of what he considers a novel proposal. But he still is not convinced.

As receptive and reflective as he is, the best he can do in such a short time is start making shifts and adjustments to their original schedule. So he starts moving around the fourth and fifth weeks of their plan, substituting one topic for another. In this one session, he is not able to solve the predicament of prioritizing, let alone synthesizing, process and content concerns. Periodically he returns to content, pointing out that each theme would be used to "highlight a different issue." Rebecca provides a mild challenge to him by remarking that "at this point, . . . they [the students] are going to have a very hard time drawing a thread through these various cultures." A close look at their language reveals that Kevin relies essentially on nouns, on content, and Rebecca on verbs—on what students can do or should do (for example, drawing a thread)—as focal points for curriculum planning. Toward the end of the session, Kevin tries to pull together what he hears from Rebecca and me, remarking that "the interesting problem of incorporating the social sciences in the HEP thing is the matter of social process as opposed to texts." Although I don't find his statement completely convincing in the context of the rest of our conversation, I am struck by his willingness to try to think differently, to focus more seriously on process issues.

Reflection Session

One year after our first meeting, Rebecca, Kevin, and I meet to discuss their course, which they taught the previous term. I have prepared a set of questions to find out what happened. I begin by asking if they did indeed "throw out" one of the texts that they had decided to discard at the original planning workshop. Kevin answers that they realized that the "students had to be grounded in what constitutes culture. And they needed a thorough and complete introduction to the character of culture, as well as society and ethnocentrism and a variety of other issues. . . . I thought about what was the best way of introducing it to them . . . and although there were lectures on this material, I felt they had to read about it as well." He explains that they wanted their students to read about what anthropologists actually do and that one of their original textual choices did just that, so they kept it in their syllabus but "pared down" other readings. Kevin lectured and read directly from a book eliminated from their required list so that their students "didn't lose that piece theoretically or in terms of content. . . . It was one of those books that I had gotten attached to and didn't really want to let go."

Later, when I ask them what pleased them most about the course when they look back a year later, Kevin expresses satisfaction with the "whole thing. . . . We profited from teaching together and getting an opportunity to make use of not just standard lectures and materials but to be able to branch out. And also I think the real luxury is if something catches fire you can stay with it. . . . There were things that we did and things that we eliminated in part because of where things were going."

Rebecca adds that although the two liked to know where they were going and had the whole semester plotted out, they wanted to shake their students up too: "Well, one thing that really shook them up was . . . the stuff about the Incas and the work the Spanish did, the devastation that they created in South America." Kevin cites a report of an eyewitness account of what actually happened on the ground when the Spaniards arrived. The team taught about this "not just as grand history regarding important conquistadors and kings but rather as a cultural issue. And what surprised them [the students] about this was first of all the availability of this information. . . . When they think about the Spaniards coming in and conquering Peru and the Incas, they presume that's the end of the story, that one culture like a giant tidal wave just washed over what was there, and it was all destroyed."

Rebecca turns to their students' reactions, remarking that they think of the conquistadors and what happened as benign: "They don't think of it as destruction. . . . They think of it as discovering, not conquering. They don't think of the bloodshed . . . of the destruction. And they were asking questions like, 'Why did the Spaniards do this?' And then we talked about religion, about the role of Christianity; we talked about politics; we talked about economy; we talked about gold and gender and the nature of European, quote, discovery. And we didn't really talk about native cultures on the North America continent . . . but they made the connection."

Shortly after, Kevin adds, "Oh, and then . . . I got to do the material culture and sculpture stuff." He goes on to describe the materials that he "personally developed specifically for that course that ordinarily I don't teach. . . . One of the things I did was develop a slide lecture and some adjunct to our discussions on culture and material culture in the physical world. And as part of that I did this thing on the relationship of museums and traditional African sculptures from the Congo, and I think that went well, and I enjoyed having the opportunity to sort of stretch out, so to speak, explore areas that I'm concerned with that tap into the topic of class."

Rebecca picks up on Kevin's scholarly enthusiasm, commenting that "those were areas that I'm interested in too . . . primitive art and the use of the primitive in modern art . . . and in postmodern art. One of the things Kevin did was go back and forth between . . . African sculpture and a contemporary craft artist who's had his work exhibited at the Philadelphia Museum of Art. And, um, that was the kind of stuff I looked at in my dissertation and postdoc at the Smithsonian. And it was interesting. . . . I watched the students, and . . . there were some that were on the edge of their seats going, 'This is really interesting' and 'Nobody ever's talked about this before.'"

Later on, when asked what they think their students came away with, Rebecca simply and quickly answers, "a different worldview." Speaking about their original goal of helping their students become less myopic, Kevin remarks, "No, we don't give them any chance; they're going to have to confront who they are and the preconceptions they carry with them. And at least the way we structured it, they could not avoid those kinds of things. In other words, from a very basic level, from who they are to how they recognize their world to their basic preconceptions of the world, this course as well as cultural anthropology overall forces them to do that." But he emphasizes that this was just one major goal: "If you recognize difference, then you'll recognize cultural diversity; an ability to see that diversity only comes from a recognition of your own starting point."

Rebecca adds that "that in itself cultivates a garden where critical thinking can grow. It's like working the soil." She describes a videotape that they used from a PBS series produced by an anthropological research group concerned with the survival of indigenous people. The principal researcher "pairs the New World against the Old World." Describing an anthropological expedition to South America, the film raises a myriad of ethical questions "that concern not just issues of discovery, conquering, and development but also ethical questions that deal with their own profession of anthropology and culture contact. . . . We probably talked about it for two entire classes. We kept having to talk about it."

In Kevin's words, the film "raises all the issues of presuppositions and starting points. In other words, before you can apprehend or come to terms with another group, you have to recognize and be sensitive to your starting points. . . . What kinds of cultural presuppositions, perhaps even ethnocentrisms, might you bring to the problem, such that if you ultimately are successful in establishing some sort of contact with another group, will you be able to apprehend that group?" He wants to know if his students will be able to take in information about the character and nature of another group and their culture, given that they take for granted their own cultural groups. The film, he believes, forces them to look at that issue: "Before you establish contact with a group, whether it be distant or near, you have to look at, well, how do my presuppositions, how do my ways of thinking, beliefs, worldviews affect things even before the contact takes place? And the answer . . . is obviously, you have to recognize your starting points."

Attempting to capture the ways that the team helps students understand their own presuppositions, Rebecca begins to describe their writing assignments. "Well, see, the writing assignment made them . . . ask themselves . . . who am I as a cultural being? How do I operate within a culture? And most of them had never . . . thought about this before."

The two now spend some time recalling specific activities and responses from students that indicated that they gradually were becoming more conscious of the ways that cultures and subcultures shape the way they perceive the world. The pair keep stressing the point that before students can understand other cultures, they have to understand their own presuppositions. This involves helping them concretize culture by starting with behaviors rather than with broad, abstract principles. Rebecca refers back to what she said a few minutes earlier when she remarks, "By forcing them [students] to think differently, that's what I mean by cultivating the ground for critical thinking. . . . It forces them to think differently about themselves, the environment, and to make different assumptions, to question the assumptions they have about the world."

At my instigation, the conversation turns to critical thinking; Kevin expresses their joint commitment to turning "the students themselves into minianthropologists, which is to take some aspect of their life experience and put it under the same sort of examination process. . . . We asked them to [write] about themselves and their cultures and . . . to talk about where they thought American life was going. . . . So I think one of the answers to your question is that I have the confidence that based on the diversity of experiences that the students currently have, particularly here at CCP, that it's immediately applicable. They can begin to . . . look at their world in terms of cultural difference and their place in relationship to it. So that's how you . . . operationalize it. . . . I assume that the students are ready and able to look at their own world."

When the question comes up about whether knowing oneself necessarily leads to understanding other people, Rebecca doesn't hesitate: "Where you find out about your own culture is by looking at other cultures. That's why it's not enough just to read British and American literature or British or American history. Because you don't get the distance from yourself. So in a course like ours, it's happening simultaneously [understanding selves and others], and they are intertwined and cannot be detached from one another. They are absolutely locked together."

A little later the team focuses on how they help students develop ways of understanding other people by applying cultural categories and interpreting cultural artifacts. Kevin once again points out that the whole semester consists of "talking about the other . . . about what culture is," that they keep looking at "varieties of cultural expressions." Rebecca cites course readings on Gypsies, Hasidic Jews, the Amish, and Black-Jewish relations. She speaks about one novel that was extremely difficult for their students but says that she would teach it again: "I think that struggle is really important. . . . We want them to struggle intellectually."

Toward the end of the session, in response to my asking if they would do anything different next time, Rebecca replies, "We thought about that. . . . Instead of doing South America, maybe doing Australia. . . . Oh, I would simplify the first writing assignment; I would not make them deal with who am I as a cultural being plus all of Gauguin's questions. . . . I do have the habit of making writing assignments that are just too tough."

Returning to their planning meetings the previous year, I ask them if they centered their design on the selection of texts, activities, and topics. Kevin replies that "it was much more organic. . . . We oscillated between themes, whole books, fiction, nonfiction; we moved between that and overarching themes. And then . . . we started to put them together. . . . We probably settled more on the themes than on the books, and negotiated the books as best we could according to what we wanted to do. . . . These books address certain key themes."

Rebecca ends the conversation by emphasizing once again that she was "really conscious of wanting to give students readings that are going to stimulate them . . . what's going to excite them. . . . See, that was one of the great things about what I would call here the HEP experience for us. . . . Because in a way for us it's kind of a playful thing. And the students saw us at work at that intellectual play. And it taught them that they could play at intellectual work too. . . . They . . . need to discover that intellectual work can be deeply satisfying and enjoyable."

Reflection Session Analysis

At the reflection session, it becomes even clearer than at the early planning meeting that Rebecca and Kevin's conception of teaching is in harmony with HEP's broadly defined commitments. The only tension that I can discern is a minor one, compared to what I find when I work with the second team in this study. Kevin still tends to talk in terms of key issues or topics, but less because they constitute "anthropology" and more because they are essential to what he wants students to be able to do intellectually. Except for two brief moments cited later, Rebecca remains focused on process, speaking in terms of what is happening to her students.

During the course of the interview, Kevin's language undergoes a subtle shift. He begins by explicitly stating that when planning the course, they both gave a great deal of thought to the need to ground students in "what constitutes culture," and he reminds Rebecca that after their first session with me, they went back and "pared down" their readings. But very soon, he comments that the luxury of teaching collaboratively and in an interdisciplinary situation is that "if something catches fire, you can stay with it."

Rebecca's response that "we like to shake them up" is typical of her inclination to use active verbs to describe what she wants to see happening. Describing her students' initial response to learning about the Spaniard's conquest of Peru, she remarks that "they think of it as discovering, not conquering." She is pleased that eventually they are able to make the connection between what happened in South America and what happened to native peoples on the North American continent. I remember her observation last year that students are able to thread ideas together.

When Kevin recalls that he "got to do the material culture and sculpture stuff" in the course, I am reminded of his stance at the last session. He enthusiastically describes materials that he developed, including a slide lecture. He is happy to have been able to explore areas that he is interested in that also "tap into the topic of the class." I am surprised, however, when Rebecca responds with equal enthusiasm about her own content interests:

"primitive art, the primitive in modern art, and postmodern art." She recalls that this "was the kind of stuff" she looked at in her dissertation and her postdoc at the Smithsonian and so she is particularly pleased to have been able to introduce it in class. This is one of the few times that she turns her attention away from process concerns.

An interesting, if familiar, metaphor that Rebecca uses is the cultivation of a garden; unlike Rousseau, however, she is not thinking of cultivating children but rather working the soil of the intellect so that critical thinking can grow. Similarly, Kevin's description of how the videotape of an anthropological expedition to South America laid the foundation for students to think about their own cultural presuppositions sounds much like Rebecca's concern for self-knowledge. His comment, "You have to recognize your starting points," is one of many signs that he has become comfortable with the language of intellectual growth. This becomes explicit when he speaks about turning "the students themselves into minianthropologists." He describes a writing assignment that asks them to locate themselves within their culture and then to speculate about where they thought American life was headed. He stresses the importance of helping his students look at their world "in terms of cultural difference and their place in relationship to it."

The last part of our discussion is telling about both the pair's synchronization with HEP's central goals and their occasional return to content concerns. When Rebecca reviews the extensive course readings, she describes a particularly difficult text that she would teach again, in spite of student complaints, because she wants them to struggle intellectually. So I am somewhat taken aback when in answer to my question "Would you do anything different next term," she replies, "Instead of doing South America, maybe doing Australia." I don't want to make too much of this, particularly since she returns immediately to thoughts about modifying the first writing assignment to make it more accessible. But I find it an odd initial response, given everything else she says.

When I ask them to recollect their planning discussions during the previous year to learn more about what they focused on (such as the selection of texts, activities, themes), Kevin replies by stressing the organic nature of those talks. But by organic, he still means content: "We oscillated between themes, whole books, fiction. . . . We moved between that and overarching themes." Rebecca modifies Kevin's remarks by insisting that they didn't try to cover everything in cultural anthropology or folklore. She once again reminds me that their goal was to stimulate their students by concentrating on "what's going to excite them." They end their reflections with the metaphor of intellectual play and the hope that their students find "intellectual work deeply satisfying and enjoyable."

After reading and rereading the transcripts of our conversations, I am surprised that the tension I detected earlier between content and process has amounted to so little. Kevin clearly has made a significant, if still tentative, shift toward merging concerns about critical themes and topics with activities designed to enable students to broaden their understanding of themselves and their cultures. I think that their work is in harmony with, even paradigmatic of, HEP's approach. Their tacit assumptions and explicit convictions about the contingent nature of culture, Rebecca's consistent focus on student growth, and Kevin's movement toward process language all provide a close fit with HEP's commitments.

John and Laura

Laura is a part-time English teacher at the college and has an interesting and varied background. Years ago, she taught A-level (advanced) students in Asia who were preparing for British universities; currently, she teaches at both the college and developmental (remedial) levels at CCP. After speaking to a number of HEP instructors, she expressed an interest in joining the program. Laura chose a partner who shared her avid interest in teaching Shakespeare, and the two decided that they would devote much of their HEP link to reading at least two of his plays. After she learned that her partner would not be able to teach with her, Laura contacted John, another experienced HEP instructor, who agreed to step in. John has been an active member of HEP since its inception in 1985 and has taught with at least four other partners. An English teacher, he has a strong interest in classical literature. Like Laura, he is in his middle years.

Planning Session

Before I meet with a new HEP team, they usually work together a few times to share preliminary ideas. In this case, because of the sudden change in partners, Laura and John have spoken to each other only briefly. What follows is their first real planning session. After a short conversation about a few HEP administrative details, Laura begins to describe her interest in teaching Shakespeare. She thinks that this would fit in with HEP because the "Elizabethan world picture is definitely a window into the thought, the history, the philosophy of that period, and we could use that as a hinge in developing the history side." She recalls that her first partner wanted to contrast the Elizabethan worldview with a more modern one and mentions T. S. Eliot. She asks John if he thinks they should "focus on a contrast of social ideas, the decline of religion. . . . We no longer have a great chain of being; we no longer believe in authority; we no longer believe in classification." When John interjects, "Some of us believe in that," Laura exclaims,

"Oh, I do! I do! And I'm saying, that's the trouble; that's why I want to stay in the Elizabethan period."

A little later, still thinking about introducing contemporary texts, Laura comments, "There are some interesting comparisons . . . the idea of authority . . . the idea of what a community is today compared to the world picture then, where everybody had his place and was meant to be in that place. If you broke out of it, that's when evil [occurred], as Shakespeare shows." Picking up on this, John suggests that they "do something about democracy," that it is usual HEP procedure to move from some early period to a more contemporary issue or source.

At this point the conversation turns to whether choosing two contrasting periods is an intrinsic part of HEP and to the official commitments of the program as written in the brief statement summarized earlier. I stress the importance of process and suggest that content is a matter of individual choice, that it is instrumental to the process. We review the commitment to the careful interpretation of primary texts, to close, slow textual interpretation, and to writing groups using heuristics.

A short while later, John asks Laura if she thinks students would be able to handle Shakespeare. She replies that the plays are not difficult and that she always gives assignments that require performance: "That's when they come to life, when they have to be the people, rather than just see it on the page." She speaks about spending no less than six weeks, two hours a day, on one play when she taught in Asia and describes the process of reading, of walking students through almost all the parts: "You are, as a teacher, . . . discovering new things and finding ways of helping them interpret a passage. . . . I know you have to go slowly." John concurs. He says that he tells students that it is their first college English course, and "whatever you read is teaching how to read. . . . Don't be scared. . . . We're just reading any text; this one's a good one, and we're reading very closely and we'll learn how to read. . . . We can take whatever we want; it's still your first college class in reading and writing."

Laura adds that "it's really crucial that we pick a text that we believe we can make come alive for them." Toward the end of the session, she asks, "what is the ratio of culture to history" in HEP classes? John replies indirectly by mentioning that on the first day [of class], he tells his students that the Individual in Society history course . . . is cultural history . . . that we won't be doing kings and queens and battles. . . . There will not be a chronology. . . . We will be doing more of what they would think of as sociology or political science."

Laura is interested in the idea that they will be teaching cultural history and once again alludes to the Elizabethan world picture as a "history thing" that provides students with a sense of a period. She cites Mumford's claim that cities have "broken down the sense of community, hierarchy, commitment, all those things." She relates this to Shakespeare's interest in exploring the city (in his Roman plays), and through this, his own institutions, community, and the Elizabethan worldview. She again stresses the importance of teaching the Elizabethan worldview and indicates that she would like to introduce more modern work to "offer an equivalent of the Elizabethan world picture."

Planning Session Analysis

One of the more surprising moments I have had in studying teachers' deliberations occurs when Laura laments that we no longer believe in authority and in the great chain of being, and John adds that "some of us believe in that." I do not know how to respond; I am not taken aback by Laura's essentialist beliefs, but rather by her up-front assertion in the context of a HEP planning session. I am curious to see how she will negotiate her way through the program. There is a real predicament here, but I'm not sure to whom it belongs or how to characterize it. So far, Laura has attended only one HEP staff meeting, but I assume that she has spoken to a number of other participating faculty. On the other hand, I understand that we have never written a statement of our philosophy but have depended instead on the poststructural stance implied by the four pedagogical commitments described previously and the frequent use at meetings of certain terms associated with the movement (for example, *hegemony* and *constructivism*). The situation is complicated by the fact that John has worked in harmony with many other HEP teachers, yet here he is indicating that he shares Laura's essentialist commitments. Does he recognize a conflict? In practice, does he subjugate his own values to the HEP process? Does he try to move in both directions at once? If the two don't realize that they share conceptions of curriculum incompatible with HEP's, who should tell them? How?

It is evident from the start that Laura views HEP as a double course in cultural history and literature. She comes to our first meeting with a clear curriculum focus: She would like to teach Shakespeare. She sees a literature "side" and a history "side" and thinks that the Elizabethan world picture is perfect for HEP because it serves as a window to the thought, the history, and the philosophy of the period. She is open to bringing in work reflecting a modern worldview because it would serve as a contrast.[16] Such a contrast, she suggests, would enable John and her to focus on the loss of religion and authority. Her agenda seems clear-cut.

John, although indirectly concurring with Laura's basic values, keeps moving back and forth between what he interprets as HEP's priorities and Laura's desire to focus on the ideals of the Elizabethan period. He always has maintained that the program should select materials from different time periods. The two of us have always disagreed about this issue, and over the years, I have come to take for granted, without much reflection, that John pedagogically is at the more conservative end of the HEP continuum. I see the continuum not only in pedagogical but in political terms as well. What is more pertinent here is that John is participating in the deliberations as a spokesman for what he perceives as HEP's goals. He is willing to try Shakespeare but is most concerned with whether or not our students would be able to handle the plays.

John's emphasis on the careful analysis of texts becomes obvious when he explains that he tells students that regardless of what the chosen text is, they still are "just reading any text" and that they're going to learn how to read. Later, he adds that he always tells them that the course is more like sociology or political science than traditional history. In the sense that he pays such close attention to careful reading, he places himself securely within the HEP spectrum. What is unclear here, and never really clarified during our discussions, is how he defines close reading; I don't know if he tries to help students make good interpretations based on internal evidence and external contexts, or whether he helps them to search for the "meaning" of a text.

This is all new to Laura, and she works hard throughout the session to hear what we are saying. It has become obvious to me that she knows very little about HEP's values and guiding assumptions; we have not been as intelligible or as direct as I had thought. Yet I begin to see openings for her to develop a merged perspective. I am encouraged, for example, by the fact that she says she always gives assignments that require performance to make a text come alive for students. She also expresses an interest in finding ways to help them interpret difficult passages. Nevertheless, it is impossible to ignore the fact that she keeps returning to the idea of contrasting a "good" worldview with a more problematic one, and that toward the end of the session she asks, "What is the ratio of culture to history" in HEP classes? She wants to "provide" her students with an appreciation of a better period and speaks wistfully of how contemporary cities have broken down the sense of "community, hierarchy, commitment, all those things." I leave the session wondering if Laura and John will teach a course at cross-purposes with HEP's commitments, or if Laura will move closer to John's position, and somehow the two will design a conservative rendition of what the program tries to do. Either way, I see predicaments, the first obviously more serious than the second.

Reflection Session

When I meet with Laura and John after they have taught together, I learn that their collaboration has gone smoothly. When asked what they consider to be the most successful aspect of their work, John replies that he had never dealt with "the recitation" before but that he and Laura had had a great deal of success in getting students to memorize and recite forty to fifty lines of Shakespeare. By the end of the term, almost every student in the course had been able to recite from *Henry V.* Laura adds that this assignment enabled students to tackle a task, finish it well, and get closure. She describes the short performances that resulted when selected pieces were put together for a collegewide Shakespearean celebration.

In answer to what else pleased them in terms of student accomplishment, they cite improvement in essays but don't elaborate about what methods or approaches they used. Rather, they speak about their grading system and then mention that they lost many students along the way, "particularly ones on the weaker side." They both express regret and bewilderment about losing students over the course of the semester. Speculating about their dropout rate, Laura thinks that they should have started with *Macbeth* and then turned to *Henry V,* rather than the reverse, because *Macbeth* was more difficult, time was running out, and the class was tired and not prepared for the close reading required. They had moved rather quickly through selected monologues of *Henry V,* being primarily interested in acquainting students with the period: "the culture . . . the perspective of the Elizabethans, the idea of the king." Laura remarks that their students had been unable to make the transition from the level needed for reading parts of *Henry V* to the "rigor in reading and writing" required for studying *Macbeth.*

John adds that it wasn't so much the rigor but that "students just can't stay that long" on one piece of work. He thinks that it's very "wearing" for students who aren't in the habit of studying "something closely for something like a month . . . and this doesn't seem to be in their experience; everything is shorter. . . . So either we would have to consider shortening or saying, 'No . . . you have to get used to this. We're going to get every inch out of this. We're going to wring it dry, one time, one play, even if it's your first semester in the school, as a practice for anything else.'" He tells his students on the first day that different teams do different things in different semesters. He wants them to understand that the primary enterprise is "simply some really advanced reading and writing. So regardless of whether it's Shakespeare one time or the Enlightenment another . . . we're going to take something that will simply develop your reading skills and your writing skills, and this time it happens to be the Elizabethan world picture and some Shakespeare stuff. So that regardless of the materials, we're still talking about skills." Laura qualifies John's statement by explaining that they try to make students see relationships between social setups at the time of Shakespeare and contemporary American thinking. She wants them "to look beyond the text to see parallels between totally different texts or totally different time periods, to see relationships that were not just within a particular text."

Later, talking about how they view their link as unique, John notes that the two seemed to be "of like mind" from the very beginning. Laura adds, "John and I found . . . that the values that were important to one of us were also important to the other. . . . I mean, we were doing a comparison and contrast of two ages, one of which was an age committed to a theology or a worldview that was perhaps nearer to our own in some ways than contemporary values. . . . And I think there was a lot of silent agreement about a lot of the material and where the emphasis might be and what we wanted the students to see and think about." She moves to "the whole question of order," acknowledging that the two valued "having a hierarchy and an ordered environment and observing that order." Speaking about the scene in *Macbeth* in which Macbeth hears of his wife's death, she suggests that John would be the kind of teacher who would view the humanity of that situation as "a kind of theological humanity. I'm being very abstract at the moment, but he would want that pointed out to the class. He would want them to hear, in the tone of voice and in the language, a man with a soul. Because he believes in souls, and it's important to bring the idea of a soul into a classroom discussion. Now I can think of a number of different classes where you wouldn't even mention soul."

In response to my comment that she is indeed correct, that many HEP classes would take an antifoundational or relativist approach, she quickly responds, "That's right. And we are not deconstructionists." We all laugh, and she quickly adds that she feels that her values are a part of her teaching. John notes that those values come out "also in the manner as well as the content" and remarks that their partnership was the closest "melding" of teaching he's had so far in HEP. When I ask him if this is because their outlooks and their values are so closely aligned, he replies, "Sure," and as an example explains that he worked with Shakespeare not to be generous to Laura but because he enjoyed it. Laura cites her appreciation that John introduced contemporary literature (such as work by J. D. Salinger) and comments that they were learning from each other "things we both wanted to learn."

Later, Laura speaks at length about the importance of teaching Shakespeare as a value in itself. Slowly, and sometimes haltingly, she tries to explain her rationale: "I think that for a student to enter into a Shakespearean world of language and outlook and character, it's as much a break from his routine and his norms as it would be for him to get on a plane and go to a totally different cultural environment and that, just as when he might go to a different culture, that culture would elicit from him whole parts of himself that haven't been activated before, so will the experience of a real encounter with Shakespeare elicit parts of his brain and his personality and his imagination that haven't been called upon before. And . . . we might say, well, OK, that happens with a lot of literature, and I think that's true, but I think it's more extreme for Shakespeare, and I don't think a student can halfway relate to Shakespeare. Either he's really going to get into Shakespeare, or he's going to remain outside. So you do risk, when you teach Shakespeare, leaving some students behind; they're not going to cross that threshold. But I think if they do, their whole educational outlook can be altered, and often is, as to what they can do. They see that they can go beyond what they felt they can go beyond, and that is different from how they looked at *Hamlet* in high school. It is a different qualitative experience."

Toward the end of our reflection session, when asked what he and Laura think their students took away with them when they left the course, John recalls the fifty lines each person was required to memorize and recite in class; he speaks of how "it must have been refreshing and invigorating for them. . . . I mean, you can learn writing skills, and you can read better, but . . . I don't think . . . personally I could memorize fifty lines of Shakespeare and deliver it in front of class without muffing it." He then speaks about the close attention they paid to *Macbeth*: "That has to serve them well. If anything else, they read with that kind of attention to just really every scene."

At this point, Laura returns to her bafflement at losing students, this time referring to two who disappeared almost at the end of the semester. She recalls her attempts to phone one particularly promising man and expresses concern and regret about what happened: "I don't know why they felt after they had succeeded in both those things that John is talking about, papers improving and delivery of lines, [why] these students suddenly just disappeared." Suddenly shifting topics, she remarks, "If I do beat the bandwagon about anything, it's this thing about performance. . . . Shakespeare can be memorized because it is metered. It's like learning a song. It has a rhythm; it has a meter; it's so much easier to memorize than an awful lot of other things. . . . They don't realize that they have a mnemonic device built in . . . and that's one reason why I think it's a good choice, particularly [for] oral work . . . to train their memory. Also because it forces them to look at punctuation, phrasing, emotional weight behind words; it makes them think about language."

Still reflecting back on what made the course successful, the two address the issue of the environment they created. They speak about how they responded to each other, how they carefully listened to each other's comments. This, they feel, provided a model for the students. They describe the circle the class sat in each day, politely participating in discussions and asking questions. Finally, when asked about how they handled grading essays, John replies that they each graded half the class for half the semester and then switched. One of the reasons they did not follow the more common HEP practice of jointly reading each major assignment was because, "it tends to confuse the student . . . two comments in two different handwritings, and sometimes it may even be in conflict."

Reflection Session Analysis

Laura sometimes and John frequently sound like their colleagues in HEP. As he noted in their initial planning session, John is interested in getting his students to understand that what they are doing "is simply some really advanced reading and writing." He tells them that regardless of what they are reading, the emphasis will be on developing reading and writing skills; the content, he suggests, is almost incidental. Similarly, Laura indicates that an important goal is to make students see relationships between the social structures and mores of the Elizabethan world and contemporary American thinking. She does not, in this particular instance, imply that there is a hidden agenda but rather that perceiving relationships is in itself the end point.

Putting those comments in the broader context of the rest of the interview, however, raises other issues. For example, John does not define what he means by reading "skills," so we do not get a sense of how such skills might relate to the "interpretive moves" that HEP instructors often allude to. Similarly, when he later speaks of their students' difficulty staying with or concentrating on one piece of work for an extended time, he offers two possible solutions: shortening the text, or just telling them that they will have to get used to it. He mentions getting "every inch" out of the play, of "wringing it dry." The austerity of his metaphors is striking here. It is true that he is speaking about process, but in the sense of training the mind. His language conjures up memories of the doctrine of "formal discipline," a movement prominent in late-nineteenth-century pedagogical thought that maintained the mind could be developed by exercising it as a muscle.[17] Memorizing Shakespeare is so important to the two because, among other reasons, it provides students with a sense of discipline and accomplishment. Laura even talks about getting her developmental students outside of HEP to recite forty to fifty lines of Shakespeare, although they initially fought it "tooth and nail." She explains that because Shakespeare is metered and has a rhythm, it can be memorized and can thus train the memory. She does add that by forcing them to look at punctuation, the emotional weight behind words, and so forth, memorization also encourages them to think about language.

Laura's comments about enabling students to see relationships between periods become clearer later on when she indicates that the two chose to compare and contrast two ages, one "committed to a theology or a worldview" nearer to their own. She remarks that there was a lot of silent agreement about what to emphasize and what they wanted their students to see and think about. This is a suggestive point. When I ask her to be more specific, she explains that John believes in souls and in bringing the idea of a soul into classroom discussions. Laura is much more vocal and explicit about her essentialist values.

It is interesting to note that whenever she speaks for John and herself about their "shared" positions, he deflects the conversation or remains silent. Either he perceives and is uncomfortable with an inherent conflict between HEP's stance and their own, or he is conflicted himself about his own commitments and values, or he recognizes no meaningful tensions or contradictions at all; I cannot tell. When Laura notes that she and John found that "the values that were important to one of us were also important to the other," John does not elaborate. Nor does he pick up on Laura's description of his interest in a "theological humanity." He does, however, agree with her that their values are part of their teaching and that, indeed, the experience provided him with the closest "melding" of teaching he's experienced in HEP. When asked for an example, he cites teaching Shakespeare not as an accommodation to Laura but because he enjoyed it. He doesn't explain why. When Laura jokes that they are not deconstructionists, we all understand that this is an understatement, but in John's case, I am primarily reading between the lines.

John's beliefs remain fairly well hidden, emerging only sporadically and disappearing before they can be pinned down. For example, he comments that although he himself couldn't have memorized and delivered fifty lines of Shakespeare "without muffing it," he thinks that his students found the challenge "refreshing and invigorating." He appreciates the activity for the sense of accomplishment it provided his students, rather than for its intrinsic worth. But without elaborating, he immediately moves to the value of close reading, to the intense attention that they paid to *Macbeth*. Once again, it is hard to figure out just where John positions himself.

At one point in the interview, I try to highlight their differences, mentioning that John thinks it doesn't much matter what they teach, that rather it is the process that counts and that helping students formulate their own ethical and literary positions is key. On the other hand, Laura, I suggest, indicates that teaching Shakespeare in itself is valuable. I am interested in learning more about what she means and how this contrasts or is compatible with what John is promoting, so I ask her to elaborate. As I indicated previously, she slowly and with some difficulty tries to think through her tacit assumptions. The result is somewhat surprising and is indicative, I believe, of deeply hidden conflicts. When put on the spot, Laura explains her choice of Shakespeare as a way to enable students to enter into "another world of language and outlook." She speaks about this break from routine and norms as an entry into a totally different cultural environment and as a means of providing students with the opportunity to elicit parts of their brains, personalities, and imaginations that "haven't been called upon before." Clearly, she views Shakespearean plays as containing a power greater than that found in other works of literature to invite students into an alien world and thus alter their outlooks: They see that "they can go beyond what they felt they can go beyond."

Shakespeare is indeed a canonical choice for Laura, but her reasons for its worthiness are suggestive rather than definitive. I am unable to find out what she means by the transformative power she alludes to. I don't know whether she is hoping to get students to understand, appreciate, and then adopt the values of the Elizabethan worldview or whether she thinks that entering into another period, like getting "on a plane" and going to "a completely different environment," is desirable because it enables individuals to develop their own conceptions and ways to live in the world. Given everything she already has said, I suspect that she is now trying out ideas she has never been aware of or at least articulated. I wonder if more experience teaching in HEP, working with new partners, and participating in faculty workshops might encourage her to play with and eventually become more conscious of conflicting pedagogical goals. Although she is implying here that she is interested in enabling students to create new possibilities for themselves, almost everything else she says indicates that she wants to teach them canonical texts from an older, more ordered, world so that they can understand and absorb a better set of values.

When I try to imagine John and Laura's classroom, I think of the portrait they themselves have sketched. I picture a group of students sitting together with their teachers in a circle and treating each other with great respect. They ask each other questions, not for the purpose of challenging or debating ideas, but to find good answers. Thinking about John's remark that they don't jointly grade papers because seeing two different handwritings might cause confusion and conflict, I understand the great value they place on harmony and order. I imagine that their students regard them as authorities in their field, as educators who seek to help them find truth and enlightenment. I respect their intentions, am aware of their fine reputations among both students and faculty, but know that they are operating on assumptions at least theoretically in conflict with HEP's implicit commitments. As a researcher, I can point this out; as codirector of HEP, I am puzzled about what to do.

Conclusion

I think that it is rare for individuals to be able to alter their worldviews in fundamental ways. I know that people have revolted against their backgrounds after a series of painful experiences or in cataclysmal moments, but I don't believe that they make radical paradigm shifts, in the Kuhnian sense, simply when the evidence doesn't add up or when they are faced with existential anomalies; I suspect that most of us look the other way and cling to our cherished positions. Adapting to HEP was relatively easy for Kevin because he had to make only small movements away from convictions that he had thought were the norm; he really didn't come up against anything that conflicted with his belief system. He had assumed that he was expected to teach the corpus of anthropology, but it turned out that he himself really didn't think there existed an agreed-upon corpus. As the second interview demonstrates, he regarded anthropology more as a mode of inquiry, as a matter of asking certain kinds of questions in certain kinds of ways. For Rebecca, it was even easier; she had no need to confront her assumptions or tacit knowledge base at all. Her ideas personified the HEP posture.

Laura, in contrast, really didn't know what she was getting into when she joined HEP. She worked hard to make sense of the program's framework, which is admittedly general and often implicit, but she was approaching it from a distant point. If she teaches again in the program, I do not know how much change she will be willing or interested in making. She is, after all, a respected educator with carefully thought out commitments of her own. She cares deeply about her students and obviously is able to elicit enthusiastic, committed responses from them.

John remains the most problematic participant in this study for me. He appeared to be conscious of, if reticent about, his own beliefs but also seemed to adopt HEP's pedagogical commitments, at least on some level. I'm not sure that he recognized any contradictions at all. On the one hand, he indirectly indicated that he believed in authority and truth, and on the other, he engaged in practices that encouraged students to draw their own conclusions. Maybe he was hoping that good teaching and close reading would lead to a respect for truth. I don't think he would welcome my asking him about this conflict; I suspect that he would find it an invasion of privacy.

I began this essay by emphasizing the power that epistemological and ethical values play in making curricular choices. In spite of my skepticism about our willingness, let alone ability, to alter our most cherished beliefs, I place my hopes in the willingness of individuals to access and at least reflect upon them. I also assume that they will be able to understand how they draw upon those beliefs to make decisions about what to teach. As a researcher who has embraced a poststructural rejection of absolutes, I can hardly claim that I know what is "right," but I can maintain that to different degrees, Laura's and John's worldviews, with their attendant assumptions about the nature of absolute truth and goodness, do not closely fit the commitments of the program they have joined. Perhaps the problem is HEP's in that it has not been explicit enough about what those commitments entail; perhaps it has not developed a sufficiently rich and direct means to encourage teachers to examine their own beliefs and their fit with

HEP's. Perhaps, as I suggested previously, Laura needs more exposure to the program to decide whether she really can or wants to accept its premises. The former choice would demand significant movement from her, a daunting prospect. As for John, perhaps he really can separate his beliefs and values from his pedagogy, or perhaps he has found a meeting ground by focusing on the close reading of texts in a way that doesn't lead students to look for the answers that he personally knows are out there. It is even possible that he is aware of conceptual confusion at some level but is unable to characterize it or assess its influence on his students.

I don't think that John and Laura are in a unique or even unusual situation. I suspect that many educational programs with partially articulated stances and a small set of pedagogical principles are staffed by at least some faculty members who embrace incompatible or incongruent positions on both an explicit and tacit level. This creates a predicament, not only because belief systems are so deeply embedded and so resistant to change, but also because programs such as HEP do not always make their philosophies and concomitant values clear. Even if they do, they may be reluctant, if not powerless, to ensure that they are taken seriously. Philosophies and personal values are not subject to mandates.

Notes

1. Joseph J. Schwab, *The Practical: A Language for Curriculum* (Washington, D.C.: National Education Association, 1970).

2. Ian Westbury, "The Character of a Curriculum for a 'Practical' Curriculum," *Curriculum Theory Network* 10 (Fall 1972): 25–36.

3. William A. Reid, "Practical Reasoning and Curriculum Theory: In Search of a New Paradigm," *Curriculum Inquiry* 9 (Fall 1979): 187–207.

4. Decker Walker, "A Study of Deliberations in Three Curriculum Projects," *Curriculum Theory Network* 7 (1971): 118–134.

5. Lynne M. Hannay and Wayne Seller, "The Curriculum Leadership Role in Facilitating Curriculum Deliberation," *Journal of Curriculum and Supervision* 6(4) (Summer 1991): 340–357.

6. Elaine Atkins, "Exploring the Use of Tacit Knowledge in Curriculum Deliberations," paper presented at the American Educational Research Meetings, April 1995; "Deliberations of College Faculty," in J. T. Dillon, Ed., *Deliberation in Education and Society* (Norwood, N.J.: Ablex Publishing Company, 1994), 101–156; "From Competing Paradigms to Final Consensus: A Case Study of the Deliberations of a Conflict-Prone Curriculum Group," *Journal of Curriculum and Supervision* 5(4) (Summer 1990): 308–327; "The Deliberative Process: An Analysis from Three Perspectives," *Journal of Curriculum and Supervision* 1(4) (Summer 1986): 265–293.

7. Ibid.

8. Richard Rorty, *Consequences of Pragmatism* (Minneapolis: University of Minnesota Press, 1982), 164.

9. Ibid., 86.

10. Ibid., 92.

11. William E. Doll, Jr., *A Post-Modern Perspective on Curriculum* (New York: Teachers College Press, 1993), 134.

12. Michael Polanyi, *Personal Knowledge: Towards a Post-Critical Philosophy* (Chicago: The University of Chicago Press, 1962), 62.

13. Although I use the terms *postmodern* and *poststructural* interchangeably, I want to point out that the former usually (but not always) refers to a gestalt, a broad spectrum of attitudes and styles in public culture, as well as to theoretical constructs in academia, and that the latter term refers to specific intellectual movements and traditions, particularly in the social sciences and humanities. Although it is beyond the scope of this chapter to do so, I would argue that a hermeneutical approach fits within the constructs of poststructuralism as well as postmodernism.

14. Students in this double course meet for six hours per week for a fifteen-week semester; the maximum number of students in each section is twenty-two.

15. Michael Hardy and Elaine Atkins, "Summary of HEP Self-Study Conducted in the Spring of 1995," unpublished paper, September 20, 1995.

16. I'm not sure that she would make a distinction between modern and postmodern positions.

17. As characterized by Edward Krug in *The Shaping of the American High School: 1880–1920* (Madison: The University of Wisconsin Press, 1969), 207.

8

The Complexities of Portfolio Assessment

KATHRYN H. AU
SHEILA W. VALENCIA

Classroom-based assessment occupies a prominent position in discussions about educational reform. As a result, many districts, schools, and teachers are trying to implement portfolios. But as they quickly learn, implementation is challenging at best and unworkable at worst. Rather than simply requiring teachers to administer new or better tests, successful implementation of classroom portfolios requires deeper, second-order changes[1]—fundamental shifts in knowledge, beliefs, and practices. To deny the problems and dilemmas inherent in such change is to doom portfolio assessment to failure. We believe that would be a tragic mistake.

Over the past six years, we have gained firsthand knowledge of the benefits, the problems, and the dilemmas of classroom portfolio assessment.[2] In particular, we have worked alongside teachers in grades K through 6, as they struggled to implement portfolios for assessing students' progress in learning to read and write, as part of two projects. The purpose of the first, the Kamehameha Elementary Education Program (KEEP) in Hawaii, was to improve the literacy of Native Hawaiian children. The second, the Bellevue Literacy Portfolio Project in Washington state, was designed to improve teaching and learning and to use classroom evidence for reporting students' achievement. Both projects had a history of strong, ongoing professional development, and both operated under excellent conditions for change. In addition to the sustained effort of each project, a group of KEEP and Bellevue teachers also came together to observe in each other's classrooms, to learn about the use of portfolios in another setting, and to score portfolio contents. Yet even with this long-term commitment and support for portfolio assessment, difficult issues surfaced.

In this chapter, we explore the complex problems and dilemmas that arise as educators create, implement, and use portfolios. We use the term *problems* to refer to issues that can be addressed and perhaps resolved over the long run. In contrast, the term *dilemmas* connotes perplexing issues that strike at our basic beliefs about how assessment reform should look, who should be responsible, and what criteria should be used to determine success. We are aware that others may judge some of our problems to be dilemmas, and vice versa. Certainly, problems in one setting may prove to be dilemmas in another. The main point, we believe, is to gain a better understanding of the many problems and dilemmas created by portfolio assessment. Ultimately, portfolio assessment involves making lasting changes in teachers' knowledge and beliefs and in educational systems. Those deep changes are the most difficult and important to achieve.

We begin with a brief description of the rationale and practice of portfolio assessment and a model for thinking about a portfolio system. Then we discuss the problems and dilemmas associated with each of the components of the system. We close with a plea for thoughtfulness, optimism, and hard work to sustain an effort that can make a difference in the lives of teachers and students.

Rationale and Description of Portfolio Assessment

Interest in portfolio assessment emerged from two areas of the educational community—teaching and learning, and assessment. From the teaching and learning community came a paradigm shift from behaviorism to constructivism, which profoundly altered educators' thinking about the nature of teaching and learning in areas such as the language arts, mathematics, and science.[3] Behaviorist theories are associated with a skills orientation to teaching in which the teacher is assumed to transmit knowledge to the students, who are regarded as passive recipients. In the constructivist orientation, students are assumed to construct actively their own understandings, with the guidance and support of the teacher. The metaphor for the skills view of learning is a conduit, through which knowledge flows from teacher to student. The metaphor for the constructivist view of learning is the conversation, in which knowledge is created by students as they interact in discussions with the teacher and their peers.[4] Coupled with this shift from behaviorism to constructivism was a series of reforms that emphasized the "thinking curriculum" and high standards for student performance.[5]

Educators were concerned with the quality of what students were learning as well as how that learning was facilitated.

Many in the area of teaching and learning recognized that multiple-choice, standardized tests were inadequate in the context of constructivist approaches and rigorous standards. Those tests could neither assess the broader goals prominent in constructivist approaches nor test students' abilities to think deeply and apply skills and strategies to challenging tasks. At the same time, the shift placed more responsibility in the hands of teachers, who had to rely less on prescribed materials and more on their own instructional decisionmaking. With the power of instructional decisionmaking came the responsibility and need for teachers to implement classroom assessment that would align with their curricula and provide feedback about teaching and learning.

The assessment community also began to address some of the problems of existing testing programs.[6] Assessment experts, concerned about the mismatch between existing tests, on one hand, and constructivist forms of teaching and more rigorous learning goals, on the other, called for new and better forms of assessment. However, they also took seriously the negative consequences of many large-scale testing programs. The prominence of standardized tests was leading to a narrowing of the curriculum, inappropriate instruction, artificially inflated scores, and antagonistic teacher attitudes toward assessment. Tests were being used to control teachers and curricula rather than to improve teaching and learning. Assessment experts found these consequences of the existing approach unacceptable. They called for different types of assessment to provide information to different audiences and, in particular, revived the importance of classroom-based assessment.[7] They too acknowledged the power of teachers to improve learning and the importance of making classroom assessment a more useful and essential piece of the assessment system.

Portfolios gained popularity as a strategy for implementing classroom-based assessment. They are conceptualized as both an evaluation product and a classroom-based assessment process. As an evaluation product, they are a purposeful collection of samples of student work and records of progress collected over time. Because work is generated as a natural part of classroom life, portfolios are better able than tests to reflect constructivist approaches and more challenging curricula. Although portfolio contents may be shaped by guidelines, they are rarely narrowly prescribed—a stance that makes them consistent with constructivist teaching and learning. Teacher and student choice play an important role. In addition, portfolio contents can demonstrate student growth over time, a feature missing from most norm-referenced tests. As a classroom-based assessment process, portfolios are used by teachers and students to evaluate learning, inform instruction, and set appropriate learning goals. Portfolios are more than folders. They require active participation by teachers and students in creating, selecting, and evaluating work. The assessment process is viewed as a crucial aspect of instruction rather than simply as a demand of policymakers. With portfolios, assessment becomes part of the ongoing cycle of teaching and learning, rather than a rare, isolated event that results in a score.

The rationale behind portfolio assessment and the resulting definition reveal why portfolios are best understood as a curricular innovation. Portfolios require teachers to extend, refine, and enact their understanding of subject matter, pedagogy, assessment, and learners. Teachers must determine what is "significant and worthwhile"[8] to teach, how to help students learn, how to collect evidence to assess their performance, and how to adjust instruction to further learning; this is knowledge in action, to be sure.[9] Unlike reforms of the past that tried to "fiddle" with changing the official curriculum or the tested curriculum by altering printed curriculum guides and test items, portfolio assessment gets to the heart of the taught curriculum and the learned curriculum, where action is required and real change is likely to occur.[10]

A Portfolio Assessment System

As with any complex innovation, many factors shape and influence the implementation of classroom portfolios.[11] As shown in Figure 8.1, our work suggests five components that operate in a complex interactive portfolio assessment system.[12]

Each of the five components must be in place for the system to operate, and each exerts an influence on the other components in the system. For example, professional-development experiences interact with both portfolio evidence and the evaluation process. As teachers participate in long-term professional networks, they enhance their understanding of teaching, learning, and assessment. They are encouraged to use personal classroom experiences and portfolios, their practical knowledge, to reflect on their own understanding. As a result, over time, teachers are more likely to develop a commitment to reflective practice, as shown in efforts to improve their teaching rather than simply to collect portfolio evidence. In turn, the quality of their students' portfolio evidence is more likely to represent high-quality teaching and learning, and teachers' judgments about student performance are likely to be more thoughtful and reliable.

As implied by Figure 8.1, a portfolio assessment system does not operate in a vacuum but is highly influenced by internal conditions (the local conditions within each school or district) as well as by the external conditions (across states and the nation) under which assessment reform is taking place. Internal and external conditions are likely to be beyond teachers'

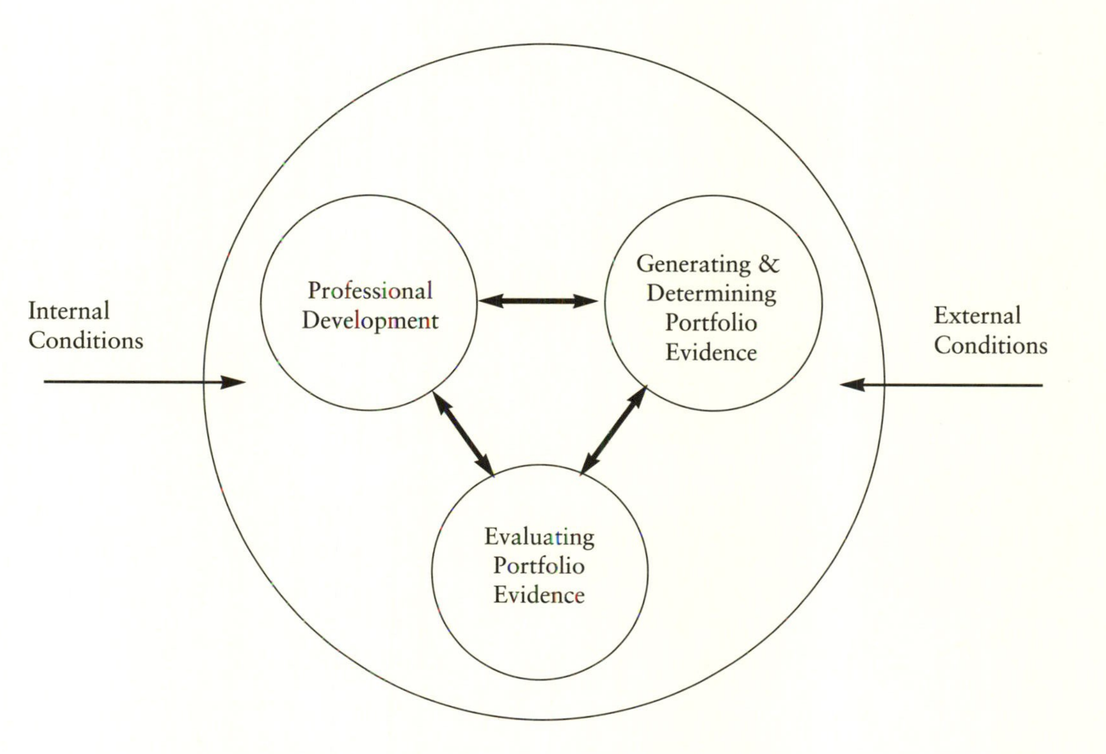

FIGURE 8.1 A Portfolio System. This figure is adapted from one that appeared in S. W. Valencia and K. H. Au, "Portfolios Across Educational Contexts: Issues of Evaluation, Professional Development, and System Validity." *Educational Assessment* 4 (1, 1997), 1–35. It is republished with permission of Lawrence Erlbaum Associates, Inc.

control, but they exert great influence on the lives of teachers and students. For example, internal, school district conditions determine how much time, money, and support is allocated for teachers as they experiment with and implement portfolio assessment. External conditions shaped by those outside the classroom and the district (such as policymakers, states, assessment experts, and community members) create contexts and expectations that facilitate or hinder portfolio assessment. Problems and dilemmas are inherent in every part of the system. The way we, as concerned educators, deal with them determines whether we achieve real systemic change in teaching, learning, and assessment. We now turn to those problems and dilemmas.

External Conditions

External conditions exert enormous pressure on portfolio assessment; the judgments and support of external constituencies can and will influence whether portfolio assessment succeeds. Although policymakers, assessment experts, and educational reformers have argued convincingly for the value of portfolio assessment in improving teaching and learning, they continue to grapple with how to evaluate its success.[13] Traditional testing designed to monitor educational programs and large groups of students is judged in terms of its reliability, validity, efficiency (cost and time), and comparability from year to year. Given the format and purpose of traditional assessments, those criteria seem reasonable. However, measurement experts have begun to rethink the criteria against which performance assessments, including portfolios, should be judged.[14] They are concerned that evaluating new assessments against traditional views of measurement may only reinforce unfavorable comparisons with standardized tests. Nevertheless, most portfolio assessment efforts continue to be evaluated against criteria developed for traditional tests.

A dilemma is created because existing criteria are a poor match for the form and purposes of portfolio assessment. For example, portfolio assessment is regularly compared to standardized testing in terms of cost, time, and reliability. Portfolios inevitably fare poorly in those comparisons. Portfolios cost more to implement and score, take longer to evaluate and implement, and have lower reliability coefficients than multiple-choice and even open-ended standardized tests. Similarly, traditional assessments have been viewed as objective and secure, protected from "subjectivity" of judgment, or "corruption." Portfolios fail to measure up here as well because teachers and students are intimately involved with collecting portfolio evidence, and they know in advance what will be evaluated and how it will be judged. Ironically, we now know that standardized assessments are neither as objective nor as secure as once thought.[15] Still, concern about the subjectivity of classroom portfolio evidence remains.

When portfolio assessment is viewed as a curricular innovation, rather than as a substitute for standardized tests, we acknowledge that it requires considerable time to take hold and significant professional development. Similarly, as a curricular innovation, portfolio assessment should be judged by criteria different from those applied to standardized tests. For example, portfolio assessment might be valued because it has influenced changes in teachers' views of curriculum, instruction, and assessment. Or it might be judged by the quality of student work in portfolios, the array of evidence that reflects students' opportunities to learn, or student motivation and engagement in learning. Although those criteria are consistent with portfolio assessment as a process, they are not the ones employed in traditional approaches to evaluation.

Reverting to existing, inappropriate criteria for evaluating portfolio assessment is not acceptable, but creating and winning acceptance for new criteria will be a lengthy process. Many questions need to be addressed in the creation of new criteria. What should be the basis for the criteria? What purpose or purposes should portfolio assessment serve? Who will make the decisions about the criteria? Who will determine if the results are worth the effort, time, and money? Developing new criteria will require collaboration among policymakers, assessment experts, and classroom educators—a collaboration that has only recently been forged. Those stakeholders will need to negotiate their requirements and expectations for assessment information. Whether they can find common ground is yet unknown.

Another dilemma is created by the fact that external audiences need and deserve information about students' performance that is not easily or immediately available from portfolios. They need data on large numbers of students across a wide range of contexts in an easily understood form. Although portfolio assessment was not designed to replace standardized tests or to yield norm-referenced information, many hoped that portfolios would be able to provide some kind of information useful to external audiences. The results thus far are equivocal.[16] In the meantime, however, external audiences cannot be expected to go without information on student performance. What information can be provided while portfolio assessment is under development? How long are external constituencies willing to wait to evaluate the results of this effort? Are external audiences likely to support portfolio assessment if they can't get the kind of information they think they need or are accustomed to getting? Can multiple approaches to assessment coexist in terms of time, money, and demands on teachers and students?

Unlike researchers, policymakers, school board members, and the public at large have not been asked to consider new criteria for evaluating portfolio assessment. They are operating from a traditional assessment paradigm reflecting long and deeply held beliefs about testing. Several years ago, a school board member made statements to this effect: "I appreciate how much teachers and students get out of portfolios. That's great. But why should we continue to support portfolio assessment if you can only get interrater agreement of .7 when standardized tests usually have reliability of .9? Why don't we have someone else develop the things that go into the portfolio and send them out to be scored?" External constituents have different expectations for how long it should take to see results of portfolios and what those results should look like. If portfolios cannot meet those expectations, they are unlikely to win the financial and political support they need to take hold.

Internal Conditions

The internal conditions for the implementation of portfolio assessment are provided by the district and the school. The internal context must support teachers in specific ways if portfolio assessment is to be successful. Factors contributing to a favorable climate for change include the expectation that teachers will be moving toward portfolio assessment and support for teachers to develop the knowledge and skills needed to implement portfolios. In addition to commitments of time and money, the district and the school must create social support for the change to portfolio assessment. Support is needed for networks of teachers, across and within schools, who can meet on a regular basis to discuss portfolio assessment. Staff in the district and the school must commit time to establishing those networks, conducting meetings, distributing readings, and maintaining communication among members.

Internal conditions surrounding portfolio assessment often lead to the dilemma of high expectations but low support. Typically, the district or school has high expectations for the implementation of portfolio assessment but fails to provide adequate support for the process of change. For example, the district issues a mandate requiring all teachers to implement portfolio assessment. One or two workshops on portfolio assessment are provided. However, following the workshops, little or no help is available for teachers as they work with portfolio assessment in their classrooms.

The district and the school may begin with the intention of providing teachers with adequate support for implementing portfolio assessment but then fail to provide this support for a number of reasons. In times of tightening budgets, money may be needed to carry out existing programs, rather than to proceed with innovations. Furthermore, the district or the school is likely to have underestimated the amount of time and money required for teachers to make the change to portfolio assessment. Funding for teacher development in portfolio assessment may be discontinued at the very time when the foundation for change is finally in place and teachers are ready to move forward. Then the failure of portfolio assessment may erroneously be attributed to weaknesses in the approach to assessment rather than to the need for further support for professional development.

A disturbing finding from our work with portfolio assessment is that indicators of change become visible only after a minimum of three years of focused professional development. The question is whether those changes will be valued by outside audiences. In Bellevue, teachers worked in professional-development teams for three years before starting to implement portfolios in a systematic way. In research at KEEP, portfolio assessment proved to be the most difficult component for teachers to implement within a constructivist literacy curriculum.[17] Although KEEP teachers received assistance from consultants based at their schools, they needed about five years before they achieved full implementation of portfolio assessment.

A dilemma for the district or the school centers on whether to make teachers' use of portfolio assessment mandatory or voluntary. The most direct approach to change appears to be that of declaring that teachers will implement portfolio assessment and insisting on compliance with this directive. The expectations underlying such a mandate are that everyone will move forward together and that all teachers can and will be able to implement portfolio assessment successfully. This approach fails to recognize that teachers enter the change process with differing levels of knowledge about portfolio assessment and differing degrees of motivation to implement it. Mandating change results in resistance from some teachers, who resent the top-down process of decisionmaking and feel that their opinions and priorities have been ignored. Other teachers comply with the mandate and attempt to implement portfolio assessment but then fail due to a lack of support. Those teachers feel that they have been betrayed by the district and the school, at first because their efforts are not supported and later because their efforts fail to live up to the high expectations set.

If the district or the school makes work with portfolio assessment voluntary, the strategy of "going with the goers" can be followed. This strategy involves initiating the change process by working with a relatively small group of volunteers, who receive intensive training and support to implement portfolio assessment in their classrooms. One advantage of this strategy is that teachers are involved with portfolio assessment by their own choice. Resistance does not develop because uninterested teachers are not under any pressure to make changes. Another advantage is that resources are focused on the teachers who are most likely to make changes on the basis of what they have learned, for example, from participating in network meetings or workshops held during the school day. When all the teachers in a district or a school are involved at once in implementing portfolio assessment, resources are spread too thin to make a difference. At KEEP and Bellevue, the strategy of going with the goers proved effective in guiding volunteer teachers toward the successful implementation of portfolio assessment.[18]

Despite the advantages, most districts and schools shy away from the strategy of going with the goers. The strategy may strike a district or a school as slow and cumbersome, in contrast with the seeming efficiency of mandating change and compelling the involvement of every teacher. Because a considerable amount of resources will be invested in a relatively small number of teachers, the strategy may seem expensive and undemocratic. The strategy assumes the gradual spread of portfolio assessment to an ever-widening circle of teachers, a process that may seem chancy. Few schools and districts have the confidence and patience to undertake a strategy that depends on teachers' taking the initiative to implement portfolio assessment, in their own time and at their own pace.

Innovations such as portfolio assessment, which depend on teachers' professional judgment, run counter to notions of control of the curriculum based on scientific-managerial principles.[19] Those who favor a scientific-managerial view worry about the inconsistency and variability that may be introduced into the curriculum if teachers are empowered to make decisions about instruction and assessment. They prefer the standardization of curriculum that comes with the use of commercially published programs, such as basal readers, and standardized tests. As Shannon points out, the application of scientific-managerial principles to literacy instruction has not yielded the anticipated gains in student achievement.[20] The dilemma is that although the scientific-managerial approach has failed to produce the desired outcomes, this approach is still endorsed by most districts and schools, as well as by policymakers and the general public, making it difficult for other views to gain ground.

Participating in Professional Development

As shown in Figure 8.1, professional development is one of the five components of our model. Along with many other people, we believe that the goal of professional development efforts should be to enable teachers to become reflective practitioners. Reflective practitioners have the ability to see the implications of portfolio assessment and other innovative ideas for their own teaching. They can analyze and improve their own practices in classroom-based assessment and other areas. They can explain the reasons for their practices. Reflective practitioners see themselves as learners and are aware that classroom teaching is a process of learning for both teacher and students.

In this view of professional development, teachers are given the opportunity to understand and interpret portfolio assessment for themselves. If teachers are to develop a deep understanding of portfolio assessment, they must have flexibility to decide what portfolio assessment might mean for their classrooms, the specific form that portfolio assessment might take, and the process by which it might be introduced to students. This flexibility or autonomy is bounded by teachers' understanding of their responsibility for improving students' learning and for being accountable to various publics. Portfolio assessment and classroom work must make sense and be useful to teachers in their classrooms, or neither will enhance teaching and learning. This view emphasizes teachers' abilities and autonomy as they fulfill their professional obligation to provide useful information to audiences inside and outside the classroom.

A dilemma is created when teachers recognize that the change process will take time, but the district and the school expect that change will take place quickly. To implement portfolio assessment, teachers must have the time to deal with issues of content knowledge, pedagogy, and assessment. They must have the time to try out portfolio assessment in their classrooms, to experiment with different procedures, and to work out difficulties. Time is required for change in teachers' attitudes, from viewing assessment as an occasional event, such as standardized testing, unrelated to classroom life, to viewing assessment as an ongoing activity embedded in the life of the classroom.

The view that professional development is an ongoing process creates a dilemma for teachers and teacher educators. The dilemma is that reflective practice is an attitude about self-improvement and not a particular outcome. In this view, teachers' ability to implement a particular model of portfolio assessment, while perhaps recognized as a worthy goal, is not considered an end in itself. Rather, what counts is teachers' ability and willingness to reflect upon their implementation of portfolio assessment and to adjust what they are doing to meet the goals they have set, such as having students reflect upon their learning through the portfolios. Conflicts occur when districts and schools stress the importance of portfolio assessment as an evaluation product or outcome rather than a professional-development process or an attitude. This difficulty is compounded because portfolios are both an evaluation product and a professional-development process, and the product may be highly important to districts and schools interested in aggregating scores and demonstrating the usefulness of portfolios for the purpose of large-scale assessment. The pressure on teachers to work toward the same product or physical form for portfolios may create situations in which there is the appearance of change but not a real change in teachers' attitudes toward assessment. This situation existed in the first three years of KEEP's work with portfolio assessment; consultants and paraprofessional aides collected materials for students' portfolios with little teacher involvement or understanding of this new approach to assessment.

A related problem resides in teachers' belief that answers to their questions about portfolio assessment are readily available from outside sources. In their eagerness to obtain answers, they may look to outside experts, other districts and schools, or readings, hoping to find an existing system of portfolio assessment that they can implement in their classrooms. This view reflects an initial emphasis by teachers on portfolios as an evaluation product rather than a professional-development process. In both the KEEP and the Bellevue projects, teachers began by expecting ready-made answers from us as teacher educators and from outside sources. At first, they did not understand that we expected to engage in a process of working together to discover the procedures for portfolio assessment appropriate to their classrooms. Gradually, as the teachers realized that we were learning along with them, their attitudes changed. They gained confidence in their own ideas about portfolio assessment, turned to other teachers for assistance, and took control of their own learning with respect to portfolio assessment. In Bellevue, the shared interest in portfolio assessment contributed to the creation of a community of learners among the teachers, who participated in monthly network meetings.

Our view of professional development is associated with the idea of empowering teachers as professionals able to exercise sound judgment over matters such as portfolio assessment. To some teachers, such a view is liberating. They feel prepared to make decisions about the content and form of the classroom curriculum, including assessment. Other teachers are not ready or willing to accept this degree of responsibility. An empowerment orientation to professional development poses another dilemma. Are we willing to give all teachers the freedom to develop their own curricula and assessments? What about teachers who are inexperienced, who lack the professional knowledge needed to make informed judgments, or who are less than conscientious? Clearly, this view of professional development makes assumptions about teachers' professional knowledge and motivations that do not hold in the case of every teacher.

In our work with portfolio assessment, we did not make the assumption that all teachers could or would successfully implement portfolio assessment in their classrooms, especially at the beginning. In our projects, we worked with volunteer teachers who were willing and able to gain the professional knowledge needed to implement portfolio assessment. Our successes with portfolio assessment resulted to a large extent because those particular teachers had the ability and motivation to take abstract ideas and translate them into workable classroom practices.

On the one hand, a dilemma in our approach is that it implies a hierarchical system of professional development, in which some teachers are privileged to act as decisionmakers, while others are not. Creating such a hierarchy poses an inconsistency, in that teachers themselves do not control their own decisionmaking ability. Rather, teachers' ability to make decisions, with regard to such innovations as portfolio assessment, is determined by an external authority, in our case, by administrators and teacher educators.

On the other hand, working with too large a group of teachers may cause an innovation to fail. This was the case with KEEP's early attempts to implement portfolio assessment. At first, the use of a constructivist literacy curriculum and portfolio assessment did not lead to gains in student achievement.[21] During this period of initial failure, the KEEP staff worked with about 150 teachers. The decision was then made to offer extensive professional development opportunities to just a few teachers, thirteen in the first year and twenty-nine in the second year. With the support of the KEEP staff, those teachers were able to achieve full implementation of the curriculum and of portfolio assessment, as documented by means of monthly observations. With full implementation, dramatic improvements were seen in students' achievement, especially in writing.[22] Early attempts had failed because the constructivist curriculum and portfolio assessment had not been fully implemented, not because those innovations were inherently flawed.

The example of KEEP highlights the dilemma posed by portfolio assessment as a complex and challenging innovation. If all teachers in a district or school have the same decisionmaking opportunities with portfolio assessment, especially in the early stages of its introduction, portfolio assessment may well fail. If professional-development opportunities are restricted to a few teachers, those who are most likely to be successful, portfolio assessment may be implemented successfully. However, this success will have been achieved at the possible cost of creating a hierarchical and inequitable situation among teachers, in which an external authority has limited some teachers' decisionmaking opportunities. The trade-off appears to be between deep, narrow change and widespread, superficial change. Despite its difficulties, we believe that deep, narrow change involving portfolios is more likely to lead to the desired results. Deep, narrow change provides the basis for continuing efforts with portfolios, beginning with a small group of well-informed and highly committed teachers, who help to spread the innovation to other teachers. Superficial, widespread change merely continues the tendency of districts and schools to follow the latest fad, with no group gaining the knowledge or commitment to sustain portfolios as a curricular innovation.

Generating and Determining Portfolio Evidence

We turn now to a discussion of another component of the model, portfolio evidence, the second circle shown in Figure 8.1. In general, portfolios contain examples of the work that students have completed as part of daily classroom routines. In this sense, a portfolio serves as a mirror, reflecting the nature of students' classroom experiences. On the one hand, if students regularly prepare written responses to the novels they are reading, samples of those written responses appear in the portfolios. On the other hand, if students are regularly completing fill-in-the-blank worksheets, those will be collected in the portfolios. Simply having portfolios does not guarantee that high-quality curriculum and instruction are in place.

One of the problems with portfolio assessment is that it cannot be pursued as an end it itself but must be part of a larger process of curricular change conducted from a constructivist perspective. In situations in which an attempt is being made to implement portfolio assessment, teachers will range along a continuum with respect to their orientations toward curriculum, instruction, and assessment. Some teachers may be at the traditional-skills end of the continuum, whereas others will be at the constructivist end. The majority of teachers are somewhere in between. They are motivated to incorporate new activities, such as literature discussion circles, in their curricula but are not interested in understanding the philosophy underlying those activities.[23] This lack of interest in the why of curriculum is consistent with a scientific-managerial perspective, in which teachers are treated as implementers but not developers of curricula and assessment.

In constructivist curricula, what is to be assessed has changed. If reading and writing are viewed as complex psychological processes, they can no longer be accurately assessed by means of multiple-choice tests that do not allow students to develop their own interpretations of text or to create their own texts. Furthermore, tests do not reflect the social contexts of the teaching and learning in which students engage every day. From a constructivist perspective, it is students' performance in those contexts that yields information about their learning and how their instruction might be improved. Portfolios attempt to address the weaknesses in traditional test procedures by allowing teachers to look at classroom products, such as students' written responses to literature, that show the use of complex psychological processes in the social context of the classroom.

Teachers who accept constructivist views of literacy and instruction often see the value of portfolio assessment in addressing important literacy outcomes and providing detailed information about the performance of individual students. However, one problem is that teachers still find it difficult at first to trust their own professional judgment in designing portfolios and analyzing and interpreting their results. The information that they gather about students, day in and day out, still initially strikes them as "subjective" and "unscientific" in contrast to standardized test scores. The problem is compounded when administrators do not perceive portfolios as "real" assessment. Portfolio evidence may be seen as "just everyday work" and less informative and more difficult to interpret than test results. It is difficult for teachers to justify the time and effort required to develop rich collections of work, when that work is not valued by administrators.

Tensions between the skills and constructivist perspectives pose a dilemma for portfolio assessment. The dilemma arises because a portfolio can serve as a mirror, providing an accurate reflection of what is happening in the classroom. The danger lies in the fact that portfolios, as collections of work, can just as easily exist in a skills-oriented classroom as in a constructivist one. This situation is possible when the implementation of portfolios has taken place at a superficial level, and portfolios are seen only as an evaluation product and not as a classroom-based assessment process. Portfolio assessment appears to be in place, but the contents of the portfolios reveal that the curriculum has retained its skills orientation. In this event, portfolios may well show us work, such as skill sheets, that is not what we want to see. Although portfolios are present in the classroom, teachers have not changed their instruction or their views of assessment. Portfolios, then, do not end up assessing the new, constructivist goals for student learning.

Another dilemma posed by portfolios is that they reflect the general environment of the classroom and not necessarily individual learning. For example, in the KEEP portfolios, evidence was collected of students' ability to edit their own writing. In some classrooms, teachers taught minilessons on editing and required students to edit their drafts and to have a peer review their editing. Only then could students sign up for a conference with the teacher. In other classrooms, teachers did not require students to edit their drafts or to review their peers' editing. Those teachers, or paraprofessional aides, did the editing for the students. In the first set of classrooms, it was possible to find evidence of editing ability in the portfolios of all, or nearly all, the students. In the second set of classrooms, evidence of students' editing ability was rarely found, even in the portfolios of students who were seen to be capable writers. Clearly, the differences in the portfolio evidence between the two sets of classrooms were largely attributable to differences in instruction and opportunity to learn.

This situation raises the question of whether portfolios provide good evidence of the learning of individuals. A study comparing portfolios from KEEP and from Bellevue showed that evidence in some categories was consistently missing in the classrooms of certain teachers.[24] For example, some of the KEEP teachers had focused on documenting their students' progress in writing and had not collected much evidence of students' progress in reading. We might conclude, then, that portfolios are better seen as measures of what is taught, how it is taught, and what information is collected, rather than of individual learning.

To the extent that this conclusion is valid, it points to another dilemma. We believe that the contents of portfolios have their greatest value in providing teachers with opportunities for reflection. Yet because portfolios so accurately mirror what has happened in the classroom, they may readily be used for the purposes of evaluating teachers. Evaluation may be helpful, if it is part of a supportive professional-development process. But evaluation is more likely to be harmful to the process of teacher reflection and to innovation, if it is of a high-stakes variety, with funding or other consequences for schools, teachers, and students. The dilemma, as we see it, is that portfolios, as a mirror of the classroom, may end up promoting the evaluation of teachers, rather than teacher reflection, as was their original purpose.

Evaluating Portfolio Evidence

Evaluating portfolio evidence is the third circle in Figure 8.1 and the final component of our model. Portfolio evidence can speak to a number of audiences. Teachers are the audience to which we have most often referred, and another audience is certainly the students themselves. By reflecting upon the work in their portfolios, students gain a sense of their own progress and of the goals they might have for themselves as learners. Parents are another audience for portfolios, which provide them with a close, detailed look at their children's progress. However, whereas teachers, students, and parents may value portfolios because of the evidence they provide of individual learning, other audiences may want portfolios to serve a different purpose. As discussed earlier, principals, other administrators, policymakers, and the general public may value portfolios primarily as a way of meeting the demands of accountability. In this event, means must be developed to reduce and aggregate the information available in portfolios, so that conclusions can be drawn about the achievement of groups of students.

Giving each portfolio a score or a set of scores is an obvious means of reducing the data. However, scoring leads to a number of problems. Because it is generally implemented in efforts to use portfolios for the purposes of accountability, scoring can easily become an end in itself. When scoring is a requirement imposed from the outside, teachers are trained to score portfolios for the sake of arriving at scores. As a result, they gain little or no understanding of the reasons underlying the scoring system or of the instructional implications growing from the scores. This approach is in contrast to treating scoring as part of the professional-development process. In this case, scoring is not seen as an end in itself but as a means of helping teachers to gain a deeper understanding of portfolios, in relationship to standards or outcomes that cut across classrooms. As they score portfolios, teachers gain ideas of how they can improve their teaching and better document their students' learning. This was the approach taken in Bellevue, where teachers participated in the development of the scoring system.

A dilemma inherent in scoring portfolios is that the richness of information on individual students is lost in the process of aggregating the results.

What was once a full picture of the student's progress as a learner has been reduced to a number or a set of numbers. The work of students and teachers may be discounted as accountability concerns become paramount. At KEEP, the overall ratings of portfolios were useful for purposes of program evaluation, in determining the number of students who were performing above grade level, at grade level, and below grade level in various aspects of literacy. However, the overall ratings were not useful to teachers or students. For teachers, the overall ratings masked differences among students that needed to be recognized for instruction to be effective. Teachers who work with portfolios may find themselves in a difficult situation. Because of their knowledge of the curriculum and of the nature of portfolio evidence, those teachers are in the best position to score the portfolios. However, they are also in the best position to recognize the richness of information being lost when portfolios are reduced to scores.

Another dilemma is that the process of evaluation does not address the needs of low-achieving students. Because portfolios show progress, they can be a way of keeping expectations low; students may show growth but still remain far below the standards for their grade level. Scoring portfolios can tell us which students need help because they have not yet met certain outcomes or standards. However, scoring generally does not indicate the type of help students should receive. Portfolios, like other forms of evaluation, may have the effect of documenting failure without providing information about how success can be achieved. This dilemma may be addressed to the extent that portfolios avoid the assumptions of standardized tests, in which the distribution of scores follows the normal curve. To improve educational opportunities for low-achieving students, portfolios need to follow the logic of criterion-referenced tests in assuming that all students, with proper instruction, can meet high standards of achievement. Portfolios must be seen as tools for promoting rapid growth for low-achieving students, more than a year's gain in a year's time. Results at KEEP indicate that such gains are possible.[25]

There are those who take the position that using portfolios for accountability purposes defeats the whole purpose of having portfolios in the first place. Scoring portfolios and aggregating information across portfolios works against the use of portfolios to develop ownership[26] or to have students explore their own identities as readers and writers.[27] The point of portfolios, in this view, is that they help students gain insights about their own lives. It can be argued that we have lost the essence of portfolio assessment, the richness of individual learning, when we try to make portfolios serve accountability purposes. Our experience does not support such an extreme view. We have found that teachers benefit from learning to score portfolios, because the process helps them clarify their own standards for student learning. However, teachers continue to worry about the possible misuse of scores derived from portfolios.

Can portfolios be the basis for a complete assessment system, serving all the necessary purposes? This is a question that cannot yet be answered. On the one hand, we want portfolios to be rich sources of evidence that permit students to reflect upon their progress and teachers to make informed decisions about instruction. On the other hand, we want portfolios to contribute to evaluation, to present an accurate picture of student achievement within constructivist curricula. This requires that the evidence in portfolios be structured to permit reliable scoring. If portfolios cannot be used for accountability purposes, we run the risk of encouraging districts' continued overreliance on standardized tests, with all the negative consequences associated with those tests. Portfolios are not meant to serve the same purpose as standardized tests, but they can contribute to an expanded view of students' achievement.

Conclusion

We wonder what history will make of this effort to implement portfolio assessment. More immediately, we wonder whether the effort will be supported long enough to give it a fair chance to work through the varied challenges of implementation and eventually to bear fruit. Surely, there are enough problems and dilemmas to test anyone's patience and endurance.

Throughout this chapter we have highlighted the tension between portfolios as professional-development process and portfolios as evaluation product. When portfolios are seen as a process, they are a central part of long-term professional-development efforts aimed at helping teachers to become reflective practitioners. When portfolios are seen as a product, they are viewed in terms of their potential to provide information useful for evaluating groups of students. In this view, the aim is not to build teachers' expertise but to implement a new form of assessment that provides information useful to policymakers, administrators, and the public. We have discussed the many problems and dilemmas raised by portfolio assessment that grow from this tension.

Given all the difficulties, it is reasonable to ask, Why bother with portfolio assessment? Some will tire and conclude that the dilemmas are intractable; others will send us back to the drawing board in an effort to get it "just right." Neither alternative is attractive. In the realm of "the practical,"[28] which is the realm of schooling, problems and dilemmas are assumed to be workable, and they must be attended to sooner rather than later. Problems cannot wait until model building has produced a perfect portfolio system; there always will be problems to solve. Knowing the problems and dilemmas that portfolios present should serve to inform our efforts with portfolios, rather than to distract or discourage us from this work.

We believe it is important not to give up on portfolio assessment. Confronting the problems and dilemmas can give us a better understanding of the conditions under which portfolio assessment can take hold and contribute to teachers' professional development and to students' achievement. We have faced all of those challenges in our work yet have experienced considerable success with portfolio assessment. In the KEEP and Bellevue projects, we helped teachers in their work with portfolios for six years. We have seen support for portfolios wax and wane, and we have seen teachers' energy wax and wane. But through it all, we have seen teachers' continuing growth in understanding what they teach, how they teach, and how they evaluate and conceptualize student achievement. At KEEP, dramatic improvements in students' achievement, especially in writing, were associated with teachers' use of portfolio assessment.[29] When we brought the KEEP and Bellevue teachers together, we saw further growth in their insights about instruction and assessment. Despite the problems and dilemmas, portfolios represent a step forward in making assessment responsive to the needs of teachers and students. Furthermore, we discovered that it was possible to develop a common scoring system, so that portfolios from different sites could be compared.[30] We believe that portfolios can be responsive to issues of professional development while also providing information valuable for the purposes of evaluation. Although the tension between portfolios as professional-development process and portfolios as evaluation product cannot be eliminated, our experience suggests that, with thought and care, a middle ground can be found.

Our fear is that with diminishing budgets, changing demographics in the student population, and growing concern about student achievement, the deeper, more important, and lasting changes that could have a positive effect on education will be sacrificed for the more immediate, easily observed first-order changes. For us, the challenges of portfolio assessment come with the territory of schooling and the work of professional development. They are a way of life. With growing understanding, we can face the problems and dilemmas optimistically. We cannot afford to do otherwise. To give in to the enormity of the challenge is to give in to the status quo and to discontinue attempts to enrich the lives and learning of teachers and students. To work with, and despite, the problems and dilemmas provides the opportunity to progress purposefully and incrementally toward improved teaching and learning for all children.

Notes

1. Michael G. Fullan and Matthew B. Miles, "Getting Reform Right: What Works and What Doesn't." *Phi Delta Kappan* (1992): 744–752.

2. Kathryn H. Au, "Portfolio Assessment: Experiences at the Kamehameha Elementary Education Program," in *Authentic Reading Assessment: Practices and Possibilities,* ed. Sheila W. Valencia, Elfrieda H. Hiebert, and Peter P. Afflerbach (Newark, DE: International Reading Association, 1994), 103–126. Kathryn H. Au and Jacquelin H. Carroll, "Improving Literacy Achievement Through a Constructivist Approach: The KEEP Demonstration Classroom Project." *Elementary School Journal* 97 (3, 1997), 203–221. Sheila W. Valencia and Nancy Place, "Portfolios: A Process for Enhancing Teaching and Learning." *The Reading Teacher* (1994): 666–669.

3. Elfrieda H. Hiebert and Taffy E. Raphael, "Perspectives from Educational Psychology in Literacy and Literacy Learning and Their Extensions to School Practice," in *Handbook of Educational Psychology,* eds. Robert Calfee and David Berliner (New York: Macmillan, 1996), 550–602.

4. Kathryn H. Au and Jacquelin H. Carroll, "Current Research on Classroom Instruction: Goals, Teachers' Actions, and Assessment," in *Research on Classroom Ecologies: Implications for Inclusion of Children with Learning Disabilities*, ed. Deborah Speece and Barbara Keogh (Hillsdale, NJ: Erlbaum, 1996), 17–37.

5. Lauren B. Resnick and Daniel L. Resnick, "Assessing the Thinking Curriculum: New Tools for Educational Reform," in *Future Assessments: Changing Views of Aptitude, Achievement, and Instruction,* eds. B. R. Gifford and M. C. O'Connor (Boston: Kluwer, 1992), 37–75. Grant Wiggins, "Teaching to the (Authentic) Test: Assessment that Measures and Evokes Quality Student Performance" (paper presented at the conference Performance Based Assessment: A Bridge to Change, Santa Clara, CA, 1991).

6. Ibid. Lorrie A. Shepard, "Why We Need Better Assessments." *Educational Leadership* 46 (April 1989): 4–9.

7. Roger Farr, "Putting It All Together: Solving the Reading Assessment Puzzle." *The Reading Teacher* 46 (1992): 26–37. Walter Haney, "We Must Take Care: Fitting Assessments to Functions," in *Expanding Student Assessment,* ed. Vito Perrone (Alexandria, VA: Association for Supervision and Curriculum Development, 1991). Sheila W. Valencia, Elfrieda H. Hiebert, and Peter P. Afflerbach, eds., *Authentic Reading Assessment: Practices and Possibilities* (Newark, DE: International Reading Association, 1994). Shepard, "Why We Need Better Assessments."

8. Virginia Richardson, "Significant and Worthwhile Change in Teaching Practice," *Educational Researcher* 19 (October 1990): 10–18.

9. Donald A. Schon, *The Reflective Practitioner: How Professionals Think in Action* (New York: Basic Books, 1982).

10. Larry Cuban, "The Lure of Curricular Reform and Its Pitiful History." *Phi Delta Kappan* (1993): 181–185. Linda Darling-Hammond, "The Quiet Revolution: Rethinking Teacher Development." *Educational Leadership* 53 (March 1996): 4–10.

11. Michael G. Fullan and A. Pomfret, "Research on Curriculum and Instruction Implementation." *Review of Educational Research* (1977): 335–397.

12. S. W. Valencia and K. H. Au, "Portfolios Across Educational Contexts: Issues of Evaluation, Professional Development, and System Validity." *Educational Assessment* 4 (1, 1997): 1–35.

13. John R. Frederikson and Allan Collins, "A Systems Approach to Educational Testing." *Educational Researcher* 18 (1989): 27–32. Robert L. Linn, Eva L. Baker,

and Steven B. Dunbar, "Complex, Performance-Based Assessment: Expectations and Validation Criteria." *Educational Researcher* 20 (November 1991): 5–21. Lauren B. Resnick and Daniel L. Resnick, "Assessing the Thinking Curriculum: New Tools for Educational Reform," in *Future Assessments: Changing Views of Aptitude, Achievement, and Instruction*, ed. Bernard Gifford and M. C. O'Connor (Boston: Kluwer, 1992).

14. Linn, Baker, and Dunbar, "Complex, Performance-Based Assessment." Pamela Moss, "Can There Be Validity Without Reliability?" *Educational Researcher* 23 (March 1994): 5–12.

15. Thomas M. Haladyna, Susan B. Nolen, and Nancy S. Haas, "Raising Standardized Achievement Test Scores and the Origins of Test Score Pollution." *Educational Researcher* 20 (June-July 1991): 2–7. Scott G. Paris, Theresa A. Lawton, Julianne C. Turner, and Jodie L. Roth, "A Developmental Perspective on Standardized Achievement Testing." *Educational Researcher* 20 (June-July 1991): 12–20. Mary Lee Smith, "Put to the Test: The Effects of External Testing on Teachers." *Educational Researcher* 20 (June-July 1991): 8–11.

16. Mearyl Gearhart, J. L. Herman, E. L. Baker, and A. K. Whittaker, "Whose Work Is It? A Question for the Validity of Large-Scale Portfolio Assessment." CSE Technical Report Number 363, Center for Research on Evaluation, Standards, and Student Testing, University of California–Berkeley. Paul G. LeMahieu, D. H. Gitomer, and J. T. Eresh, "Portfolios in Large-Scale Assessment: Difficult But Not Impossible." *Educational Measurement: Issues and Practice* 14 (3, 1995): 11–16, 25–28. Martin Nystrand, A. S. Cohen, and M. N. Martinez, "Addressing Reliability Problems in the Portfolio Assessment of College Writing." *Educational Assessment* 1 (1993): 53–70. Daniel Koretz, Brian Stecher, Steven Klein, and Daniel McCaffrey, "The Vermont Portfolio Assessment Program: Findings and Implications." *Educational Measurement: Issues and Practices* 13 (3, 1994): 5–16.

17. Au and Carroll, "Improving Literacy Achievement Through a Constructivist Approach."

18. Ibid.; Valencia and Au, "Portfolios Across Educational Contexts."

19. Patrick Shannon, *Broken Promises: Reading Instruction in Twentieth Century America* (New York: Bergin and Garvey, 1989).

20. Ibid.

21. Kathryn H. Au, "Portfolio Assessment: Experiences at the Kamehameha Elementary Education Program," in *Authentic Reading Assessment: Practices and Possibilities*, eds. Sheila W. Valencia, Elfrieda H. Hiebert, and Peter P. Afflerbach (Newark, DE: International Reading Association, 1994).

22. Au and Carroll, "Improving Literacy Achievement Through a Constructivist Approach."

23. Lia Ridley, "Enacting Change in Elementary School Programs: Implementing a Whole Language Perspective." *The Reading Teacher* 43 (May 1990): 640–646.

24. Valencia and Au, "Portfolios Across Educational Contexts."

25. Au and Carroll, "Improving Literacy Achievement Through a Constructivist Approach."

26. Kenneth Wolf and Yvonne Siu-Runyan, "Portfolio Purposes and Possibilities." *Journal of Adolescent and Adult Literacy* 40 (September 1996): 30–37.

27. Jane Hansen, "Literacy Portfolios Emerge." *The Reading Teacher* 45 (April 1992): 604–607.
28. J. J. Schwab, *The Practical: A Language for Curriculum* (Washington, DC: National Education Association, 1970).
29. Au and Carroll, "Improving Literacy Achievement Through a Constructivist Approach."
30. Valencia and Au, "Portfolios Across Educational Contexts."

9

Understanding and Managing Classroom Dilemmas in the Service of Good Teaching

MAGDALENE LAMPERT

Teachers and reformers of teaching are concerned with making teaching "good." Recurring attempts to improve schools focus on improving teaching so that teachers "do the right thing" more often than not. How might we think about whether a particular piece of teaching is good? The question of whether teaching should be judged as "good" or "right" if it produces appropriate learning outcomes will not be taken up here.[1] Learning outcomes often cannot be judged in the moment that teaching and studying take place, and although we know that good teaching matters in producing learning, many questions have been raised about the legitimacy of linking particular teaching practices with particular learning outcomes.[2] For the purposes of this chapter, I assume that teaching is good if it *aims* to produce learning. Even with this more modest definition in hand, can we expect to walk into any particular moment of teaching and be able to judge whether what the teacher is doing is good? Suppose we consider the aim of turning out girls who have learned that they are at least as capable as boys at doing well in mathematics and science. What would we look for in the classroom as evidence that a teacher is sincerely aiming toward this goal? What if we sat in the classroom for ten minutes and saw a class discussion in which the teacher called only on boys, even though many girls had their hands raised?

When Is Teaching Good?

We might judge the aforementioned teacher in need of "reforming," since she seems not to be doing something that many have agreed should be happening in classrooms. But another interpretation of what we see in this classroom might be that the teacher cares about improving girls' self-image but at the time we are watching is prevented from doing something about it. What would prevent a teacher from trying to accomplish such a worthwhile aim? American social scientists have often characterized the work of the teaching profession as fraught with dilemmas, plagued by internal conflicts that are impossible to resolve, and hindered by essential contradictions among its aims.[3] Ann and Harold Berlak have developed a taxonomy of those conflicts, relating them to the ambiguous role that schools play in social change.[4] Perhaps the teacher we are observing faces just such a conflict, wherein she has multiple goals and cannot address all of them at once.

One way to think about what teachers do in the face of such conflicts is to assume that practitioners choose—between children and subject matter, between childhood needs and adult norms, between social equality and academic excellence. Much of what is written about teachers' work suggests that such choices are not only common but inevitable. The psychological theories that predominate in building models of teacher thinking also assume that teaching involves making dichotomous choices.[5] Yet choice between mutually exclusive alternatives may not be the only course of action a practitioner can take to cope with a pedagogical dilemma. And furthermore, teachers may not perceive the same dichotomies in their work as those that trouble social scientists. As Richard Shavelson and Paula Stern observe in their review of the literature on teacher thinking, judgment, decisionmaking, and behavior, description of how teachers choose one practice over another based on the bilateral decision trees of cognitive information processing can describe only limited aspects of teacher thinking because "this formulation ignores multiple, potentially conflicting goals which teachers have to balance daily."[6]

Conflicting Goals in the Classroom Context

We may think of the classroom as a workplace full of potential "goods," full of ideals to be realized. In the actuality of teachers' work, however, the practices intended to realize those ideals are often incompatible. In this sense, the classroom is a microcosm of the larger social world. In the words of William James, "The actually possible in this world is vastly narrower than all that is demanded; there is always a pinch between the ideal and the actual which can only be got through by leaving part of the ideal behind."[7] The question is, which part? Which of the teacher's goals can be sacrificed? Which is the higher good? Can rules be made a priori to help teachers decide what goals to sacrifice and what goals to meet? James concluded that such rules might be helpful but that intuitions about the immediate situation are more so: "For every real dilemma is in literal strictness a unique situation; and the exact combination of ideals realized and ideals disappointed which each decision creates is always a universe without precedent, and for which no adequate previous rules exist."[8]

James's conclusion is congruent with analyses of what occurs during teachers' interactive decisionmaking. Plans are brought to the teaching situation that relate teacher actions with desired outcomes. But those plans do not suffice to determine what a teacher does or should do in the course of instruction.[9] Because teachers work in a web of social relationships, and because the commitments of their students to the goals to be accomplished are both crucial and uncertain, teachers must weigh continually changing evidence and make moment-by-moment choices about how to proceed, continually creating what James calls a "universe without precedent." Because teachers are personally present over time in classrooms in which conflicts arise, they have the capacity to alleviate conflicts using strategies that are unavailable to those intervening in practice from the outside.[10]

What happens when teachers face choices between equally desirable but conflicting practices? What can we learn about good teaching from looking at instances in which teachers cope with such choices? In this chapter, I consider three particular cases in which teachers face the incompatibility of their ideals as they recognize their consequences for conflicts in practice. The teacher, in each case, invents a set of strategies that enables her to avoid the contradictions among her goals while she practices in a way that maintains an ongoing productive relationship with students. The purpose of this study, then, is to conceptualize a particular aspect of teachers' work: coping with the conflicts among aims, all of which would be recognized as "good" to accomplish.

By writing about teachers' strategies for managing contradictory ideals, I do not seek to define a set of mechanical tools that can or should be used by all teachers in all situations. Instead, my intention is to explore the *kinds* of actions teachers might take when they are confronted with contradictory aims. My purpose in presenting case studies is to provide examples of what is possible rather than models of "correct" teaching practice. Conflicts among professional ideals and social norms are managed by people in the context of their idiosyncratic experiences.[11] The case studies that follow are examples of ways conflict can be managed, not illustrations of the best or only way to manage it. We might then construct a more subtle judgment of whether a particular piece of teaching is good, considering whether and how the teacher copes with dilemmas.

Conflict from the Teacher's Point of View: Methodological Issues

To study the many and potentially conflicting facets of teachers' perspectives on their work, as well as the actions teachers take to manage dilemmas, it is necessary both to observe teachers' actions and to explore how they make sense of those actions in different contexts over time. Conflicts in the way teachers view themselves and their work emerge only as teachers present themselves in the stories they tell about their work to different people and in different settings.[12] Such activities as journal keeping and stimulated recall can give only a partial picture of the multifaceted self of each teacher as he or she works. In fact, when teachers are asked to represent their thoughts, judgments, or decisions in any form for review by researchers, distortions may be caused by the assumed value of consistency and rationality.[13] In reconstructing an interactive decision ex post facto, therefore, teachers might leave out conflicting aspects of themselves that they could not accommodate in their actions, or they might be reluctant to admit that the action they decided to take was inconsistent with one of their goals or with a prior action observed by the researcher.

To address those methodological problems, I have used a variety of strategies for collecting and analyzing the cases reported here. I recorded discussions among a group of seven elementary school teachers talking weekly over a two-year period with one another, as well as with researchers, about the problems in their work. The tendency in such a group for the teachers to respond to researchers' expectations was restrained by the presence of several other practitioners. I also observed the same seven teachers at work in their classrooms over a three-year period, interviewed them individually and in small groups, and read journals they kept over the course of the project. I analyzed the data simultaneously with collecting it to discover patterns and relationships in the teachers' perspectives on particular classroom incidents. The analyses were continuously tested against later expressions of the teachers' points of view on the same incidents. From this large set of data, I have drawn several case studies of teachers managing dilemmas in their classrooms, three of which are considered in this chapter.

The data I collected from this group of teachers are complemented by data from another source less familiar to scholarly research. I also work as a teacher and keep a journal of my reflections on my practice. Autobiographical analysis has not been widely used as a technique for doing research on teaching, but it is particularly appropriate to the question in this study. Being both a teacher and a researcher on teaching provides opportunities for scholarly deliberations that must meet two sets of criteria for legitimate knowledge: those that obtain in the world of practice as well as those determined by academic research.[14]

The weekly discussions of teaching that I observed occurred in the context of an experimental teacher-development project.[15] The teachers who attended were volunteers who agreed to come together to examine their own assumptions about learning and teaching. They worked in large and small urban neighborhoods. They were all women, but they ranged considerably in age, years of experience, and educational background. Most of their classrooms were traditionally organized, but two of them taught in alternative, "open" structures. My autobiographical data were collected while I taught fourth-, fifth-, and sixth-grade mathematics in a private elementary school. The children I taught came primarily from middle- and upper-class families living in the city and the suburbs. They ranged in academic competence from below average to very talented.

Case Studies

The Strategies of Social Reorganization

In the school at which I taught, students were grouped for mathematics instruction according to their ability. I had just begun teaching the "high-ability" group what it means to multiply and divide fractions, and they had seen several strategies for doing the complicated computations. I thought it would be useful to observe the children's facility with such computations, so one day I gave the class several problems to work on, and my assistant and I walked around the room watching them and answering their questions. Once they got settled down to their work, I decided to glance at their homework papers. The assignment revealed that although most of the class had a good sense of what fractions meant and how to compute with them, four children had some confusion. On closer inspection, I recognized that the errors of two students would be easy to clear up, but the other two students were in need of considerable help.

My teaching goals led to a practical conflict at this point because of the character of the two students needing help. Noel and Terry, the boys who were confused about fractional computation, also have especially fragile egos. And both of them are likely to react destructively if their sense of themselves as competent students is threatened. One of my goals was to enable them to focus on their studies. The other boys in the class, in a manner typical of fifth-graders, were always ready to pounce on Noel, who was the slowest problem solver in the group and particularly vulnerable to their scapegoating. Terry was among the brightest students in his class, and math was his favorite subject. He had extremely high expectations of himself, and the other boys often looked to him for help. But he was a perfectionist; if he was "caught" by someone in even the slightest mistake, he became silent and unapproachable. So singling out Noel and Terry for help would also make them unteachable.

I devised a strategy of social reorganization to avoid the potential conflicts involved in the choice between singling out Noel and Terry for help and ignoring their difficulties in favor of classroom peace and emotional security. Instead of calling on only those students who had made errors on their homework to receive special attention at my desk, I changed my position to a less-conspicuous corner of the room and called each member of the class there one at time, in no particular order, for a discussion of the homework papers. As I took each paper in hand, I chose one element of the conceptual or procedural content on which to focus a question to the student who had produced that paper. By checking over everyone's homework individually, I would not call anyone's attention to the special help I needed to give to Noel and Terry, but I also cut down the time that would be available to clear up their confusion. I had not planned to run the class this way, but it seemed to be an appropriate way to manage my dilemma.

The pedagogical thinking required in this case involved redefining the problem to be solved rather than finding a solution to my original difficulties. What I chose to accomplish was a goal different from the goal of Terry and Noel understanding fractions or the goal of reducing their social and emotional vulnerability. The problem to be solved became how to present myself to all of my students in a way that communicated that I valued everyone's privacy. Without drawing special attention to Noel's or Terry's difficulties, I conveyed the message to them that they were indeed confused and prepared them for the fact that they would need to find a way to clear up their mistakes at some point. I was also able to collect more information about what they did and did not understand. Their positions in the class group remained precarious, however, and I needed to continue to carefully monitor their interactions to avoid the eruption of major disorder in the classroom.

One way to characterize the thinking I needed to do in this situation is as "reframing."[16] By removing myself from the conflict of choosing between one goal and another when those goals would clearly lead to conflicts in practice, I was able to construct a strategy that would move me closer to my goals while not accomplishing them completely. The personal significance of this reframing of goals is that I did not need to give up either of my concerns. Choosing one accomplishment over the other would have required me to redefine myself in a way that would disregard goals that were important to my sense of professional identity. By changing the meaning of the situation to myself, I was able to put the choice between those goals aside and find a way to practice that was appropriate to the situation, maintaining my identity as a teacher who was concerned both about students' learning the subject matter and about maintaining their personal integrity. I did not act in a way that denied that both of those outcomes would be good to accomplish.

The Strategy of Negotiation

Suzanne is a fourth-grade teacher. This case focuses on a teaching incident in which she had been working with one of the boys in her class, whom I will call Andre. She had been teaching her class how to use prepositional phrases to elaborate on the action in a sentence. To assess the students' understanding, she wrote a simple sentence up on the blackboard ("The lady ran") and asked her students to add to it using prepositional phrases. The class went to work, and Andre presented her with the following sentence: "The lady with the red hat ran to the parking lock to get her car." Suzanne reported that she was particularly pleased with this piece of work because Andre was usually reticent both in speaking and in writing. She said she expressed her satisfaction to the boy, but she also told him that he had one word "spelled wrong."

Because she usually had difficulty getting Andre to say or write anything, Suzanne perceived a contradiction in the work she needed to do here: She wanted to praise the boy for producing a long and complex sentence, but she also wanted to correct him for his misuse of the word *lock*. She worried about how he might respond to a mixed message from his teacher about the quality of what he had produced. She was concerned about being in any way critical of his use of the English language because one of her goals was to encourage him to write and speak *more,* yet she also had as a goal for him to learn to write and speak *correctly*. How could she teach in a way that would sidestep the seeming incompatibility of those two educational "goods"? The two goals that Suzanne had for Andre, that he would spell words correctly and that he should feel comfortable taking risks with the processes of writing and speaking in the classroom, are not necessarily in conflict with one another. However, in this particular moment of teaching and learning, they were perceived to be in conflict by this teacher. She saw her job at this point as trying to find a way to do two things that seemed to be in contradiction.

The first thing that Suzanne tried was to ask the boy if he knew which of the words in the sentence was "spelled wrong." She was collecting information about what the boy knew rather than assuming she understood his abilities from what he had put down on paper. Instead of judging Andre directly, she asked him to judge his own work. If he recognized which word was spelled incorrectly, her conflict would go away. She would not need to say anything that might discourage him from trying again on the next assignment. Suzanne's strategy engaged her student as a partner in the correction of his own work. By doing this, she hoped to avoid the continuing conflict in her classroom identity between her role as supporter and her role as judge and to deflect the possibility that the student see her in only one way or the other. The way he sees her would affect his response to her and thus also affect the sort of learning that could occur in future interactions. Thus, by using the aforementioned strategy, she might succeed in preserving a productive relationship with Andre that would affect his future engagement in learning.

As a way to accomplish both encouragement and correction, however, Suzanne's strategy turned out to be a failure. Andre said he didn't know which word was spelled wrong. So she told him: "Lot. It's parking lot." But Andre did not agree; he responded, "No, it's lock." This exchange exacerbated Suzanne's conflict rather than alleviating it. She was back in the midst of the same contradiction between goals that she had faced initially. Should she insist on the correction and risk alienating Andre from the writing process? Or should she just leave him alone at this point in the hopes that she would not discourage him from writing more, even though he had used the word *lock* incorrectly? Again, there were reasons for doing both; Suzanne needed a bargaining strategy that would provide an alternate to choosing between goals.

Suzanne decided to be tentative. She did not say, "*Lock* is wrong, and the correct word to use is *lot.*" Instead she told Andre, "It was probably said, 'lot.'" By using the word "probably," Suzanne was again inviting Andre to make the correction himself rather than having it imposed by the teacher's authority. She did not bring out the full force of her authority to overwhelm whatever this student thought might be right. She also changed her opinion at this point about the nature of his error. She now was acting on the belief that he was pronouncing the word incorrectly rather than making a spelling mistake. With this change, Suzanne was moving away from a subject in which her knowledge and authority were clear (*lock* is spelled l-o-c-k) into a hazier area where determination of right and wrong is more dependent on social circumstances. Pronunciation is less determined by universal rules than spelling.

Andre did not respond to Suzanne's tentative suggestion, however. He continued to hold firm to his position that *lock* was correct. But Suzanne still avoided a direct judgment of the mistake. Instead of telling the boy he was wrong and exacerbating her conflict with him, she used still another form of negotiation. She appealed to evidence from outside the situation and continued to leave the judgment about which word was correct up to the student. She told the boy the meanings of the words *lot* and *lock* and asked him to choose which one was the more appropriate word to follow *parking* in his sentence. Giving him this information could be seen as a further attempt to engage him in partnership to correct his mistake. But Andre was not moved, and this time he mustered some evidence to support his argument that *lock* was correct. He said, "Well, over where I live, it's parking *lock,* l-o-c-k, parking lock."

Andre was now drawing some boundaries that served to defend the original integrity of his written work. By qualifying his assertion with "where I live," Andre inferred that *lot* might seem right *to her,* or perhaps *lot* was right *in school,* but he was not wrong to use the word *lock* because that's what was said in his neighborhood. (Perhaps he lived near a parking lot sign that said "Park and Lock.")

Andre and Suzanne did not need to decide what word was *absolutely* right or wrong, but what word was appropriate to a given setting. Their interaction had the character of a negotiation. Suzanne struck a bargain with Andre: "It's okay with me if you want to say 'parking lock' at home, but here in school, I expect you to say 'parking lot.'" She did not give him any reasons for her expectation. She did not say he should say it that way because she was the teacher or because that was the correct way to say it or even because that was how most people said it. She had respected his point of view, and now she was expecting him to respect hers. She left Andre feeling that he was right to say "parking lock" at home, but she also got him to write "parking lot" on his school assignment.

Suzanne recognized, in her conclusion of the story about her interaction with Andre, that the contradictions among her goals would remain even though she had managed them in this particular interaction. She said:

> The boy accepted *lot* and wrote it on his paper, yet I wonder if he really believed me and if he will continue to say "parking lock" at the place where he lives.
>
> There's a difference between *his* language and how *I* expect kids to spell words. They've learned their spelling rules, but they're not spelling the same words as I am. He wasn't making a spelling error. It wasn't an error; it's part of his life.

Whether Andre learned that *lock* was wrong and *lot* was correct remains an open question. But through this negotiation, Suzanne maintained the possibility of keeping Andre interested in the writing process because she did not directly criticize his work. She maintained her identity as the person in the classroom with the power to "correct" students' errors, but she did it with some degree of subtlety and grace, also allowing Andre to maintain his integrity. She might have ignored the problem, choosing in favor of Andre's fragile self-esteem, or she might have been unambiguously authoritative. As the teacher, she had the power to choose either of those options. But instead, she hedged her correction in a way that expressed the complexity of her relationship with her students.

This way of thinking about classroom problems suggests that a certain inconsistency on the part of the teacher may be necessary to get the job done. Suzanne was unyielding about the standard usage of *parking lot,* and she persisted until her student got it down on his paper. But at the same time, she also engaged him as a fellow human being in the struggle involved in following such rules. She cajoled him to go along with her and was sympathetic with his resistance. Willard Waller recognizes the centrality of expressing such ambivalence in teachers' work:

> The teacher must alternate his roles because he is trying to do inconsistent things with students. . . . He is trying to maintain a definite dominance over young persons whose lives he presumes to regulate very completely. This requires of the teacher aggressiveness, unyieldingness, and determination. If persisted in, this attitude would exterminate in students all interest in subject matter and would crush out every faint inclination to participate in the public life of the classroom. . . . Before this reaction has been carried through to completion, one says, "But I am a human being and I try to be a good fellow."[17]

If Suzanne had been absolutely authoritative in her correction of Andre, it would not be hard to imagine that she would have widened rather than narrowed the gap between his acceptance and his belief, exterminating, as Waller suggests, any further interest on this boy's part in learning the rules of formal language.

Structural Reorganization with Negotiation

Vicki is a first- and second-grade teacher in an urban school. The dilemma I describe here arose when she was teaching her students to add three-digit numbers. She had two instructional goals for these lessons: One was to have the class learn how to record their answers when the total in any column was more than 9, and the other was to have them learn to judge the correctness of their own answers by checking the additions with groups of base-10 blocks. The class had been working successfully on adding numbers when no "regrouping" or "carrying" was required, for example, in the addition problem

$$\begin{array}{r} 326 \\ +143 \\ \hline \end{array}$$

As long as there were no sums larger than nine, the students could treat each of the columns as a separate problem, and it did not matter whether they began working in the hundreds column, the tens column, or the units column.

The students were using blocks representing units (each measuring a cubic centimeter), blocks representing tens of units (ten cubic-centimeter blocks attached together in a "rod"), and blocks representing hundreds of units (ten rods attached together to make a "flat" block one centimeter by ten centimeters by ten centimeters). The students would first represent each of the two numbers to be added as a pile of units, tens, and hundreds blocks, then push the two piles together, and finally count out the total of units, tens, and hundreds, writing the total of each kind in the appropriate column on the paper.

When two of the boys finished all of their sums correctly, Vicki decided to give the problem of finding the sum of the problem

$$\begin{array}{r} 309 \\ +309 \\ \hline \end{array}$$

She wrote the problem on a piece of paper between the two boys and went off to check the other students' work. The boys counted out two piles, each containing three hundreds blocks and nine units blocks. They put the two piles of hundreds blocks together and wrote a 6 under the two 3s and a zero under the two zeros so their paper now looked like this:

$$\begin{array}{r} 309 \\ +309 \\ \hline 60 \end{array}$$

Then they pushed the piles of unit blocks together and set to counting them. They came up with a total of 18. Under the two 9s they wrote a 1, so the paper now looked like this:

$$\begin{array}{r} 309 \\ +309 \\ \hline 601 \end{array}$$

At this point, the teacher asked, "How did you get that answer?" One of the boys told her about the eighteen units blocks and said there wasn't room to write 18 in the units column.

Vicki said she felt a conflict between her goals. She did not want to tell the boys the conventional solution to this problem of "not enough room." She wanted them to notice that the answer they had written down (601) was not the numeral that matched the total number of blocks (618), and she wanted them to figure out a way to make them match. Vicki believed that if she simply told them the conventional regrouping procedure, they would easily forget it or misuse it. But she also worried that if she did not tell them how to "regroup" eighteen units into tens and units, they would continue to struggle and waste a lot of valuable classroom time.

Berlak and Berlak would call Vicki's difficulty the "personal knowledge versus public knowledge" dilemma:[18] The public knowledge that Vicki would have liked these boys to have is that the eighteen units need to be regrouped as one ten and eight units, and the total, therefore, written as 618. Yet she also strongly believed that this regrouping needed to make sense to the boys personally as a way of solving their own problem with the blocks. She saw her conflict in this way: "Maybe I need to give them more direction than I do. Maybe it's not fair to make them struggle when I know how to help them. Yet at the same time, it can be so rewarding if they do figure out something for themselves. I know from past experience, if *they* figure it out, they will always be able to use it and not forget it."

Vicki's mind was not made up. As she told me about the incident the day it happened, she was arguing with herself about what to do.

The major strategy that Vicki constructed to manage her dilemma was used in the math lesson the next day. She made several structural changes in the way the lesson was presented. Instead of simply asking the children to make informal "piles" of units, tens, and hundreds blocks, she gave them charts and instructed them to place the blocks they were adding in the appropriate boxes. She also told them: "Trade up whenever you have more than nine units or nine tens, and make sure the blocks match the numbers you write down on your papers *exactly*." By rearranging the work space and giving more precise directions on how to use the materials, Vicki invented a tool for mediating between the public knowledge she wanted to teach and the private knowledge the boys would derive from solving their own problems with the blocks.

One of the boys who had been having problems the day before with 601 versus 618 worked through two or three more sums, and Vicki noticed him becoming frustrated with the mismatch between what he had on paper and the blocks he counted on his chart. After watching him for a few minutes, Vicki noticed that he did the appropriate trading with his blocks but had no way to record the trading on his paper; he did not simply write the total number of blocks after trading and counting. He treated the blocks and the paperwork as separate endeavors. On the paper, he always began by adding the hundreds column first and made the same recording error he had made the day before. One of his additions looked like this on paper:

$$\begin{array}{r} 538 \\ +216 \\ \hline 741 \end{array}$$

However, on his chart, he had seven hundreds blocks, five tens blocks, and four units blocks. He did not know why they did not come out the same.

Vicki did not judge his answer immediately. Instead she made a few suggestions while he worked about how he might record what he was doing with the blocks on paper. In both tone of voice and content, these were clearly not directives. She left it up to him whether to use the suggestions in his work. The student continued to work, and the teacher watched. Once the boy noticed that his written sums were beginning to match the total number of blocks, he loudly announced to the other children at his table, "Hey, I just found a supereasy way to do my math." He had learned what the teacher wanted him to learn, and yet he took credit for "finding" the way himself.

Vicki restructured *the materials of instruction* so that she would not need to confront her students with their errors directly. By creating a way to use the math materials that brought out the problem of the students' recording system, Vicki did not need to assert her authority as the one who knows how to do math. She was able to teach and yet foster independent discovery. In her interactions with this learner, Vicki used suggestion rather than direction. She did not tell her student what to do, but she made a solution available for him to choose, which he could then feel some sense of owning. The management of Vicki's dilemma depends on an interaction between the child's concerns and her own. She assesses those concerns and responds to them, not by constructing abstract resolutions of potential conflicts and contradictions, but by constructing practical interactions like those just described—balancing, mediating, trying one thing or another, and monitoring the child's response. The management of the dilemma emerged for her in practice, whereas its resolution had been elusive to her when she told me about her dilemma the day before.

Common Features of Dilemma-Managing Strategies and Their Implications for How We Think About Good Teaching

These three cases illustrate three strategies teachers might use for coping with potential dilemmas that result from conflicts among their aims: social reorganization, restructuring the materials of instruction, and negotiating with students. There are no doubt many other possible strategies that could be considered, as there are many other potential conflicts among teachers' aims. This list of strategies is not meant to be a complete taxonomy with clear borders between categories; rather, it is meant to be a set of illustrations of an aspect of teachers' work that merits further exploration.

What can we learn from these case studies about the practical meaning to teachers of seemingly unresolvable conflicts? What do the strategies analyzed here tell us about how to judge the quality of a particular piece of teaching? The instances of teaching practice described in this chapter have several common features. Those features suggest the sort of thinking that is required to do the work of "dilemma management," and they yield an image of the teacher at work that has important implications for how we go about improving practice.

In each case, the teacher accomplishes an instructional goal, but it is different from the goals she had set out to accomplish at the start of the interaction described. This *change in goals* is not a whimsical disregard either for the plans established for a given lesson or for the importance and appropriateness of her original goals. Rather, practice in these cases involves an on-the-spot *reassessment of the means available to achieve the desired ends.* When the cost of achieving those ends becomes too dear in any particular moment of the teacher's work, the problem to be solved needs to be redefined according to the means available for solution. In the case of teaching, the means available to the teacher include students; the knowledge and attitudes they bring to a lesson are among the resources a teacher calls upon to get her job done. But students' knowledge and attitudes are not only largely unknown quantities, they are also constantly changing as a result of forces over which the teacher has little control. So the teacher must take into account not only which problems should be solved in a particular teaching interaction but also which problems can be solved given the information she gains along the way about the resources available to her. Although the teachers' initial goals in all these cases were attractive and desirable, they were not feasible. After I looked at the homework papers and assessed the volatility of certain relationships in my math class, I needed to define an instructional problem that could be solved using what I had to work with in the way of student attitude and knowledge that day. Vicki similarly readjusted her goals in teaching addition to take into account the information she was gaining about a particular student's difficulties. Suzanne continually redefined the problem to be solved as she negotiated with her student about the correctness of the writing he had done. This sort of teaching enables learning in light of what the teaching itself reveals to be probably realizable.

The strategies that these teachers used to move forward *led them toward their goals in endless tiny increments.* The teachers did not initiate large-scale classroom reforms designed to accomplish their goals once and for all. They moved toward recognized aims small step by small step, because taking larger steps when goals were in conflict would have pushed them further away from other equally desirable and appropriate aims. The actions taken in the instances of practice described in this chapter were not intended to achieve the somewhat utopian ideals that inform teachers' thinking about what should be done; instead, the teachers' orientation was toward coping with difficulties in a commonsense manner and recognizing contradictions endemic to the work situation that will not be resolved. The point toward which they are moving changes constantly as they redefine where it is possible to go. Such mechanical devices as behavioral objectives give one the illusion of final accomplishment, often by equating quality with quantity, but in these three teaching situations, such objectives would only mask the underlying contradictions with which the teachers described had to actively cope.

Not only do the teachers in these examples redefine problems and move incrementally toward elusive and ever-changing goals, they also do teaching that is *exploratory*. Actions are taken that have the capacity to produce new and useful information, both about what has been accomplished and about what can be accomplished next. The definition of what is possible and what is desirable emerges from the give-and-take of teaching students. Each of the teachers described had a different sense of what she could do and what she should do after she actually did something. The purpose of many of the choices the teachers made about what to do was to postpone action or judgment until more information could be collected.

This relation between action and reflection in the context of teaching presents a view of teacher thinking that is broader than "decisionmaking." The teacher is not only confronting choices about how to use means to arrive at desired ends but continuously redefining what those ends can be. In this redefinition, the nature of teaching itself is being determined. This quality makes teachers' thinking "personal," as defined by George Herbert Mead: The demand of the context (social norms) and the teachers' actions together contribute to the possibility of what can be done.

If teachers are considered to be persons in Mead's sense rather than simply role incumbents whose actions should be determined by the environment in which they work, they can be thought to manage the tensions in their work through their personal presence in situational acts of teaching. In each of the cases presented in this chapter, we can see a teacher acting responsibly in a morally defensible way, even though she is not directly pursuing an aim that we would agree is important. Seen in this way, teachers' thinking is not enhanced by the creation of logically correct solutions constructed outside of the situation in which a problem arises, and teaching practice is not improved solely by the invention of stable universal theories of professional decisionmaking. This perspective suggests that it might be appropriate to think about good teachers as people who act responsibly in the face of multiple and conflicting goals rather than in terms of good teaching observed in particular instances of practice in relation to single dimensions of reform.

Notes

An earlier version of this chapter appeared in *Advances of Research on Teaching*, The Proceedings of the Second Annual Conference of the International Study Association on Teacher Thinking, Tilberg, The Netherlands, 1986 (M. Ben-Peretz, R. Bromme, and R. Halkes, eds.).

1. For a thorough investigation of this question, see Fenstermacher, G. (1986). Philosophy of Research on Teaching: Three Aspects, in M. C. Wittrock, Ed., *Handbook of research on teaching, Third edition.* New York: Macmillan Publishing Company (pp. 37–49).

2. See, for example, Oser, F., Dick, A., and Patry, J. L. (1992). Responsibility, Effectiveness, and the Domains of Educational Research, in Oser, F., Dick, A., and Patry, J. L., Eds., *Effective and responsible teaching: The new synthesis.* San Francisco: Jossey-Bass Publishers (pp. 3–13); Shulman, L. (1992). Research on Teaching: A Historical and Personal Perspective, in Oser, F., Dick, A., and Patry, J. L., Eds., *Effective and responsible teaching* (pp. 14–30).

3. Waller, W. (1932). *The sociology of teaching.* New York: John Wiley and Sons; Bidwell, C. W. (1965). The school as a formal organization, in James G. March, Ed., *Handbook of organizations.* Chicago: Rand McNally; Dreeben, R. (1970). *The nature of teaching: Schools and the work of teachers.* Glenview, Ill.: Scott-Foresman; Jackson, P. W. (1968). *Life in classrooms.* New York: Holt, Rinehart, and Winston; and Lortie, D. C. (1975). *Schoolteacher: A sociological study.* Chicago: University of Chicago Press.

4. Berlak, A., and Berlak, H. (1981). *Dilemmas of schooling: Teaching and social change.* London: Methuen.

5. See for a schematic description of these models: Clark, C., and Peterson, P. (1986). Teachers' Thought Processes, in M. C. Wittrock, Ed., *Handbook of research on teaching, Third edition.* New York: Macmillan Publishing Company (pp. 255–296).

6. Shavelson, R., and Stern, P. (1981). Research on Teachers' Pedagogical Thoughts, Judgments, Decisions and Behavior. *Review of educational research* 51, p. 471, fn 2.

7. James, W. (1969). The Moral Philosopher and the Moral Life, in Roth, J. K., Ed., *The moral philosophy of William James.* New York: Thomas Y. Crowell Company (p. 183). (Originally published in *International journal of ethics* 1, April 1981, pp. 330–354.)

8. James, W. (1969). The Moral Philosopher and the Moral Life (p. 187).

9. Leinhardt, G., and Greeno, T. (1983). The Cognitive Skill of Teaching. Paper presented at the annual meeting of the American Educational Research Association, Montreal.

10. Lampert, M. (1985). How Do Teachers Manage to Teach? *Harvard educational review* 55(2), pp. 178–194.

11. Mead, G. H. (1934). *Mind, self, and society*, Ed., Charles W. Morris. Chicago: University of Chicago Press.

12. Hammersly, M. (1979). Towards a Model of Teacher Activity, in John Eggleston, Ed., *Teacher decision-making in the classroom.* London: Routledge and Kegan Paul.

13. See Festinger, L. (1964). *Conflict, decision, and dissonance.* Stanford: Stanford University Press; Ericcson, K. A., and Simon, H. A. (1980). Verbal reports as data. *Psychology Review* 87, pp. 215–251.

14. See, for a description of deliberation as a model of scholarly inquiry, Schwab, J. (1983). The Practical 4: Something for Curriculum Professors to Do. *Curriculum inquiry* 13, pp. 239–265; Shulman, L. (1984). The Practical and the Eclectic: A

Deliberation on Teaching and Educational Research. *Curriculum inquiry* 14, pp. 183–200.

15. See, for a description of the project and my role in it, Lampert, M. (1984). Teaching About Thinking and Thinking About Teaching. *Journal of curriculum studies* 16(1).

16. Watzlawick, P., Weakland, J. H., and Fisch, R. (1974). *Change: Principles of problem formation and problem resolution*. New York: W. W. Norton and Company.

17. Waller, W. (1932). *The sociology of teaching*. New York: John Wiley and Sons (pp. 385–386).

18. Berlak, A., and Berlak, H. (1981). *Dilemmas of schooling: Teaching and social change*. London: Methuen.

Other References

Braybrooke, D., and Lindblom, C. E. (1963). *A strategy of decision*. New York: Free Press.

Hofstaedter, D. R., and Dennett, D. C. (1982). *The mind's I: Fantasies and reflections on self and soul*. New York: Bantam Books.

Lindblom, C. E., and Cohen, D. K. (1979). *Usable knowledge: Social science and social problem solving*. New Haven: Yale University Press.

March, J. G., and Olson, J. P. (1979). *Ambiguity and choice in organizations*. Bergen: Universitetsforlaget.

Wiezenbaum, J. (1976). *Computer power and human reason: From judgment to calculation*. San Francisco: W. H. Freeman and Company.

10

Being a Good Influence

DAVID T. HANSEN

In this chapter, I want to address a condition of teaching that has characterized the practice since its very beginnings. That condition is the gap that exists between what teachers say they want to do and what actually takes place in their work. I am not referring to the discontinuity between pedagogical intentions and outcomes that can result from the obvious fact that teachers cannot force students to think and learn in particular ways. That inability to dictate learning presents its own set of challenges to teachers. Rather, my concern is the gap between, on the one hand, teachers' aims and purposes and, on the other, their non-self-conscious actions and habits enacted in the classroom.

That gap generates an unavoidable predicament in teaching, one that accounts for much of the uncertainty, the unpredictability, and even the anxiety that often accompany the work. While all serious-minded teachers hope to have a good influence on students, they cannot control, much less fully imagine, the influence they end up having. This is in part because a teacher's pedagogical habits often operate, metaphorically speaking, with a mind of their own. They send or emit signals and messages to students that teachers are in the worst position of all to perceive and understand, because they cannot watch themselves while actually teaching.

When in the presence of their students, teachers say and do an immense number of things of which they are not mindful—things that often appear to be automatic or, in a word, habitual. This truism applies to people everywhere, and it is a permanent feature of being human. Nobody can check every step he or she takes or monitor every word he or she utters. If one tried to do so, action would quickly come to a halt, and he or she would be like a mannequin frozen in place in a store window. Or one's practice would simply unravel, as countless athletes have discovered when they shifted their focus from the game to their technique while playing: "If you ask [a golfer]," Richard S. Peters reminds us, "to pay attention so that he can tell you in what order he makes a series of movements when hitting a good drive, . . . he will probably put the ball into the neighbouring wood."[1]

Teaching is not a solitary endeavor in which one has the luxury of examining one's conduct while engaged in it. It is conducted publicly, and typically in settings crowded with learners. While actually teaching, teachers have no recourse but to look *outside* themselves, at least if they are to pay attention to what students are saying and doing and, hopefully, learning. Thus, the tension I touched on previously between intentions and beliefs, which one can ponder beforehand, and what one actually does, which one cannot "watch" in a leisured way, pervades the practice. It does so at all levels of the educational system, from preschool to graduate seminars. I believe it worthwhile to examine what, if anything, teachers can do about this state of affairs, short of simply throwing their hands up and making the best of a fundamentally indeterminate endeavor. My question can be summarized as follows: What can teachers do to shape the messages their habitual conduct may be sending to students, such that those messages complement their hopes for being a good influence?

This question takes on urgency if we grant that teachers' influence on students, for better or for worse, derives not solely from their stated purposes but from the host of little things, often habitual things, that they undertake over the course of a school year and of which they may be scarcely aware. For example, a biology teacher may want his students to appreciate the complexity and wonders of that subject. But if he is habitually brusque and impatient with students' attempts to learn, the consequence may well be that they leave their school year disliking biology. Moreover, if he is unaware of his own manner with students, he might conclude that they alone bear the blame for an unsatisfactory course. Conversely, a biology teacher who listens with care and attentiveness to what students say—to their queries, their difficulties, their pleasure in the material—may be teaching her students far more than she realizes about the marvels of that subject, if not about learning itself. Her habitual concern for her students' ideas and feelings can spark their own curiosity and engagement with the subject.

Being taken seriously by a teacher in a natural, unforced way can promote a student's own seriousness of mind and purpose. Michael Oakeshott suggests that a quality like seriousness of mind "is never explicitly learned and it is known only in practice; but it may be learned in everything that is learned, in the carpentry shop as well as in the Latin or chemistry lesson."[2] Such a quality cannot be taught directly, either. Here is Oakeshott again: "[A quality like seriousness of mind] cannot be taught overtly, by precept, because it comprises what is required to animate precept; but it may be taught in everything that is taught. It is implanted unobtrusively in the manner in which information is conveyed, in a tone of voice, in the gesture which accompanies instruction, in asides and oblique utterances, and by example."[3] The second biology teacher described above is teaching biology, not seriousness of mind. The latter cannot be a separate object of instruction. People learn to become serious-minded by focusing on things, on objects, on activities, and so forth. That is what the biology teacher is doing. She is focusing intently on her teaching, and that quality of seriousness can be seen, if one looks for it, with as much clarity as the classroom's desks, chairs, and laboratory equipment.

In short, two teachers can present the same subject and employ identical instructional plans and methods but exert a different influence on students because of their habitual ways of conducting themselves in the classroom. When cast in this light, the gap that can exist between stated intentions and enacted deeds in teaching takes on moral significance.

Teachers occupy the central role in classrooms. They do so not simply as technicians who know how to organize small-group work or how to coordinate experimental procedures in a biology lab, but as people whose view of life and whose own character infuse potentially everything they do in the classroom. Teachers' personal qualities promise to be as influential on students, in the long run, as their pedagogical know-how. Other things being equal—instructional skills, subject matter knowledge, and so forth—a teacher who esteems learning, teaching, and students themselves will have a more enduring and beneficial impact than one who does not. Those familiar facts make pondering classroom habits an important, even necessary, dimension of good practice.

The Moral Significance of Habit

If what I have said thus far is sound, one question forces itself to the front: What can teachers do to bring their stated purposes and their habitual practices into greater harmony? A first step is to reconsider the possible meanings in one's habitual ways of working in the classroom. I pose the matter in those terms because in discussions of teaching and of human conduct more generally, habit is often treated as a distant and poor cousin of principles, of stated purposes, of beliefs, and so forth. Habit is sometimes regarded as an obvious, humdrum feature of our lives and, correspondingly, as of much less importance than the things we say we believe in and want to accomplish. Habit is so very "habitual." Why care about it?

Moral philosophers since Aristotle and sociologists since Durkheim have argued that the fact that habits appear mundane does not render them insignificant. Quite the contrary. From a sociological perspective, a person's habits can help determine how and whether he or she fits into a community. For example, a person who habitually disregards the customary ways in which members of a community interact will likely be viewed as an outsider.[4] From a moral perspective, a person's habitual treatment of other people can shape decisively the kinds of influence he or she might have on them, for better or for worse—a point that recalls the differences between the two biology teachers mentioned earlier in the chapter. In a broad sense, habits of conduct embody a person's dispositions toward other people and toward the varied affairs of life.[5]

Habit refers to repetitive actions undertaken automatically, without premeditation. In this light, habits in teaching can encompass an almost numberless array of doings. They can include such things as whether teachers routinely ask questions, make regular use of the blackboard, walk around the room, or remain in one place. They can include how teachers typically use resources such as texts, overheads, films; how they usually arrange tables and chairs in the classroom; whether they take roll in the same manner each day. Habits can include whether teachers are punctual, evaluate homework in a consistent manner, greet or fail to greet students when they come into the classroom, and much more.

As I have just presented them, however, such actions constitute mere behavior. They are not personalized but generic in nature—the kind of issues, for example, that fill textbooks in teacher education. Such generic descriptions can be valuable as guides for what to do. For example, educators would agree that it is a good idea for teachers to come to class punctually. However, when habits are listed serially in the way I have just done, the person behind the behaviors cannot be seen. Put differently, anybody can enact them. Even a robot could be programmed to stand by the classroom door and "greet" students. But the concern here is not with "anybody," much less with robots. It is with the possible influence of an individual teacher, which encompasses his or her unique qualities as a person.

We do sometimes speak of acting out of "blind habit," a phrase that emphasizes how unaware people can be of their conduct. It is not difficult to conjure up images of a classroom teacher plodding along day after day with the same dull, utterly routinized lessons. But habits are never really blind, if we take that term to suggest that they are devoid of meaning. Habits always represent more than sheer behavior alone. They convey dispositions and attitudes. A teacher who leads one desultory lesson after another soon reveals himself to be a person who lacks interest in the work and perhaps in young people themselves. This same person might at one point have been enthusiastic about teaching. The fact that he may be unaware of his present conduct attests to how slowly and imperceptibly dispositions can evolve and infuse habit—for better or for worse. Oakeshott writes that the change that is characteristic of this dimension of our moral lives "is analogous to the change to which a living language is subject: nothing is more habitual or customary than our ways of speech, and nothing is more continuously invaded by change. Like prices in a free market, habits of moral conduct show no revolutionary changes because they are never at rest."[6]

Teachers' character and dispositions eventually surface in their work with students. Once we look beyond the behavioral, or the literal, and begin to view habits in teaching symbolically, as expressive of individual qualities, the person who occupies the role of teacher comes to the fore. To understand who that person is, as well as what her influence on students might turn out to be, means considering not only her values and beliefs but her habitual conduct when in the presence of students. We begin to note not just the fact that the teacher remains standing lesson after lesson, but also how she does so—whether she looks around frequently, talks with students, listens to them, acts engaged, or acts bored. We begin to attend not just to whether the teacher asks questions and what kind of questions, but to how he does so—in an apathetic way or with actual interest in what students might have to say.

Those habitual but personalized ways of conducting oneself in the classroom constitute what can be called a style of teaching. Teachers' styles encompass their habitual tones of voice, gestures, body movements, and more, all of which can be highly expressive of their attitudes and orientations toward students and what they say and do.[7] In behavioral terms, a teacher's style can be dramatic, even histrionic. Conversely, it can be mild-mannered, even subdued. A teacher might enact both styles, behaving in dramatic ways in some circumstances, in others remaining cool and low-key. However, turning from behavioral to moral terms, which are of much greater significance for how teachers influence students, we observe that a teacher's style can express warmth or coldness, friendliness or hostility. It can exude dislike or caring for students; it can be threatening or encouraging; it can reveal aloofness or engagement—and all of this repetitively and automatically, which is to say non-self-consciously, as the core term *habit* implies. Like many readers, I have observed teachers in the classroom who are dedicated to their work. But such teachers are not trying to "demonstrate" dedication in some deliberate or self-conscious manner. Rather, they simply *are* dedicated people, and that quality is expressed through their habitual classroom practices. It is a disposition as decisive for their long-term influence on students as their instructional skills and subject matter knowledge.

In sum, the significance of a teacher's habitual ways of working extends well beyond the mechanical or the passive, terms we sometimes associate with habit. Habitual acts reveal the person the teacher is in the classroom. Students are usually attuned to the personal qualities their teachers display, regardless of whether they can articulate that awareness or not. Students at all levels of teaching care about what kind of people their teachers are because of the time they spend with them and because of the role teachers play in students' progress and promotion. There may be wisdom in the child's apparently ho-hum description of a teacher—"she's okay." The child may be summarizing in those terse terms the moral bottom line.

Reflecting on Habit

What does it mean for a teacher to reflect on what his or her habitual practice expresses in the classroom? How *does* one "reflect" on habit? As we have seen, specific behaviors per se are not the issue. The upshot of my argument is not some formulaic rule that all teachers should spend half the class standing and half the class sitting. Behavior alone is not the crux of the matter. What is at stake are the dispositions and attitudes toward students and toward learning itself that teachers express through their everyday conduct. Exploring this concern is comparable to asking how one can become more attuned to one's own character—whether one is respectful and just, for example, in one's dealings with other people. Bringing such matters into awareness is no simple affair. This is particularly true with habits, which are doings we tend to take for granted. Because of that, they are often hard to picture clearly. They are often opaque to the very person who enacts them. "Our deepest-seated habits," says Dewey, "are precisely those of which we have least awareness."[8]

Moreover, pondering what habits one might be expressing to students carries risks. What a person may uncover about himself as teacher might be troubling, or possibly even worse. He may realize that his habitual ways of working have become a convenient way to ignore certain questions about what he is doing and why. Another risk is that the process can become self-absorbing, in the literal sense of those terms. A teacher I know once said that she did not want to know what her style of teaching was—her tones of voice, her gestures, and the like. She did not want to think about those habits because she worried that doing so would distract her from thinking about her students. She feared that opening the issue of habit would lead her to become too self-preoccupied, too engaged in watching herself rather than attending with care to her students' doings. This is a real danger in reflecting on the moral dimensions of one's teaching. A person can become so self-conscious about her influence on students that she becomes pedagogically anxious, unable to act with confidence and vigor. Dewey warns of this possibility when he points out that excessive concern with one's character and actions can "hamper and paralyse conduct" and can even lead to "a mania of doubt."[9]

Still another reason why reflecting on habit can be risky is that it may not yield tangible or immediate results, an outcome that can prove discouraging. A teacher may endeavor to be more patient and attentive in the classroom. But students may not respond to that change, at least not right away. Moreover, there may be no reliable way of judging whether students have benefited from it or whether they have been led by it to become more patient and attentive themselves with others. One reason for this possibility is that self-awareness lags behind habit. Typically, we become conscious of our habitual attitudes and behaviors only after we have already formed them. "We learn by doing," Aristotle says of the habitual way we take on moral virtues. "We become just by the practice of just actions, self-controlled by exercising self-control, and courageous by performing acts of courage."[10] Only later, Aristotle tells us, are we in a position to reflect upon and perhaps question what is involved in being just or self-controlled. Thus, an additional obstacle that may dampen the inclination to reflect deeply on moral matters—including what one's habitual practices may be expressing in the classroom—is that such reflection may not yield an immediate, perceivable result in terms of student conduct and learning. Teachers may not detect much change in their students, at least not at first, despite their efforts to improve the quality of their own human presence in the classroom.

Two replies to the concerns raised by those risks come to mind. The first is that the idea of a reward or a payoff for trying to be a better teacher, in the moral sense of *better,* is strange. Nobody joins the practice to be rewarded for their virtues. Teaching is a form of service, and virtue its own reward—an instance in which that cliché has genuine meaning. Second, few serious-minded teachers believe they have no influence whatsoever on their students. They could hardly teach without that belief. They may not know precisely what makes their impact a positive or enabling one, but they have no doubts that students are at least to some degree well served by their efforts to teach.

The challenge becomes how teachers can shape their habits and what they express so that they complement rather than work against the teachers' deliberate attempts to be a force for good. To spell out how that might be done, I turn to Dewey's analysis of the habitual aspects of moral judgment. I also make use of Iris Murdoch's notion of paying moral "attention" to other people.

Dewey notes that many immediate reactions of approval and disapproval can legitimately be called "intuitive." "They are not based upon any thought-out reason or ground," Dewey writes. "We just admire and resent, are attracted and repelled."[11] This can be true of our immediate responses to people ("What a fine thing she did") or to objects ("What a beautiful painting"). But Dewey argues that such responses are "the results of *prior* experience, including *previous* conscious thinking, [that] get taken up into direct habits, and express themselves in direct appraisals of value."[12]

Dewey means that present habits of judgment are shaped by past experience and thought. Much of what we might now spontaneously value or disvalue was at one point perceived as new, as something requiring choice and reflection rather than a habitual response.

For instance, a teacher who habitually attends to the smallest signs of student effort may at one time have overlooked or simply not perceived them. He may have been more concerned with his own performance than with that of his students. But somewhere along the way, a change took place. He began to notice students' reactions to his teaching as well as their reactions to one another. He began to see the look of delight that lit up a student's eyes or the look of worry that knit a student's brow. He began to hear the note of curiosity or of frustration in a student's comment. In short, through experience, reflection, and time, his conduct has changed. He now notices and reflects upon such matters regularly. In other words, his emerging awareness has become *embodied* in his now habitual alertness to his students' doings. His focus on signs of growth has become a non-self-conscious element of his conduct. He does not say to himself, as if he were carrying around a prompt card, "I must pay attention; I must pay attention." He now just does so. The daily question he faces is not whether to attend to students—that disposition has become embedded in his classroom habits—but rather how to do so in each particular context.

Every teacher, as soon as she walks through the door of the classroom, responds to students and to the environment to some extent spontaneously and non-self-consciously. This is inevitable, given the human beings we are and given the ways in which we take on habits of perception, judgment, and appraisal. It is inevitable because of the nature of character itself. Character can be understood, in part, as a person's habitual way of regarding and treating other people. It spotlights whether the person enacts qualities such as honesty, patience, respectfulness, and so on. Character is also difficult for the person to envisage clearly. People tend to find it difficult to perceive their own character in a many-sided fashion, as Ludwig Wittgenstein implies when he writes: "It is as impossible to view one's character from outside as it is *one's own handwriting*. I have a one-sided relation to my handwriting which prevents me from seeing it on the same footing as others' writing and comparing it with theirs."[13] To paraphrase Wittgenstein's analogy, it is as impossible for a teacher to perceive her own character from the "outside" as it is for her to fathom the imprint she has made on a class. That imprint is left as much by her habitual ways of working—which, as we have seen, are expressive of character—as by her deliberate, self-conscious acts.

In brief, teachers' classroom habits can be as difficult for them to perceive as their own character. However, Wittgenstein's remark raises the possibility that once people become aware of habit, they are at least on the way to thinking about its significance and what it may be signaling to other people.

They may be on the way to changing what that habit might express, even if they cannot, as Wittgenstein emphasizes, stand outside themselves. The sheer act of bringing into view a habit may imply that a process of change has already begun.

Beginnings are one thing, of course, but bringing to life their promise is another. Returning to Dewey's analysis, his enabling insight is that a person's habits can be "funded" by past experience and reflection.[14] Habit can be informed by thought rather than merely by custom and unexamined assumption. Over time, a teacher's thinking can unawares begin to infuse his habits with greater meaning and value—meaning and value that, I have argued, will find expression in his everyday practice. The key is to ponder one's daily efforts continually, guided by the belief that that reflection will, over time, begin to shape or "fund" one's daily classroom presence. Just as habits form over a fairly long period of time, so what is expressed through them can be altered only over time. We cannot "make" our habits of teaching express commitment, concern, interest. Only with reflection and time can those qualities become a part of who we are and find expression in our everyday, non-self-conscious work with students.

How might this process of "funding" habitual conduct with prior reflection appear in actual practice? To answer the question, I turn to Murdoch's distinction between "looking" and "attending." We "see" or "look" at other people and at things in the world all of the time. Much of our looking is neutral, disinterested, unengaged. However, according to Murdoch, to "attend" to another person is a moral act. It is to look at the other person with the intent and desire to understand her, to connect with her, perhaps to assist her in some way. Attending involves actively resisting easy interpretations of the other person's position or difficulty; it involves counteracting facile, prejudiced conclusions. It implies turning things over in the mind, trying to see beyond one's own possible interests and to recognize those of another person. In brief, it means trying to see other people as they are, rather than how we expect them or want them to be.

Those remarks apply directly to teaching. All serious-minded teachers want to understand their students' individual abilities, capacities, interests, and so on. In addition, those teachers hope that when they are called upon to make classroom decisions that affect their students, they will conduct themselves well. They hope that when they have to act immediately, *to do something now,* their spontaneous response—which often means their habitual response—will be enabling rather than damaging to students. Here is how Murdoch surveys the issue:

> If we consider what the work of attention is like, how continuously it goes on, and how imperceptibly it builds up structures of value round about us, we shall not be surprised that at crucial moments of choice most of the business of choosing is already over. This does not imply that we are not free, certainly not. But it implies that the exercise of our freedom is a small piecemeal business which goes

> on all the time and not a grandiose leaping about unimpeded at important moments. The moral life, on this view, is something that goes on continually, not something that is switched off in between the occurrence of explicit moral choices. What happens in between such choices is indeed what is crucial.[15]

Murdoch's claims suggest that becoming a good influence in the classroom results from more than the specific values, beliefs, and knowledge a teacher might hold and attempt to teach students. Rather, it derives, in part, from what Murdoch calls the "work of attending," the habitual ways in which the teacher ponders his students, his work with them, his aims and hopes for them, and so on. When Murdoch contends that the "business" of choosing actually takes place between moments of choice and decision, she underscores the importance of everyday, serious-minded reflection on one's teaching. To recall Dewey's language, that reflection can "fund" the teacher's conduct such that he can act better than he otherwise might when the chips are down—for example, at all those unpredictable, often startling moments of immediacy in the classroom, when students are all of a sudden upset, excited, arguing with one another, and so forth and when there truly is no time for a leisurely look at what is going on. Murdoch helps us reconsider the question, What is it that informs or guides what a teacher does in such moments? Part of the answer, she suggests, resides in the nature and extent to which the teacher ponders his everyday ways of working with students in between the periods of actual teaching.

To reflect on teaching and to "attend" to one's students can infuse all of one's day-by-day classroom practice with greater moral awareness, sensitivity, and understanding. "As moral agents," Murdoch concludes, "we have to try to see justly, to overcome prejudice, to avoid temptation, to control and curb imagination, to direct reflection."[16] Over time, this contemplative process[17]—which can itself become a kind of habit if engaged in steadfastly—can work its way into the messages and signals that teachers' classroom habits send to their students.

Conclusion

The viewpoint I have outlined in this essay parts company with some widespread assumptions about what it means for a teacher to have a good influence on students. Some of those assumptions are explicitly moral—for example, that being a good influence is a matter of helping students determine right from wrong. For some educators, that means telling students how and what to think; for others, it means helping students understand what they are doing when they are debating moral matters. Other assumptions are explicitly pedagogical—for example, that being a good influence means teaching the curriculum successfully, or motivating students to work hard, or effectively managing the classroom. Despite some major differences, however, those moral and pedagogical assumptions share the view that being a good influence boils down to implementing a particular set of identifiable actions. They are actions, moreover, that can be specified in advance, at least in broad outline, before so much as stepping into the classroom.

This chapter has charted a different direction. Being a good influence is not solely a matter of having a battery of appropriate instructional techniques available for use. Nor is it purely an issue of having a clear, articulate picture of right and wrong with which to engage students. Rather, being a good influence requires thinking about the habitual nature of much of what one does as teacher when in the presence of one's students. It means thinking about habits and the messages they send. It involves steady soul-searching and an ongoing inner dialogue, terms that recall Murdoch's notion of moral "attention." Soul-searching means pondering one's motives and interests as teacher, mindful that students are individuals with motivations and interests of their own. An inner dialogue means, literally, conversing with and questioning oneself, a process that brings one's beliefs and values into view and also helps in better understanding students' responses to teaching and to subject matter more broadly.

Being a good influence also entails faith in the idea that unpredictability and uncertainty in teaching are not synonymous with failure or a lack of expertise. The former are conditions of teaching. I use the term *faith* mindful of the point elaborated on previously, that one cannot watch oneself while actually teaching. Such self-consciousness about one's habits while *in* the act of teaching is not fully possible. It would also be counterproductive. As the teacher whose concerns I mentioned earlier said, it would take the focus away from its proper place, namely students. However, by reflecting today on their own hopes, values, and actions, teachers can build confidence in *not* having to watch themselves tomorrow. They can build trust in themselves, that whatever their habits may be, they are expressing positive and enabling messages to students rather than their opposites.

The gap between aims and beliefs on the one hand and habitual practice on the other can never be fully closed. That predicament comes with practice. Teachers can never quite know what they are doing or what influence they are having while actually teaching. And they *must* never know such things, for otherwise they would be attending to themselves rather than to their students, and teaching would become a detour to the self rather than the moral practice it has always been.

Notes

1. Richard S. Peters, "Reason and Habit: The Paradox of Moral Education," in Israel Scheffler (Ed.), *Philosophy and Education*, Second Edition (Boston: Allyn and Bacon, 1966), 257.

2. Michael Oakeshott, "Learning and Teaching," in Timothy Fuller (Ed.), *The Voice of Liberal Learning: Michael Oakeshott on Education* (New Haven: Yale University Press, 1989), 61.

3. Ibid., 61. For a useful discussion of the teacher's "manner" and how it can articulate with pedagogical method, see Gary Fenstermacher, "The Concepts of Method and Manner in Teaching," in Fritz K. Oser, Andreas Dick, and Jean-Luc Patry (Eds.), *Effective and Responsible Teaching: The New Synthesis* (San Francisco: Jossey-Bass, 1992), 95–108. Fenstermacher's view of manner bears a family resemblance to what I call "style" elsewhere in this essay. Both of those uses echo Oakeshott's claim quoted in the paragraph in which this note is cited.

4. For a comprehensive review of sociological analyses of habit and its place in social life, see Charles Camic, "The Matter of Habit," *American Journal of Sociology*, 91 (1986): 1039–1087.

5. John Dewey has elaborated on this claim in detail. See, for example, his *Democracy and Education* (New York: Free Press, 1966 [first published in 1916]); *Human Nature and Conduct* (New York: The Modern Library, 1930 [first published in 1922]); and *Theory of the Moral Life* (New York: Holt, Rinehart, and Winston, 1960 [revised edition first published in 1932]). For a recent study of Dewey's viewpoint, see Suzanne Rice, "Dewey's Conception of 'Virtue' and Its Implications for Moral Education," *Educational Theory*, 46 (1996): 269–282.

6. Michael Oakeshott, "The Tower of Babel," in Oakeshott, *Rationalism in Politics and Other Essays* (Indianapolis: Liberty Press 1991 [essay first published in 1962]), 471.

7. See Philip W. Jackson, Robert E. Boostrom, and David T. Hansen, *The Moral Life of Schools* (San Francisco: Jossey-Bass, 1993) and David T. Hansen, "The Moral Importance of the Teacher's Style," *Journal of Curriculum Studies* 25 (1993): 397–421.

8. John Dewey, *Experience and Nature* (New York: Dover Publications, 1958 [first published in 1929]), 311.

9. John Dewey, *Theory of the Moral Life*, 13.

10. Aristotle, *Nicomachean Ethics,* trans., Martin Ostwald (New York: Macmillan, 1962), 34–35 [Bekker pages 1103a33–1103b1].

11. John Dewey, *Theory of the Moral Life*, 124.

12. Ibid., 125 (emphasis supplied).

13. Ludwig Wittgenstein, *Culture and Value*, trans., Peter Winch (Chicago: University of Chicago Press, 1980), 23e.

14. John Dewey, *Theory of the Moral Life*, 125.

15. Iris Murdoch, *The Sovereignty of Good* (London: Routledge and Kegan Paul, 1985 [first published in 1970]), 37.

16. Ibid., 40.

17. For a discussion of contemplation as it pertains to teaching, see Margret Buchmann, "The Careful Vision: How Practical Is Contemplation in Teaching?" *American Journal of Education*, 98 (1989): 35–61.

About the Book

Teaching is a complex and challenging endeavor. Teachers are continually faced with difficult choices in which competing values are in tension with one another. The interests of all students and of other groups and constituencies can rarely be served at the same time. Different educational goals, each desirable in and of itself, often place incompatible demands on teachers, especially in light of the limited resources and time available to most of them. Of course, teaching does have its satisfaction and fulfillment, but increasingly, those rewards must be sought in the context of challenges that reflect the competing expectations society places upon educators.

This book tackles important aspects of the complex, often conflicted contexts of teaching. Each chapter focuses on a different aspect of teaching, offering candid analysis of the difficulties and trade-offs inherent in teaching practice, while suggesting ways to productively address a given conflict. Together, the chapters speak honestly to the realities and challenges of teaching, without downplaying the ideals that draw teachers into education in the first place.

About the Editors and Contributors

Elaine Atkins is coordinator of curriculum development and professor of English at Community College of Philadelphia. Her research focuses on the fusion of American pragmatism and hermeneutics in education and on curriculum deliberations. She teaches the curriculum theory course at the University of Pennsylvania's Graduate School of Education.

Kathryn H. Au is an associate professor in the College of Education at the University of Hawaii. Her research interest is the literacy learning of students of diverse cultural and linguistic backgrounds. She is president of the National Reading Conference and has been a vice president of the American Educational Research Association.

Robert Boostrom is assistant professor of teacher education at the University of Southern Indiana and is the U.S. editor for the *Journal of Curriculum Studies.* He is interested in moral education and particularly in how conceptions of teaching as a moral enterprise may be used to assess teaching practice and to shape teacher education. He is coauthor, with Philip W. Jackson and David T. Hansen, of *The Moral Life of Schools.*

Nicholas C. Burbules is professor of educational policy studies at the University of Illinois–Urbana/Champaign. He is also currently the editor of *Educational Theory*. He has published numerous articles on the philosophy of education, critical social and political theory, and technology issues in education and is the author of *Dialogue in Teaching: Theory and Practice.*

Robert E. Floden is professor of teacher education and educational psychology and director of both the Institute for Research on Teaching and Learning and the National Center for Research on Teacher Learning at Michigan State University. His work has addressed educational issues in teaching, teacher education, philosophy, measurement, and policy. He is currently studying connections between educational policy and teaching practice.

David T. Hansen is associate professor in the College of Education, University of Illinois–Chicago. He serves as coordinator of Secondary Teacher Education and teaches courses in the philosophy and practice of teaching. He is the author of *The Call to Teach* (1995) and coauthor of *The Moral Life of Schools* (1993).

Magdalene Lampert is a teacher, teacher educator, and researcher on teaching. She is professor of education at the University of Michigan, where she directs the Investigating Teaching Project. The project examines the use of multimedia records of practice for the study of teaching.

Nel Noddings is Lee Jacks Professor of Child Education at Stanford University. She is the author or coeditor of nine books, among them *Caring*, *The Challenge to Care in Schools*, *Educating for Intelligent Belief or Unbelief*, and *Philosophy of Education*. Her latest book (coedited with Suzanne Gordon and Patricia Benner) is *Caregiving* (1997).

Jo Anne Pagano is professor of education at Colgate University. She has published numerous articles on feminist theory and curriculum theory. She is the author of *Exiles and Communities: Teaching in the Patriarchal Wilderness* and, with Landon Beyer, Walter Feinberg, and James Anthony Whitson, *Preparing Teachers as Professionals*.

Sheila W. Valencia is associate professor of curriculum and instruction at the University of Washington–Seattle. Her teaching and research focus on literacy instruction and assessment, with an emphasis on classroom-based assessment. She has served on the advisory boards of several national, state, and professional assessment projects, including the National Academy of Education, the National Task Force on Assessment, and the Joint Committee on Assessment of NCTE and IRA.

Index